Router Joinery Workshop

Router Joinery Workshop

Common Joints, Simple Setups & Clever Jigs

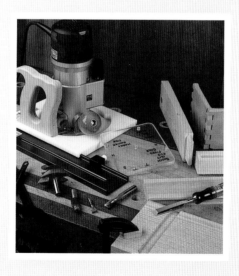

Carol Reed

Editor: Andy Rae

Art Director:
Susan McBride

Production:
Charlie Covington

Photographer:
Sandor Nagyszalanczy

Cover Designer:
Barbara Zaretsky

Illustrator:
Frank Rohrbach

Assistant Editor:
Veronika Alice Gunter,
Rain Newcomb,
Heather Smith

Proofreader:
Michele Drivon

Production Assistance:
Shannon Yokeley

Editorial Assistance:
Delores Gosnell

Library of Congress Cataloging-in-Publication Data

Reed, Carol.
    Router joinery workshop : common joints, simple setups & clever jigs / by
Carol Reed.—1st ed.
      p. cm.
    Includes index.
    ISBN 1-57990-328-2 (pbk.)
    1. Routers (Tools) 2. Joinery. 3. Jigs and fixtures. I. Title.
  TT203.5.R44   2002
  684'.08—dc21

                         2002030169

10 9 8 7 6 5 4 3 2 1

First Edition

Published by Lark Books, a division of
Sterling Publishing Co., Inc.
387 Park Avenue South, New York, N.Y. 10016

© 2003, Carol Reed

Distributed in Canada by Sterling Publishing,
c/o Canadian Manda Group, One Atlantic Ave., Suite 105
Toronto, Ontario, Canada M6K 3E7

Distributed in the U.K. by Guild of Master Craftsman Publications Ltd.,
Castle Place, 166 High Street, Lewes, East Sussex, England BN7 1XU
Tel: (+ 44) 1273 477374, Fax: (+ 44) 1273 478606,
Email: pubs@thegmcgroup.com, Web: www.gmcpublications.com

Distributed in Australia by Capricorn Link (Australia) Pty Ltd.,
P.O. Box 704, Windsor, NSW 2756 Australia

If you have questions or comments about this book, please contact:
Lark Books
67 Broadway
Asheville, NC 28801
(828) 253-0467

Printed in China

1-57990-328-2

Table of Contents

Introduction

We all know that choosing the right joint and milling it accurately are the key elements of fine woodworking. But how many of us feel that we have a firm handle on the joint-making process? Novices marvel at the projects and skills of more proficient woodworkers and wonder, "How do they do it?" On the other hand, many skilled woodworkers know there must be an easier way. Others decide it's time to learn a new joint. And everyone wonders which is the best tool for the job.

It's to all of these woodworking folk that I offer this book. It presents the router as the tool of choice for making joints accurately, quickly, and consistently. Inside you'll find practical joint-making instructions, including the tools and jigs you'll need, with sequential instructions and over 200 photos and illustrations that make each process clear.

As The Router Lady, I've been teaching students the ins and outs of the router for many years through woodworking colleges, woodworking shows, guilds, and in my own shop. My own skills didn't come easily. When I first learned of the router over 20 years ago, the machine nearly defeated me. But I became determined to master it. When I later became an instructor, I discovered my students had the same frustrations, and so through the years I developed and refined simple and proven jigs and techniques. Now I have the chance to share them with you.

Router Joinery Workshop is divided into four sections. The first section contains advice on choosing the best router, bits, and other router tools—and essential techniques for using them. In addition, there are numerous jigs you can make for more efficient and accurate joints. You'll also find special holding systems for securing your work predictably and safely.

Section Two covers methods for cutting common woodworking joints with a router. Look for rabbets, dadoes, grooves, slots, box joints, mortise-and-tenon joints, and dovetails. There's even a chapter on making joints with special bits, including drawer-lock joints, lock-miter joints, and cope-and-stick joinery for door making, with instructions for making raised panels as a bonus.

Section Three is offered as "dessert." Here you'll find special template-routing techniques at which the router excels. You'll learn how to make multiple, irregular-shaped parts and join complex curved pieces using template routing and complementary template routing. Plus you'll find out how to fix defects or decorate a plain project using router inlay.

The fourth and last section includes practical projects that let you practice your new joinery skills, as well as make some pretty fine furniture. You'll find all the information you need for making a fancy breadboard, a box, a bookcase, a table, and a cabinet with trays, drawer, and paneled door. As practice projects, the pieces are small and manageable, but they're designed so you can scale them up if you choose. Build them so you can try the joints in the book, and consider them a primer for more challenging projects down the road.

As you practice some of the techniques in the book, you'll discover there are many ways in woodworking to do the same thing. Be open to new methods, and try a different approach if it suits you. However, keep in mind that there are only two wrong ways when it comes to doing anything in the shop: The first doesn't work; the second is unsafe. If at any point you are uncomfortable, stop and think it through. And always stay within your center of balance. Consider where your hands and fingers are—and where they'll be when a machine is turned on. Dress appropriately by removing jewelry, securing loose clothing, and tucking hair out of the way. Above all, practice first. Then hit the "on" switch.

You'll find many tools and accessories in the book. A complete source list can be found at the Lark Books website (www.larkbooks.com). Or you can contact me directly at www.routerlady.com. Can't find a jig or kit you read about? Is my written description lacking? Want to know what's new in techniques, machines, or bits? Interested in taking a class? Check my website, or drop me a line—you'll find my e-mail address listed on my site.

So come on over to The Router Lady's shop. Now that you're ready to learn how it's really done, I'll be happy to show you how to do it!

Carol Reed, *The Router Lady*
Ramona, CA

SECTION 1:
Tools, Jigs, and Techniques

Choosing a Router

There's nothing worse than spending money on a machine that frustrates you or, worse, buying one you never use. But how do you buy a router with all the options you need, and one that you look forward to taking off the shelf? To answer these questions, let's start with some routing basics. The router itself consists of a high rpm motor with a sharp cutter installed at the end of its shaft. The motor is inserted into a base that's equipped with a baseplate, which in turn provides a reference surface for contacting the work. The router works best when the baseplate is attached to a jig or utilizes one to make safe, predictable, and repeatable cuts. Rarely do we rout freehand, which means that routing is actually 95 percent setup and only 5 percent routing. Since making and using these jigs accurately and quickly is the secret to using the router like a pro, one of the key aspects to consider when choosing a router is how easily it works with the jigs you'll need. We'll talk more about jigs later.

When router shopping, whether you're a beginner or not, it's best to look for an all-purpose, do-every-thing machine. But choosing a do-all router begs the question: which should you buy? There are three types: a fixed-base router, a plunge router, and a trim router. (See photo, opposite page.) Of the three, we can weed out the trim router because it accommodates only ¼ in. bits, which severely limits your routing capabilities. Both fixed-base and plunge routers have limitations, but they also have unique features that make them desirable tools.

In the next section, we'll look at what features are available in different routers. Some features are important; others you can live happily without. For a quick look at the most useful ones, check the list on page 9. Included are some improvements you can consider to make your router more user-friendly. Once you understand the elements that make a good router, go ahead and shop for brand names. Simply make a list of the important features and see which manufacturer can offer the most, and for the best price.

Get a Collection of Collets

Some manufacturers offer ¼ in., ½ in., ⅜ in., and 8 mm collets. Why so many? You may rout for a lifetime

Pick from three. From left to right: trim router, fixed-base router, and plunge router

Features to Consider

- ¼ and ½ in. collets standard, with ⅜ in. and 8 mm available

- ⅛ to ¼ in. collet adapter available

- fixed base, able to accept a plunge base and stripped-down bases

- symmetrical screw-hole pattern in base

- 10- to 12-amp variable-speed motor

- 6 lbs. or less in weight

- flat top

- metal depth-adjustment mating surfaces

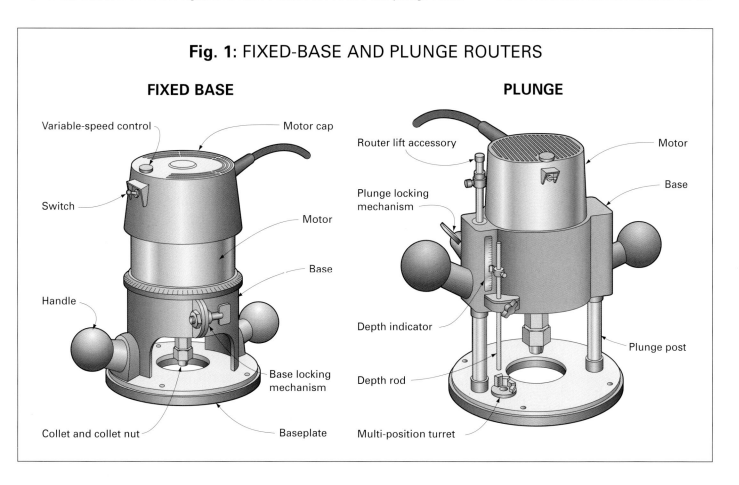

Fig. 1: FIXED-BASE AND PLUNGE ROUTERS

FIXED BASE

- Variable-speed control
- Motor cap
- Switch
- Motor
- Base
- Handle
- Base locking mechanism
- Collet and collet nut
- Baseplate

PLUNGE

- Router lift accessory
- Motor
- Base
- Plunge locking mechanism
- Depth indicator
- Plunge post
- Depth rod
- Multi-position turret

and never require more than a standard ¼ in. and a ½ in. collet. But some jigs require a bit with an 8 mm shank, such as commercial dovetail jigs. Or you may want to save money and use end mills, which are available in many more lengths than regular straight bits and are about 30 percent less expensive. End mills require odd-size collets, since they have the same diameter along their entire length. Although standard collets let you use ¼ in. and ½ in. end mills with no problem, acquiring a ⅜ in. collet allows you to use a ⅜ in. mill for mortising, a very common mortise width. Small ⅛ in. end mills can be used with an ⅛ to ¼ in. adapter for inlay work, which can save on bits that break easily. Keeping a wide variety of collet sizes on hand will provide you with more options. Add to that the opportunity to save a few bucks, and you have a good deal!

Consider Four Bases

I admit I am an unabashed fan of fixed-based routers. I find them more stable than plunge routers, since their lower handle locations keep your hands closer to the work surface for more control. The fact is, in our quest for an all-purpose router, a fixed-based machine best meets the wide variety of applications and uses we look for in a router. The good news is that several manufacturers offer router motors that accept multiple bases, including a fixed base, a plunge base, a D-handled base, and a stripped-down base designed for mounting in a router table. All four types are handy to have, and best of all, you now have the option of purchasing a combination package containing a plunge and fixed base with the same router motor. (See top photo, opposite page.)

Hold that bit securely. Get an assortment of collets and collet adapters that accept the varying shank diameters of your bits.

A fixed base locks the motor and bit to a specific depth of cut, and holds it in that fixed position while you make the cut. Setting the depth of cut with a fixed base is simply a matter of positioning the motor up or down in the base. However, you can't safely change the depth of cut on the fly (while the motor is running), such as when trying to deepen a mortise.

A plunge base does allow you to change the depth of cut with the motor running. This means you can start in the middle of a workpiece with the bit first clear of the wood, then plunge into the stock with the base firmly positioned. This action makes a plunge base an ideal mortising platform. (More on mortising later.)

A D-handled base is very handy because it provides an asymmetrical hold on the machine and usually places a trigger-type on-off switch under your finger. An asymmetrical grip means that your hands are not directly opposed to one another as with a common fixed base, which allows more control over the movement of the router. The downside is that the projecting handle makes the router prone to tipping. But the fix is easy. You can stabilize the router by making or buying an inexpensive offset baseplate to replace the factory baseplate. Or you can forgo the D-handled base altogether and make an offset baseplate with its own built-in D-handle. You won't have the trigger-type switch, but you'll have more to spend on router bits!

A table base is a stripped down version of a standard fixed base—no handles, and often no depth-setting indicator. It's an inexpensive way to get a permanent setup for quickly attaching a motor to the bottom of your router table or to other shop jigs.

One router, four bases. Clockwise from left: D-handled base, plunge base, fixed base, and a stripped-down table base

You can make any router more useful by choosing one that accepts a variety of bases, then stocking up on the specific bases you need. A number of manufacturers price their bases so your can easily afford several. Best of all, with a variety of bases on hand you can permanently mount your favorite jigs to them for quick changeovers.

Look for Baseplate Hole Symmetry

Another feature to consider when choosing a router is the symmetry of the screw-hole pattern for the screws that attach your router's baseplate to its base. Symmetrical hole patterns make jig-making much easier, as shown in figure 2. Asymmetrical hole patterns make it necessary to keep track of top and bottom, and

---

Fig. 2: BASEPLATE HOLE PATTERNS

SYMMETRICAL

Baseplate

Bit hole

Each screw hole is the same distance from the bit hole and all screw holes are equidistant from each other.

ASSYMETRICAL

Screw holes are unevenly spaced from bit hole and from each other.

left and right on the base during jig construction—a real pain. Symmetrical screw hole patterns make for a happy marriage of the base to the jig.

Buy or Make Accessories

Commercial router accessories, such as edge guides, extra collets, adapters and the like, are other important considerations when buying a router. Now that you're an informed tool buyer, you will want to know where you can get these items. Are the accessories you want easily available? Few tool stores carry all the accessories you need, simply because they're not expensive, high-volume items. Look in your phone book for power tool repair services and ask if they carry or can order accessories for you. Also check woodworking stores and mail-order catalogs, although mail-order catalogs often don't include this information. If you can't find what you need, get the manufacturer's catalog to determine which accessories are available; your local tool store often stocks catalogs and gives them away for free. Another option is to check the manufacturer's website for the information you need, or order a catalog from them via the Internet or phone.

In addition to what the manufacturers make, there are some shop-made accessories you can add or replace on your router that will make it much more user-friendly. My favorite is to substitute the standard base-locking mechanism, typically a thumbscrew or small latch, with a ratcheting lever for more positive locking action, as shown in the photo, above. Another technique is to add contrasting color to the on/off switch. For example, I adhere tape to the "off" side of the shroud on my router's switch as a reminder to keep the tog-

Friendly fixes. User-friendly improvements include adding tape to the "off" side of the power switch, replacing the standard base lock with a ratcheting lever, and using a hook-and-loop strap to keep power cords under control.

gle in the off position—especially when the router is unplugged. This small detail alerts me to make certain the router is "off," preventing the router from unexpectedly coming to life when I plug in the power cord. A third handy addition is to attach a hook-and-loop strap on the power cord. This way, I can wrap the cord into a secure loop, then nest the router in the loop on a shelf for tidy storage.

Motor Size Counts

Motor size is a key aspect of routers. A general-purpose router will have a 1½ to 2 hp rating. However, don't put a lot of stock in that rating. There are many ways to measure horsepower, and unfortunately there's no unified measurement used by all manufacturers. This makes horsepower ratings suspect. However, a number not to be trifled with is the

amperage rating of the motor. So do what the pros do: Read the fine print on the motor plate. You're looking for 10 to 12 amps, which provides enough power for all your joinery needs. The good news is that every manufacturer has routers in this amperage range. (See photo, below.)

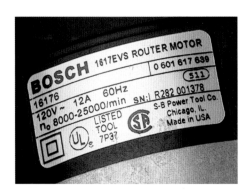

Check the amps. The best measure of power is the amperage rating listed on the router's motor plate. Look for a tool in the 10 to 12 amps range.

Motors are available with fixed or variable speeds. Since we're looking for a machine that will give us the most options, a variable-speed motor offers more versatility. Changing the speed of a router allows you to choose a lower speed when using larger bits, and lets you rout a wider variety of materials such as plastics and non-ferrous metals. While this book covers wood as the media of choice, buying a router with a variable-speed motor will give you the option of working with these alternative materials down the road.

Watch Your Weight

A good router in the 10 to 12 amp power range should weigh about 6 lbs. This is an important control issue for first-time and occasional users. A router can be very intimidating, considering the torque of its high rpm and the loudness of its motor. Keeping the weight of your router in this moderate range will help lessen these challenging factors. In fact, many pros avoid trying to control a 15 lb. hand-held router. In addition, some jigs simply can't accommodate a heavy router, such as a horizontal router-table setup (more on this later in the book).

Get a Flat Top

It's wise to choose a router with a flat head, or motor cap. With a flat top surface, a router can be placed firmly upside down on the bench with the sharp (and expensive) bit safely out of harm's way while you're busy making another setup. It's also much easier to set the bit depth when your router stands securely on its head, freeing both of your hands for bit adjustment, as shown in the top photo, right.

Plastic Versus Metal

Many inexpensive routers have a plastic motor cover that engages a plastic base. This means that as you adjust the depth of the router bit, you're turning plastic against plastic. The result is sticking. This sticking gets worse when the motor warms up and the plastic expands a little. In my classes, students find that no amount of lubrication overcomes this sticking. A sticky router makes small, finite depth adjustments frustrating and time consuming— although it does provide an opportunity for you to learn new four-lettered words. So keep your vocabulary clean, your routing experience successful and happy, and avoid routers with too much plastic.

"The Envelope, Please…"

Remember, the idea is to acquire a do-everything, all-purpose machine. With this in mind, there is no "perfect" router on the market, since no one router currently has all of the features we've talked about. Realistically, none probably ever will. What you *will* find are either commercially available accessories or those you can make yourself, which will go a long way toward making your router the best for you. Some of those jigs and accessories are right here in this book, ready for you to make.

Price can be a big factor in buying the right router, too. What should your budget be? Many first-time buyers mentally commit to spending about 75 percent of the amount needed for a quality, feature-rich router. The truth is you should probably plan to pay 25 to 35 percent more than you thought. To some,

Flat tops are better. A router with a flat top sits securely upside down on the bench and lets you work more comfortably when setting bit heights.

that's a lot of money. But it's the right amount. Spending less can seriously compromise the usability of the machine. How many times have we regretted an inexpensive purchase, when subsequent experience causes us to lament "If only I had known…?" Consider carefully how a bit more money now could prevent headaches down the road. On the other hand, there are plenty of routers on the market that will keep a true tool-junkie's wallet slim and trim, but the final truth is, when it comes to actually *using* routers, the ideal machine is the one most hauled off the shelf and put to work.

Router Bits

How to Aquire an All-Purpose, Must-Have Collection

Just as a drill needs drill bits, a router needs router bits to be useful. But router bits are quite different from drill bits. The vast majority are designed to cut from the side, rather than from the point, or end, as regular drill bits do. This side-cutting action is a significant aspect of router bit design, as you'll see.

Spending wisely on router bits is an equally important aspect. Over the years in my Router Lady classes, I've seen too many students waste good money buying inexpensive router bits. The truth is, a little more money often buys disproportionately more value. But you don't have to spend a fortune. The following information is meant to help you buy the right bits, at the right price. There are many important aspects and features you'll want to consider. You'll even find a list of specific bits I rec-

ommend for joinery, and descriptions of why you need them. (For more on some unique joinery bits, see the chapter on Special Joints with Special Bits, page 114.) You'll also want to keep your bit collection well maintained, so some tips on care and use are in order.

First, let's start by outlining the major factors that separates good bits from those that disappoint.

Carbide Only, Please

I recommend purchasing only carbide-tipped or solid carbide router bits. That's because the lifetime of a bit is determined by how long it will produce a good cut. High-speed steel (HSS) bits dull quickly, which produces an inferior cut that requires more sanding and scraping to achieve a surface ready to finish. Keep in mind that some inexpensive carbide bits render poor cuts as well.

One way to think about steel versus carbide is to ask yourself what you expect from a bit. I always take a survey when I teach a class, and one of my standard questions is, "How many of you like sanding?" In all my years of asking, I can count the affirmative answers on the fingers of one hand. And what do you think the odds are that those few are fibbing? The point is, it makes no sense to purchase bits that make you do something you don't enjoy. Invest in carbide. It will last a long time, and your sanding time will happily diminish.

Buy Quality Bits

Now that you're buying carbide, you should look for quality bits. But how do you determine quality? My personal measuring stick has been to use the brands that manufacturers use in industrial applications. Production router bits must get the best cut for the longest period of time and at the least expense. Since routers were used first in Europe extensively before they made the trip overseas, industrial bits made in and near Europe have proved their worth.

There are also North American companies that have been making great router bits for decades. But finding out which manufacturers make qual-

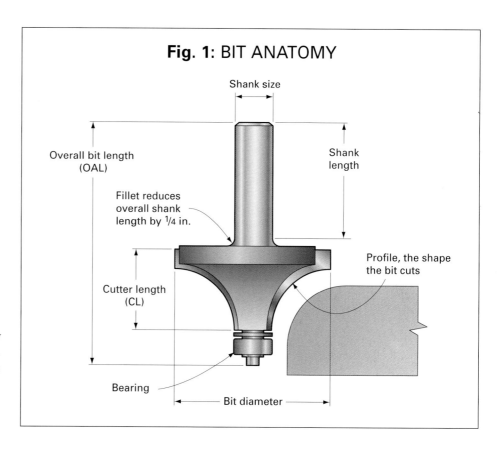

Fig. 1: BIT ANATOMY

Shank size

Overall bit length (OAL)

Shank length

Fillet reduces overall shank length by 1/4 in.

Profile, the shape the bit cuts

Cutter length (CL)

Bearing

Bit diameter

ity cutters takes a bit more sleuthing. The first clue is that the company also makes saw blades, shaper bits, and other boring or sawing cutters. The second clue is that they've been in business for at least 20 years. Be careful, though, because some manufacturers also make a secondary line of router bits they sell through building centers, and the quality of these bits is not the same.

With a little investigative work on the Internet, you can find out a company's customers. If you discover that furniture-making companies are buying the cutters you're researching, you can be sure these are quality bits. Failing that, ask professional shops where they buy. Another approach (and one that's lots of fun) is to ask questions at various woodworking forums on the Internet. Be warned: You'll get lots of opinions, so qualify your queries by asking

whose bits the opinion-giver actually uses, as opposed to what they've heard.

Router bits catalogs are another source for information on router bits. Many catalogs are masterpieces of information and can become your router bit textbooks. There are dozens available, because there are numerous brands of bits on the market. Collect as many catalogs as you can, and compare information. Acquire them by searching the Internet, visiting woodworking stores, or calling manufacturers' toll-free numbers. Not only will you find a wide selection of bits available, you'll also discover how bits are manufactured, why some are painted, and what grade carbide is used and why. Some catalogs even suggest uses for their bits, helping you to find the right bit for the job.

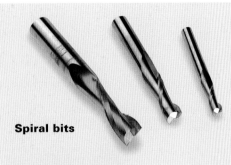

Spiral bits

Dovetail bits, including a piloted bit for a commerical dovetail jig

Rabbeting bit set

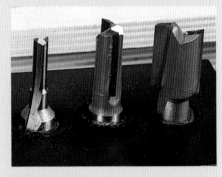

Dado bit set

A Good Starter Set

The following list of specific bits will get you up to speed for joinery work quickly and efficiently.

- ⅛ in. two-flute, down-cutting spiral bit with ¼ in. shank or ⅛ in. two-flute, left-hand end mill (requires collet adapter)

- ¼ in. two-flute, up-cutting spiral bit with ¼ in. shank or ¼ in. two-flute, right-hand end mill

- ⅜ in. two-flute, up-cutting spiral bit with ½ in. shank or ⅜ in. two-flute right-hand end mill

- ½ in. two-flute flush-trimming bit with ½ in. shank or ¾ in. two-flute flush-trimming bit with negative shear angle and ½ in. shank

- ½ in. pattern bit with short cutter length and ¼ in. shank or ½ in. two-flute flush-trimming bit with negative shear angle, ¼ in. shank, ½ in. bearing, and stop collar

- ½ in. 14° dovetail bit with ¼ in. shank

- ³⁄₁₆ in. or ¼ in. roundover bit with bearing and ½ in. shank

- 45° chamfering bit with bearing and ½ in. shank

- ¾ in. mortising bit with short cutter length and ½ in. shank or ¾ in. two-flute straight bit with negative shear angle and ½ in. shank

- Dado bit set for plywood with ½ in. shanks

- Rabbeting bit set with ½ in. shank and various bearings

- Slot cutter bit set with ½ in. shank and various bearings

Mortising, or hinge, bit

Flush-trimming bit (above) and **pattern bit** (below)

Roundover bit (left) and **chamfer bit** (right)

Slot cutter bit set

Most importantly, all router bit catalogs list the overall length of the bit (OAL), along with its cutter length (CL), shank diameter, and cutter diameter. (See fig. 1.) Many show you a bit's profile and the resulting cut, often at full or actual size. This is key information for making an informed purchase.

Once you've educated yourself about bits and narrowed your focus to a particular type of bit and its vital statistics, check your catalogs yet again. The prices listed will quickly instruct you as to who the major players are. Be aware that the highest price doesn't always reflect the best quality. There are many quality brands, at various price points. Read a lot. Experiment a little.

Bigger is better. When it comes to shank diameter, it's best to choose ½ in. over ¼ in. shank bits.

Shop for Shank Diameter

The shank of a router bit plays an important role, as it is the part held securely in the router. In almost all cases, it's wise to choose a bit with a shank diameter of ½ in. over ¼ in. (See top photo, right.) Sometimes you won't have this option (certain styles of bits, such as specific types of dovetail bits, are only made with small-diameter shanks), but whenever you can, buy bits with ½ in. shanks. There are several compelling reasons why.

First, the shank circumference of a ½ in. bit presents four times the gripping surface as a ¼ in. bit, so it's more likely to stay where you put it. In addition, when you consider that router motors produce heat, you'll realize that a thicker shank has more mass to absorb and dissipate it before it reaches the cutting edge. While friction from cutting alone produces its own heat, excess heat only helps to dull sharp edges.

Another point to consider is vibration. Router motors invariably make lots of it. The larger mass of a big shank smoothes out vibration, which translates into a smoother cut and, again, less sanding. (Still no raised hands for sanding lovers?)

Last, a heavier shank is less likely to deflect under cutting forces. Deflection is caused by a combination of high rpms and the stress a cutter undergoes as it meets wood. Deflection produces an inferior cut, requiring more post-routing work to finish the surface. You guessed it: More sanding again.

The good news is that ½ in. bits generally cost the same as ¼ in. bits with the same profile. Even if on occasion you have to cough up a little more cash for certain bits, you'll still be reimbursed with bonus time on your hands by avoiding all that tedious sanding.

Cutter and Shank Length Count

The length of a router bit's shank is an important factor, as well as its cutting length. Both should be considered before plunking down your cash.

Many of us think that longer bits with longer cutting profiles are the way to go. But long cutting lengths aren't always preferable to short ones. Sometimes a longer profile is unnecessary, and is simply wasteful. But worse is a long cutter that fouls up a jig design and compromises effective routing action. A bit's cutting length should reflect the thickness of a jig or other material being used, and generally, shorter is better. Long cutters force you to use thicker jig materials, which in turn makes your jigs heavy, bulky, and awkward to use. The best approach is to tailor the length of a bit to a specific jig or routing procedure, which lets you cut joints in the most efficient and successful manner possible.

Shank length is another key aspect. Always make sure the shank of every bit you use is long enough to completely fill your router's collet. You might be surprised at how short some shanks are, especially with ¼ in. bits designed for the shorter collets of trim routers. Above all, never pull a bit partially out of the collet to create a longer cutting edge or to reach the workpiece. The reason is simple: Reduced contact on the collet means reduced holding power, and a loose bit can spell disaster—a major safety concern, not just for you, but for your work as well. Another important safety item is to check that the shank of the bit and every part of your router's collet, including its socket and the collet nut, are pristine clean.

It's easy to calculate whether a bit will fit safely in your router by factoring its shank length and the length of your collet. Unfortunately, shank length is the one criterion tool catalogs don't list. You'll have to do the math yourself, which thankfully is a simple affair. To calculate a bit's effective shank length from a catalog, find its overall length, then subtract its cutter length plus another ¼ in. (to account for the fillet between the shank and the cutter). Now measure your collet length, add ⅛ in., and you're left with the minimum shank length you can safely install in your router. Write this number on the front of your favorite router bit catalog in big, bold letters. It's a good number to have close at hand.

Types of Bits You'll Need

In my shop, router bits fall into two categories: bits used for joinery and bits for decorative work. A basic starter collection of joinery bits is listed on page 16. Save your money for decorative bits when a special project calls for them.

While there are many types of bits to consider, the one I recommend avoiding is the multi-purpose bit. These bits are difficult to set up, and it's nearly impossible to repeat the same setup the next time you use them. Also, I generally pass on bits sold in sets, as they usually have only one or two truly useful bits. The remaining bits in the set are probably slow movers when sold individually, and you'll use them seldom—if at all. However, some sets are worth seeking, as I'll describe.

Some of the most-used bits in my shop are spiral bits, a special type of straight bit with cutting edges that wrap in a spiral fashion. Spiral bits cut with a shearing action, much like a skewed hand plane does as you angle it to the grain of a board. The result of these twisting cutting flutes is a cleaner, smoother cut that's easier on the router motor, especially when cuts get really heavy or deep.

Standard straight bits are more common fare in most shops, but they don't leave a particularly smooth cut. However, some straight bits have flutes with a negative shear angle, and can rival the smooth cut of a spiral bit. I especially like this style for flush-trimming bits. Not every manufacturer carries them, but they're worth looking for.

End mills are spiral cutters with two to six cutting flutes, and they're worth getting in addition to other types of straight bits. One compelling reason is they're about 30 percent less expensive than regular router bits. They have only minor differences in cutter geometry, and produce a very acceptable cut. Be sure to purchase end mills with only two flutes, as more flutes don't leave enough room for waste removal in deep cuts. The important thing to know about end mills is that their shank size equals the cutter's diameter. Since a bit's shank must match the router's collet, this fact limits the variety of end mills you can install in your router. However, you can save money by buying ⅛ in. end mills and installing a collet adapter into your router's collet. In the same vein, I buy a ⅜ in. collet for my favorite ⅜ in. end mill mortising bit.

There are a few router bit sets that are very useful. Dado sets are one, and come with bottom-cutting flutes (as well as side-cutting) that rout super clean dadoes in plywood. These special bits are slightly undersized in diameter and produce narrower dadoes for matching the nominal thicknesses of plywood and other sheet goods. You can even buy dado cutters that are slightly oversized for thicker materials, such as some of the plastic-coated sheet material used in kitchen and bath cabinets.

A rabbeting bit set is also handy to have, and comes with a single cutter and a variety of different size bearings. This setup lets you mill rabbets in various widths, all with one cutter. These sets are worth the money, since it's like getting several bits for the price of one.

Like a rabbet set, slot cutter sets also come with a variety of bearings, letting you rout slots in varying depths.

In addition, some (more expensive) sets come with an assortment of thick and thin cutters as well as multiple bearings for milling slots of different thickness.

Take Good Care of Your Bits

Once you get the knack for buying good bits, you'll soon find your collection totals a sum far greater than the cost of your router. To give you an idea of how much, my own personal bit collection is worth about 10 times the cost of one of my routers—and we're talking about common bits used for joinery. Specialty bits can be much more costly.

The fact that your bit collection is valuable makes it worthwhile to handle and store bits in a safe manner. More bits are destroyed by improper handling than those that simply get dull. One of the best approaches is to keep your bits in a box when you're not using them—but not in an ordinary box. Make a box with a bottom that's 1½ in. thick, and into it drill a series of holes in the diameters that fit the shanks of your bits. Or buy plastic bit holders and fit them in your router box. Make sure to space your holes carefully so cutting edges can't touch each other, to prevent the brittle carbide from chipping. (See top photo, right.)

Another storage system that has worked well for me is a capped, plastic container with a shop-made plywood insert. I use the container to take bits safely to jobs outside the shop. (See photo, right.) To keep bits from clunking into each other or falling out when the container gets tipped over (it will, trust me), twist a cotton cloth into a "rope," curl it around the bits, and snap on the lid.

Bit box. The author's bit box incorporates a router cradle on top (see page 51) with two drawers below for storing bits and accessories.

A third strategy is to make plywood shelves from 1½ in. thick panels glued to ¼ in. bottoms and fit them under your bench, or in any accessible area of your shop. Make the shelves so they pull out completely for easy access, and like the bit box, drill a series of holes in them for your bits. It's an effective and inexpensive solution for safe bit storage. (See photo, page 20.)

Don't overlook cabinets as valuable storage space for bits. Like my woodworking friend who made a special cabinet for his bits, I use the Router Bit Cabinet in this book (see page 150) for storing the larger bits in my arsenal.

Bits to go. Take your collection on the road by storing bits in holes drilled into a plywood disc that fits inside a plastic container.

Bit shelves under the bench. Keep bits right at your bench by building a set of pull-out shelves. A thin plywood bottom extends beyond each shelf and slides into ¼ in. grooves cut in the case.

Once you've organized your bit collection, it's important to handle your bits safely. For example, when a bit is in the router and you're occupied with setting up the next operation, it's always best to stand the router on its top. This keeps the bit standing straight up in the air, away from potential harm such as wayward tools and other hard objects. Laying the router on its side allows stuff to be pushed accidentally into the bit, which risks chipping. And, frankly, a sideways-parked bit puts you at risk for self-inflicted surgery to arms and hands.

Sharpen or Not?

Many woodworkers wonder whether it makes sense to have router bits sharpened, or whether it's feasible to sharpen bits themselves. The short answer is a qualified no. Let's consider the facts.

Since I advocate carbide over steel, it's important to realize that this brittle and extremely hard material can't be tackled with most home-shop sharpening tools. Trying to sharpen carbide yourself will only result in frustration—and the same dull bit you started with. While there are inexpensive diamond-impregnated honing devices that do a decent job of touching up a worn carbide edge, don't expect them to truly sharpen your bits. Besides, most bits can't be sharpened without adversely affecting their geometry. Flush-trimming bits are a good example, since even a slight change in their cutting diameter, which occurs during the grinding of a worn edge, creates a cutting edge that doesn't match the bearing diameter of the bit. The result is a bit that won't cut flush, and leaves a little smidgen of uncut material right where you don't want it. Angled bits, such as dovetail bits, also change dimension with sharpening, and will no longer work with their respective dovetail jigs. Regular straight bits suffer from diminished diameters, too, and make simple joinery impractical. While spiral bits can be sharpened, their particular geometry makes it an economical nightmare, and the cost would most likely far exceed the bit's value.

One exception is bits used expressly for decorative purposes. These types of bits can be sharpened and resharpened without complicating their subsequent use. However, the chances are these bits won't get near the use and wear as your joinery bits, and with proper storage they'll last years before they need sharpening.

When you're ready to have a bit sharpened, the trick is to find someone with the necessary skills to do the job correctly. In my experience, the folks who sharpen your scissors and knives know precious little about sharpening router bits. Saw blade sharpening services are a step in the right direction, and many offer router bit sharpening. But all too often I've found that a less-than-skilled individual believes the necessary skill is to be found in his sharpening machine—not in himself. If you're lucky enough to find a local sharpening shop that specializes in sharpening, look for a talented individual who takes pride in his work. He might do wonders with your bits. Another option is to ask about sharpeners in one of the woodworking forums on the Internet or at your local woodworking guild—both are vast reservoirs of knowledge. When you do manage to find a reliable sharpening service, remember to proceed with caution—and only with your decorative bits.

Trash Damaged Bits

If you chip a bit, consider it ready for the trash, and dispose of it accordingly. A chipped bit can't be sharpened to yield the same cut as it did when new, and will leave tell-tale ridges in your work. Additionally, chipped bits can become dangerous, unbalanced chunks of metal, especially when chipping is severe. Spinning an unbalanced bit at speeds as high as 23,000 rpm—typical of router motors—puts great stress on the bearings of the router, not to mention the risk to yourself. It's best to toss damaged bits, and replace them with new ones.

The Router Toolbox

There are several essential tools and accessories you'll need for routing beautiful joints. All are hand tools or jigs of one sort or another. Many are standard woodworking items, such as chisels or squares. Some you may not be familiar with; some you can make yourself. All of them can be acquired over time, as you need them.

The first of these is the tool that holds all the other tools; namely, a portable toolbox. I own a dedicated box for all my routing tools, and I transport it wherever I'm working in the shop. Inside are all the little jigs, props, and tools I need for any type of routing work—all in one spot and right at my fingertips. While I'm routing (and making clouds of fine and annoying dust) I simply close the lid to keep the contents clean, and set the box nearby.

I've found that the handiest size box is around 18 to 20 in. long, which is big enough for all your tool needs. Look for a separate bin at the top of the box, so you can sort smaller tools from the larger ones that go in the bottom of the box. Avoid toolboxes with plastic latches—unless you enjoy picking tools up off the floor. Latches with regular metal buckles work best and are reliable.

The tools inside my toolbox are described on the following pages, arranged alphabetically. I've included the reasons why you should consider each for your kit. Most are inexpensive; some you may already have. Use the list as a reference for adding to your collection, especially if you're just starting out.

Sources for these tools include hardware stores, woodworking stores, discount/import tool stores, home centers, auto-supply stores, office supply stores, and even welding-supply stores. Don't forget to check woodworking catalogs and the Internet.

Auger File

An auger file used to be the tool of choice for sharpening auger drill bits. Today the auger bit has been replaced for the most part by brad-point drill bits. Happily, an auger file is the perfect tool to touch up brad points and keep them sharp. This special file comes with "safe" (non-cutting) edges, allowing you to file right up to adjacent surfaces without damaging them. Another useful application for an auger file is when squaring a combination square, since its slim profile lets you get into the narrow groove on the square's head. (See Squaring a Square, page 25.)

Bearings for Bits

My favorite guide for my router is the ball bearing on a piloted router bit. Eventually, you'll want to acquire more bearings in addition to the ones that came with your bits. Use them in conjunction with stop collars (see Stop Collars, page 31) for adding to router bit shanks to customize your bits for guided, or piloted, work.

It's best to shop for bearings from router bit manufacturers, since they'll come shielded and designed for high-speed applications. Before you use a bit with a bearing, spin the bearing by hand. If it feels even slightly rough, replace it immediately. It's amazing how fast they can fly apart, ruining your cut. (You were wearing your safety glasses, weren't you?)

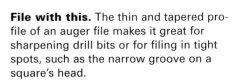

File with this. The thin and tapered profile of an auger file makes it great for sharpening drill bits or for filing in tight spots, such as the narrow groove on a square's head.

Bit Cleaner

It's important to keep your router bits clean, because dirty bits cut just like dull bits do: badly. The best approach for cleaning bits is to grab a bottle of bit cleaner. I used to regard this stuff as too expensive and ineffective. Then I learned that the oven cleaner I had been using was detrimental to the carbide on my expensive bits and blades, and besides, oven cleaner is noxious stuff to use in the first place. In contrast, bit cleaner is environmentally safe, extremely effective, and pleasant to use. A small bottle lasts a long time. I found mine in the bit manufacturer's catalog and have seen many brands at woodworking stores.

Bit Gauge

I use this handy positioning jig to accurately set the bit height or its distance from the fence. The Incra gauge shown here is my favorite, but there are several positioning devices on the market that work in similar fashion. I like the fact that my gauge is plastic, which means it can't harm the fragile carbide on my bits. One of the appealing attributes of a bit gauge is its positional settings in 32nds of an inch. This lets you make accurate,

Get your bearings. Keep an assortment of router bearings and stop collars on hand and secure them to your bits for custom cuts.

repeatable setups and cuts. Thankfully, these plastic gauges are so inexpensive that I couldn't justify the time it would take to make a similar gauge from wood.

Box Wrenches

Stackable router bits, like reversible cope-and-stick bits, slot cutters, and other specialty bits, often use a hex nut at the end of their shafts to secure the cutters. The best way to remove these nuts is with a box wrench, which has a closed jaw that won't slip and possibly damage the cutting edge. A set consisting of ⅜, ⁷⁄₁₆, ½, and ¾ in. will let you tackle most bits. For more versatility, I use a set of combination wrenches, which have a box end at one end and open jaws on the opposite end for reaching the odd, hard-to-get nut.

Brass and Nylon Brushes

These small brushes are perfect for cleaning the metal parts on routers and router bits. Their relatively soft bristles won't harm router components, carbide, or registration surfaces. First use bit cleaner on the item you want to clean (see Bit Cleaner, opposite page), let the dirty part soak for a few minutes, and then scrub it with a brass or nylon brush for quick, effective cleaning. Wipe off the dissolved dirt with a clean cloth and you're back in business.

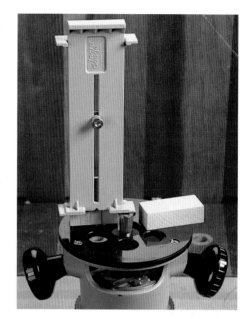

Setting bits. A commercial bit gauge and a small hardwood block make setting bit heights and depths reliable and accurate.

Wrench combo. A wide variety of wrenches and hex keys come in handy for loosening and tightening all sorts of router gear.

Butcher Knife

Every kitchen has old butcher knives no longer in everyday use. Put one in your toolbox to use as a cutting wedge to release work that's been held together with hot glue. (See The Secret of Hot Glue, page 65.) Make a scabbard to protect yourself from the sharp edge.

Calculator

Dividing and multiplying numbers, especially fractions, doesn't come easily to many of us. An electronic calculator is the answer. My favorite type can handle fractions and is solar powered. Be sure to let it out of your toolbox from time to time to catch some rays, which keeps it charged and ready to go.

Chisel

A sharp ½ in. bench chisel is handy for all sorts of shop work. It's particularly useful hanging out in your toolbox, ready for rounding the corners of square tenons, squaring the rounded end of a routed rabbet, or

Cleaning tools. Remove dirt, rust, pitch, and keep your bits, collets, and other metal accessories clean by using spray-on bit cleaner, brass and nylon brushes, fine-grit sandpaper, and paste wax.

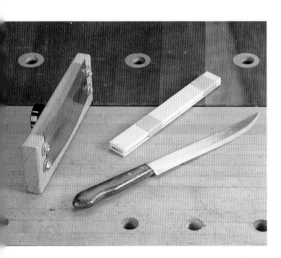

Removing glue. An old butcher's knife lets you separate parts held with hot glue and a scraper (held in a bowed position in a shop-made block) removes leftover residue.

for other small fitting cuts. I keep mine in a separate bin at the top of my toolbox where it lives safe and sharp.

Clamps

The old adage "Ain't no such thing as too many clamps" is remarkably true, especially when it comes to working with the router. C-clamps, quick-action clamps, wooden handscrews, and other small clamps do a good job of grasping and positioning fences, securing hold downs, and temporarily fastening workpieces. The handiest are the one-handed variety, which I use extensively for routing operations.

In addition to the one-handed clamp, handscrews are particularly useful, and come in a variety of jaw lengths. I use the smaller variety to fine-tune bit height when using my horizontal router table setup (see page 40), as well as for other setup tasks. These sometimes confounding wooden clamps feature jaws that quickly move into unparalleled alignment—especially when you don't want them to! While moving the jaws out of parallel is handy for grasping tapered work, the secret to keeping the jaws parallel or at a steady angle is simple. First, position the jaws in the plane you want (tapered or parallel to each other), then grab the handle closest to the clamping end with one hand and, while keeping that hand stationary, rotate the other handle around the stationary hand. It may sounds complex, but your hands will quickly get the knack.

Combination Square

This is a specific type of square with a ruled blade and a sliding head. A knurled brass nut loosens the blade and allows you to slide it to an exact dimension in relation to the head. This feature lets you take measurements directly from the work, or you can lay out and mark work without reaching for a tape measure or ruler. The most useful are 6 and 12 in. models, where the number refers to the length of the blade.

Take heart: you don't have to spend a fortune on a decent combination square. I buy inexpensive squares from discount/import tool stores, well aware that they don't come particularly square, then I square them myself back at the shop. (See Squaring a Square, right.)

Craft Knife

When marking has to be absolutely precise, nothing beats a knife. I find the blade on a penknife is generally too thick, while the razor-thin and pointed blade on a craft knife is super sharp and replaceable. If you lose the cap, poke the blade into a dry wine cork when storing it in your toolbox.

Squaring a Square

Squares are often the most "assumed" tool in the shop. We assume them to be square, and often they're not, even when purchased new. Yet there is no more vital tool in the shop than a reliable square. Some years ago a timber framer showed me how to square a combination square, and I've never looked back. The process is simple and requires few tools, as shown in the drawing. Once you have a truly square square, you can use it to check all the other squares in your shop.

Step 1: Determine the Problem

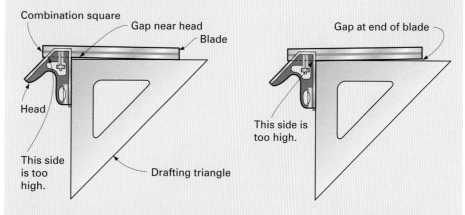

Combination square — Gap near head — Blade — Gap at end of blade — Head — This side is too high. — Drafting triangle — This side is too high.

Step 2: Remove the Blade and File the Head

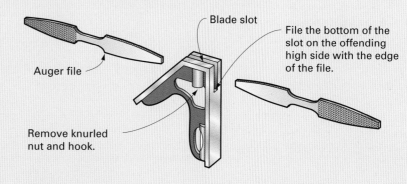

Auger file — Blade slot — File the bottom of the slot on the offending high side with the edge of the file. — Remove knurled nut and hook.

Step 3: Test the Square

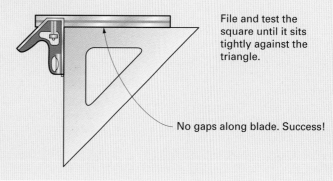

File and test the square until it sits tightly against the triangle. — No gaps along blade. Success!

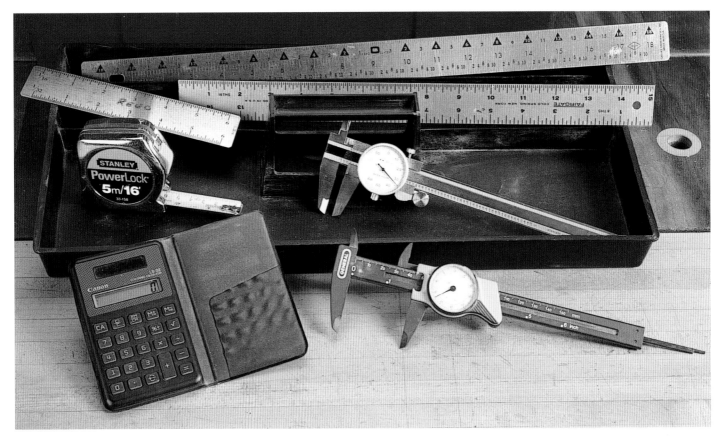

Measure with accuracy. Important measuring tools include a calculator, a tape measure, 6 and 12 in. steel rules, a centering rule, and metal and plastic dial calipers.

Dial Calipers

There are two types of dial calipers I use on a regular basis to take all sorts of precise measurements. One is made from a durable plastic and has fractional and metric markings. However, the one I use most for routing is a machinist's dial caliper, which measures in thousandths of an inch. It's an indispensable device for tuning and setting up tools, or for measuring stock when making fine adjustments. The internal jaws measure inside areas, such mortise lengths. The external jaws measure outside work, such as router bit shank diameters or the thickness of tenons. A bar at the end of the tool extends to measure depth, such as the depth of mortises or other holes. (See fig. 2.) A machinist's dial caliper

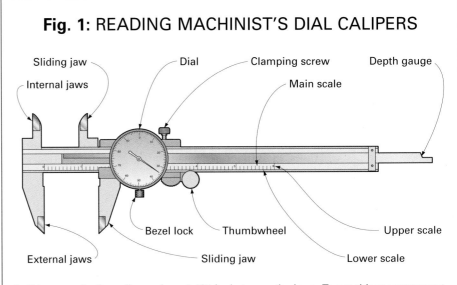

Fig. 1: READING MACHINIST'S DIAL CALIPERS

Sliding jaw — Dial — Clamping screw — Depth gauge

Internal jaws — Main scale

Bezel lock — Thumbwheel — Upper scale

External jaws — Sliding jaw — Lower scale

In this example, the calipers show 1.434 in. between the jaws. To get this measurement, start by reading the number on the upper main scale, which is the digit in front of the decimal point. Now read the number on the lower main scale to get the first number after the decimal point. Finally, read the dial to get the last two numbers.

Square and miter. Combination squares let you check for square as well as measure lengths. A large drafting triangle and an adjustable triangle allow you to measure and set up fixed or intermediate angles.

doesn't have to be expensive, and a 6 in. model is the most useful in the shop. I get mine at discount/importer tool stores.

Dial calipers take a little getting used to. The trick is to learn how to use them, and how to read them. You can rotate the thumbwheel to open or close the sliding jaws for measuring inside or outside areas. This action simultaneously extends the depth gauge, which lets you measure into holes by inserting the gauge into the crevice while keeping the end of the tool on the work surface.

Measurements are expressed in decimals to three places, or in thousandths of an inch. Once you've taken a reading for a particular setup with the calipers, you use a gauge, such as playing cards (see Playing Cards, page 29) or a feeler gauge (see Feeler Gauge, this page), to correct

the setting. This process is precise and allows you to fine-tune your setups very accurately with little chance of mistakes. You'll see plenty of setups in the book showing where to use this method of measuring.

Drafting Triangle

A trip to the office- or art-supply store will yield plastic drafting triangles—highly accurate and very inexpensive tools for joinery work. I recommend getting two, a large 45°/45°/90° triangle (or a 30°/60°/90° triangle) and an 8 in. adjustable triangle. You'll wonder how you ever got along without them.

Use the 90°/45°/45° triangle to square squares, set saw blades square or to a perfect 45° angle, check for perpendicular layout, confirm the position of jigs, or any of the gazillion things that need squaring or

mitering in the shop. A triangle with 30° and 60° angles will increase your measuring abilities. The adjustable triangle helps you determine those elusive 22½° angles needed for octagons, as well as other finite angles.

Feeler Gauge

Sometimes called a blade gauge, this measuring tool consists of a set of super-thin metal fingers in graduated thicknesses. Individual fingers or pairs of fingers can be used to measure very fine settings and adjustments on jigs, such as when making dovetails and box joints. Like hex keys, feeler gauges are available in folding sets. The most useful for routing is a 26-blade set that starts at an incredibly thin 0.0015 in. and goes to 0.025 in. thick. You'll find them at auto parts stores.

Glue Gun

A glue gun and a supply of hot-glue sticks are just the ticket for quickly mounting work to jigs and other fixtures (see The Secret of Hot Glue, page 65).

Glue and slice. A ½ in. chisel is handy for all sorts of quick paring jobs; protect the sharp edge with a chisel guard. A hot glue gun is great for temporarily tacking work together.

Hex Keys

When I was a kid, these were called Allen wrenches, but today most suppliers call them hex keys for their six-sided shape. Hex keys are useful for all sorts of fastening jobs that involve hex screws or bolts. The set screws in stop collars (see page 31) and the cap screws in piloted router bits can only be adjusted with hex keys, and often these screws are metric. Common sizes to get are 1.5 mm, 2.5 mm, 3 mm, and 3⁄32 in.— tiny ones to be sure. Because of these small sizes, I prefer to buy folding sets rather than individual keys. The sets are compact, provide plenty of leverage for each key, and there's a bonus: your smallest keys are neatly contained, where you'll never lose them. This is another item found at the auto parts store.

Inlay Kit

An inlay kit is similar to template guide bushings (see page 32) and consists of a guide that screws into the center hole of a router's baseplate for inlay work. A removeable bushing grips the collar of the guide when routing the mortise for the inlay. You then remove the bushing to rout the inlay. Some inlay kits are made of brass, which won't harm the 1⁄8 in. steel or carbide bit that pokes through the guide.

Paste Wax

Ordinary furniture paste wax is the best lubricant for woodworking tools in the shop. It's available everywhere—even at the grocery store—and, in addition to keeping router plunge posts, baseplates, and other paraphernalia well lubricated, you can use it to finish your projects.

Pencils

Of course, everyone knows the value of pencils for marking your work, so why mention them? I consider pencils important because good joinery is dependent on careful marking and layout, and the more accurate your mark, the better. An eraser comes in handy for revisions. Keep your pencils sharp, or try mechanical pencils with 0.5 mm thick leads that never need sharpening. Keep several on hand, ready to go. I swear they evaporate before my very eyes!

Driving and tapping. Combination screwdrivers (left) allow you to drive an assortment of screw types, while film canisters hold your specialty screws. A tap and the appropriate sized drill bit (right) let you cut threads in wood and other materials.

Permanent Markers

Buy two markers with fine tips, one in black and one in red. They're great for permanently marking information right on your jigs, and the contrasting colors make different levels of information really stand out.

Playing Cards

You probably have an ordinary deck of playing cards lying around the house. Now's the time to devote a pack to the shop. Did you know that Federal regulations require them to be 0.010 in. thick? This is a useful fact to know. After you've measured your setup or workpiece with a machinist's dial calipers (see page 26), you can divide that measurement by 10, and you'll have the number of cards you need to make up that measurement. If there's a remainder, simply add the correct thickness of feeler gauge, and then make your adjustment. One tip: If you're liberating a used deck from the house, make sure to trim the frayed edges to keep your measurements accurate.

Ring Pliers

Some router collets have a retaining ring, sometimes referred to as a snap ring, which holds the nut on the collet. To clean the collet, you'll have to remove the ring, which is where retaining ring pliers come in. There are two varieties: inside and outside pliers. You'll need external retaining ring pliers, although many auto parts stores carry combination pliers, providing you with both types in one tool.

Clever clamps. One-handed quick-clamps are great when your other hand is busy. A wooden handscrew grips securely and can be adjusted for grasping tapered work.

Gauges, punches, cards, and bushings. Template and inlay guides (left) are great for routing patterns and inlays. Transfer punches (right) help with laying out parts. A feeler gauge (right, foreground) and an ordinary deck of cards are indispensible when making ultra-fine measurements.

Router Wrenches

Several manufacturers supply decent wrenches with their routers. Others give you wrenches made from stamped steel. They're often sharp at the edges; fix them by filing them smooth when possible (some wrenches are made from heat-treated metal that's too hard for filing). Wrap the thin handles in electrical tape to give them a better grip, or slip rubber or plastic tubing over the handle. Another option is to replace a cheap wrench with a regular open-ended wrench.

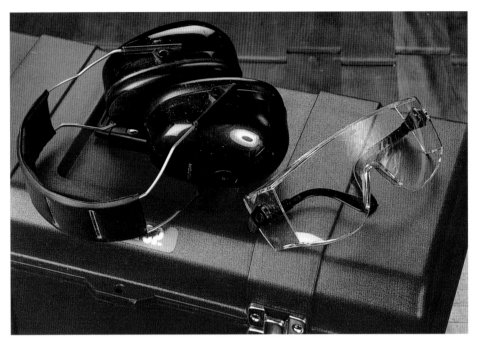

Protect your eyes and ears. High-quality, comfortable earmuffs will protect your hearing; safety glasses keep your vision intact.

Be advised that some routers use metric wrenches, and telling the difference between these and standard Imperial wrenches can be troublesome. To keep your sanity and your collection in good order, try painting all your metric wrenches with a stripe of red.

Safety Gear

Safety is paramount in routing, and safety gear should be a standard part of your toolkit. High router rpms and decibel levels present real hazards to the eyes and the ears. This makes safety glasses and ear protection a must.

Unlike some woodworkers, most metalworkers I know suffer no delusions about the threat of flying objects to their eyes, which is why you should shop at a welding-supply store for a variety of great safety glasses in many styles and fits. They'll work equally well for woodworking.

Your ears are as precious as your eyes, making hearing protection just as important. Consider that routers are one of the loudest tools in the workshop, then add the fact that many of us keep our heads up close to watch bit action, and it's clear that you'll need serious ear protection. I suggest you shop for hearing muffs that have the highest decibel rating. Check with a gun shop for some of the highest-rated muffs.

Take the time to find comfortable gear. Like you, I can offer an endless stream of excuses for not wearing uncomfortable safety glasses and hearing muffs, but I quickly don the necessary gear when it fits well.

Sandpaper

Most of us keep an assortment of sandpaper in the shop. For router work, be sure to keep some 600-grit, silicon-carbide sandpaper on hand, also known as wet/dry sandpaper.

Use it to control the fine rust that may form on unused collets, especially if you live in a humid climate. Cut a sheet into quarters, fold the quarter into thirds, and rub lightly to remove surface rust without affecting the fit.

Scraper

A scraper is an important tool for many woodworking applications, but the reason it's in the toolbox is for removing hot glue residue. Make or buy a holder for it to make it easier to use.

Screwdrivers

I keep two combination screwdriver sets in my toolbox. I like combination screwdrivers because they're compact and offer multiple sizes in one package. The first set has Phillips-head drivers, and the second has Torx, or star, drivers. Both types are good to have on hand.

My Phillips drivers get the most use. Even though my particular set comes with straight blades for standard slot-

Fine marks. Use a mechanical pencil or a craft knife for accurate lines on your work. Red and black permanent markers let you label your tools and jigs clearly and legibly.

THE ROUTER TOOLBOX **31**

ted screws, I almost never use them. It's too easy to slip on a slotted screw's head, ruining the screw as well as the driver. Instead, I customarily replace all slotted screws with Phillips screws. The reason is simple: Phillips screws provide a more positive purchase. While many of my students initially hate Phillips screws, citing slippage and difficulty in driving them, the truth is that they're guilty of using the wrong size driver. If you experiment, you'll find that often a smaller driver works better than the big one in your hand. For example, a #6 or #8 Phillips screw requires a #2 driver. Smaller screws, such as a #5 or #4, work best with a #1 driver.

The star driver is a necessary "evil" because manufacturers have recently been using star screws on their baseplates and in other areas on their routers and accessories. A star screw is similar to a Phillips screw, except it has additional edges against which a screwdriver can bite. This makes them even easier to drive. However, while star screws may be superior in design, I confess that I replace them regularly with Phillips screws, purely in an effort to keep continuity in my shop. Be warned: Don't try to remove a star screw with a Phillips driver, or it will bugger the head.

Small Hardwood Block

Make a ¾ x 1 x 2 in. maple or birch block and keep it on hand for all sorts of setup checks. Use the block to gauge router bit heights, so you can see directly how much material you're about to remove. Another method is use

Pliers for routers. A pair of external retaining ring pliers is just the ticket for removing the ring on your router's collet to allow for easy cleaning.

the block as an aid when bringing a bit flush with a work surface or to a piece of hardware.

Soft Hammer

There are certainly many ways to make adjustments, but let's face it, every so often we reach for a hammer to get the job done. Better than a standard carpenter's metal hammer is a soft hammer, which is any hammer that has a soft face on its head. I especially like small, plastic deadblows. Surprisingly, a deadblow can deliver small, positive taps. It's my adjustment tool of choice when I need focused force without fear of damage to the part I'm hitting.

Special Screws

Like sandpaper, you're sure to have screws in the shop. But routers require special screws for mounting jigs and other accessories to their bases. Shop for Phillips flat-head machine screws, in the unplated variety. Avoid plated screws; the plating peels off and they rust. I keep several lengths of machine screws in 35-mm film canisters, including metric varieties. Make sure to buy them in extra long lengths so you can fasten jigs that require longer mounting screws. I wrap red tape around my metric screw canisters. Know why? The color matches the red marks on my metric router wrenches.

Steel Rules

There are three rules I find handiest. The first is the shirt-pocket variety that's 6 in. long and measures in 64ths of an inch. Of course, I need a magnifying glass to read the darn thing, but it's very precise. The second rule is 12 in. long and measures in 16ths of an inch. The third rule is a centering rule. This last one I could not do without. Marking stock often requires you to find the center, and a centering rule makes it a snap to find. The best kind of rulers have measurements marked from the very ends of the rule, with no dead space. This feature allows you to butt the rule directly against a part for an exact reading.

Stop Collars

Stop collars are just the ticket for keeping a bearing on the shank of small-diameter bits for piloted work. Keep in mind that sometimes you'll need to position a bit and its collar adjacent to the edge of a jig that the bearing is following. If the set screw in the collar is too long, it will gouge or destroy the surface of the jig. When necessary, replace the screws in your stop collars with shorter set screws from your local hardware store.

Tools of persuasion. An ordinary claw hammer is useful in the shop, and a plastic deadblow is even better when you need a forceful blow that won't mar your work.

Tape Measure

Here's a tool many of us take for granted. Check yours. It may be ready for retirement if the hooked tip is bent, the markings are rubbed off the edges, or it sports kinks in the tape. I use a tape measure for stock preparation, and consider it a rough measurement tool compared to my metal rules. But it's an indispensable tool that needs to be as accurate as possible.

Taps

You'll need a ¼-20 tap for cutting threads in wood and plastic for some of the jigs in the book, plus a #7 drill bit to drill the necessary clearance holes for the tap. Although taps are designed for threading metal, you'll find they work great in hard or dense materials like hardwoods and plastics. You can buy taps as a set, with

the appropriate drill bit matched to a specific tap. It doesn't hurt to keep a selection of different taps on hand for other general tapping jobs in the woodshop.

Template Guide Bushings

These circular metal guides are available in different diameters and fasten to your router's baseplate. Used in conjunction with a straight bit, they follow shop-made templates, or patterns, for duplicating parts. I hesitate to add these to the tool list because I prefer using bearing-guided router bits to achieve the same results with fewer headaches. Using template guide bushings require that you calculate the necessary offset between the bushing and the bit that fits inside it. This is a lot more complex than the direct reading you get from

the bearing on a router bit that matches the bit's profile.

While my template guides have migrated from my router toolbox to the back of the tool drawer, the common dovetail jig still requires them. Usually the jig includes the necessary bushing, but you'll have to acquire these accessories if your dovetail jig is missing one or your bushing is worn out or abused. Although you can certainly buy an entire kit, I suggest getting only the bushing you need. Be aware that some router manufacturers have a proprietary system and require that you use their specific template guides. However, adapters are available that let you use inexpensive, more easily available guides in a wider variety of sizes. If you do use these guides, one manufacturer offers a centering cone, an accessory that helps you align the guide accurately to the center of your router's collet.

Transfer Punches

It was a memorable day when a retired machinist introduced me to transfer punches. You'll find numerous references to them in the book. Transfer punches are most commonly used for finding the center of an existing hole to transfer to another surface, such as when locating holes for screws. I find them indispensable in jig making, and you will, too. These punches have pointed ends, and are about 5 in. long. You can buy them in sets graduating in 64ths from ³⁄₃₂ to ½ in. You'll find them at the discount/import tool store or from machinist's suppliers.

Jiggery

*J*iggery is a term coined just for this book. I use it to describe the art of designing and using jigs and fixtures. This is an important aspect of router work because, for the most part, there isn't a built-in guide system in a router. Therefore, learning to build and use jigs is essential for successful and easy routing. There are many types of jigs, each allowing you to execute specific cuts with your router. For example, a dovetail jig guides a dovetail bit in a predetermined path, so you can rout dovetails that fit precisely. Another type of jig is the router table, which allows you to rout pieces too small to handle with a hand-held router. There are many more. You'll find them in this chapter, and you'll see them used throughout the book. Some you can build quickly, some require more effort to make. Some are available as commercial kits or as complete jigs you can buy.

The premise of jigs is to confine the travel and path of the router without the possibility of screwing up. A tall order? Not really. Good jigs provide repeatability, predictability, safety, and accuracy. These four attributes are worth looking for, regardless of whether you purchase a jig, build one from someone else's plans, or design and build your own.

The jigs presented here fill that order quite nicely. They've been used for a long time in my shop, have been tested by students in my classes, and have generally proven themselves to be very useful. So go ahead and take a look, make or buy those you need, and enjoy using them. They'll certainly make your router much easier to use, increase the accuracy of your joinery cuts, and make the entire routing process more fun.

Base Marker

BITS AND TOOLS

- ¼ in. drill bit
- countersink bit
- ¼ in. dowel centers, as needed
- ¼ in. straight bit
- awl
- center punch
- transfer punch, as needed
- ⁷⁄₃₂ in. socket and handle
- router with ¼ in. collet and its various bases

MATERIALS AND HARDWARE

- clear acrylic sheet, ⅜ in. thick, cut to square and equal to diameter of your router's base-plate

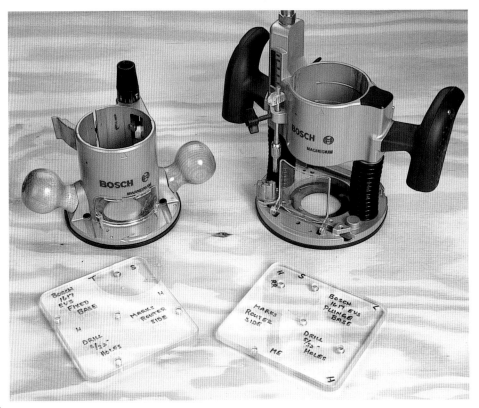

The jigs that make other jigs. These two plastic squares allow the author to quickly and accurately make and attach custom baseplates for her specific router bases.

Base Marker

This is the first jig you should make, since it helps you make every base-plate-type jig that mounts to your router's base. The base marker consists of a clear plastic plate with pointed dowel centers protruding from one side. You use it to mark the location of the bit hole and the screw holes on a jig's baseplate in order to fasten the plate to your router. This is handy, because few router bases have a symmetrical screw-hole pattern around the bit hole. The base marker lets you mount a baseplate so it's perfectly concentric with the bit for accurate cuts, and lets you orient the router to the plate so handles, switches, and the like are in the most convenient spot. If you have a lifting device on your plunge base, you can

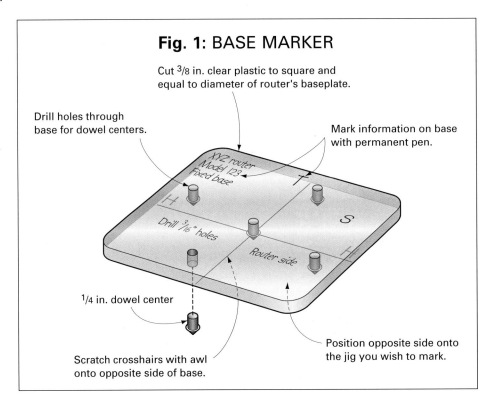

Fig. 1: BASE MARKER

Cut 3/8 in. clear plastic to square and equal to diameter of router's baseplate.

Drill holes through base for dowel centers.

Mark information on base with permanent pen.

Drill 3/16" holes

1/4 in. dowel center

Scratch crosshairs with awl onto opposite side of base.

Position opposite side onto the jig you wish to mark.

mark the location of the required adjuster hole as well.

Since router bases and baseplates differ from brand to brand—even fixed and plunge bases from the same manufacturer can be different—you'll want a base marker for every router base that you plan to use with a baseplate-type jig, such as your router table.

MAKE THE MARKER

Refer to figure 1 and cut the marker blank to size. (See Working with Plastic, page 36.) Remember to keep the router unplugged throughout this process, and leave the protective paper on the plastic until directed to remove it.

On the unprinted paper side of the plastic blank, mark a label, such as "router side." This is very important,

as it tells you which side corresponds to the router base. On the printed paper side, draw diagonals to find the center. Use a square and a sharp awl to scratch perpendicular lines into the plastic and through the center mark, as shown. Use a center punch to tap a dimple into the center, and drill a ¼ in. hole through the mark. Lightly chamfer each side of the hole using a countersink bit on the drill press.

The next step, just for insurance, is to stick small squares of masking tape next to the mounting holes on your router's baseplate and base. This ensures you know precisely which holes are mounting holes, since some routers have multiple holes for other purposes, as shown in the photo, below. Once you've marked the mounting holes, remove the baseplate and set it aside.

Clamp and punch. With the router clamped to the base marker in the correct orientation, use a transfer punch to locate the screw holes.

Insert a ¼ in. straight bit into the router and tighten it by hand. Now place the router on the "router" side of the marker blank and insert the bit into its center hole. Rotate the router until its handles are parallel with one of the blank's crosshairs, and clamp the assembly to the bench. Use a transfer punch through each hole in the router base to tap a dimple in the blank. (See photo, above.) If your router has stopped screw holes that aren't accessible from above, use a paper template instead. If you want to mark an adjuster hole location on the marker for a router-lifting device, now is the time to do it by using the template that came with the device.

Once you've marked the hole locations, unclamp the assembly, draw a circle around each dimple (tired eyes like mine appreciate this convenience), and drill a ¼ in. hole through the blank at each dimple.

Tape tells the story. Stick squares of tape on your router's baseplate and base for correct orientation of the base marker relative to handles and switches.

Working with Plastic

Acrylic sheets that you buy come covered on each face with a protective sheet of paper. One side has printing on it; the other side is usually plain. When working with plastic, always leave the paper on both sides until all the milling is done. The following procedures work with most plastics, but experimenting in scrap is always useful.

You can use the same woodworking tools that you use to cut wood to saw and shape plastic, such as saw blades, drill bits, and router bits. When cutting sheets on the table saw, use a sharp carbide-tipped blade and raise the blade so its gullets are above the work. (See photo, right.) Rabbeting and dadoing can be done on the table saw or with a router. Keep in mind that plastic sawdust is very sharp, so be sure to wear eye protection and long sleeves.

To drill acrylic, it's best to use regular HSS (high-speed steel) drill bits. For large holes, use a spade bit with sharp spurs, and drill from both sides of the stock. Regular spade bits will cause most plastics to melt and "weld" themselves to the bit. Before drilling, use a center punch or transfer punch to make a dimple at the hole location. Use the drill press for drilling—not a hand drill—and place the fresh area of a scrap board under the plastic, then

Ripping on the saw. An ordinary carbide-tipped blade works fine for sawing plastic sheets to size. Keep the protective paper on until all your machining is done.

clamp the assembly to the drill press table. If you don't back up the workpiece in this manner, you're likely to create a star-shaped fracture on the back side of the hole. Once you've drilled the hole, chamfer both sides lightly to discourage future fracturing and to aid in inserting dowel centers, steel pins, taps, and the like.

To tap a hole in plastic, drill the correct size hole and slightly chamfer both sides. I install the tap in my cordless drill, place the tap in the hole, and slowly drive it through. (See photo, left.) Once the tap exits the hole, stop and clean the plastic waste off its threads with an awl or stiff brush. Then reverse the drill and slowly back the cleaned tap out of the hole. This technique avoids drawing waste back into the hole, which quickly ruins threads.

To make edges safe and smooth, round all corners and chamfer or round over every edge. Router bits, files, and sandpaper work great for this. To make your edges look clean and professional, use a scraper to remove saw marks, then sand in successive grits from 120 through 220-grit using a sanding block. The finished edges won't be totally clear, but they'll look and feel great.

Tapping for screws. Cutting threads in plastic is easy if you install a tap in a drill and slowly rotate the cutter through the work.

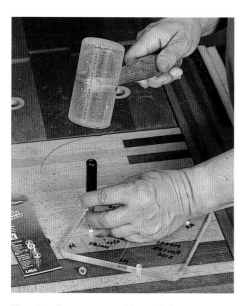

Tap in the centers. Use a ¼ in. nut driver to hold the dowel centers as you tap them into the marker.

Now peel off the sheet of printed paper (your crosshairs are on this side), stand the router on its head, and position the opposite "router" side of the blank atop the router base, aligning the holes in the blank with the holes in the router. Use a permanent pen to mark an "H" onto the marker blank at the end of each crosshair that corresponds to the router's handle locations. (Luckily, "H" is one of those letters that looks the same when viewed upside down.)

Next, peel off the paper from the "router" side of the blank and transfer the "router side" label that you previously wrote onto the plastic. Place the router and the blank next to each other on the bench, and align the router handles with their respective marks. Mark the router's switch and base or plunge lock locations onto the blank and label the make, model, and type of base of the router. In addition, measure the router's baseplate screw diameters with a dial caliper, choose the next bit size up, and mark this drilling information right on the blank.

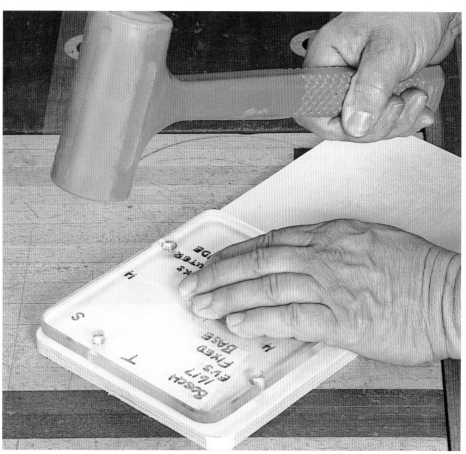

Mark the new baseplate. Using a soft hammer, tap over each dowel center to mark the new jig's baseplate for screw holes.

To complete the marker, insert dowel centers in all the holes from the crosshair side of the blank, including the center hole. Be warned: Installing the centers can be tricky. To make the job go smoothly, I use a 7⁄32 in. socket in a ¼ in. nut driver to hold each dowel center straight, and I tap the handle with a small hammer, as shown in the top photo, left. If a dowel center is loose, drip one drop of acetone (nail polish remover also works) into the hole and onto the dowel center from the "router" side of the blank. This melts the plastic and "welds" the center in place.

USING THE MARKER

Start by marking the bit hole location on the baseplate you wish to attach to your router. Position the base marker on the baseplate with the tip of the center dowel on the mark. Rotate the base marker to locate the router's switch, handles, and lock at the most convenient position. Holding the base marker firmly in position, tap over each dowel center to make dimples in the baseplate, as shown in the photo, above.

Remove the marker and drill the appropriate size screw holes through the baseplate at your marks, and countersink the holes. Finish by drilling the bit hole on the center mark. A good rule of thumb is to make the bit hole 25 percent larger than the largest bit you'll be using.

Router Table

A router table is one of the first jigs woodworkers buy or make for their router, and for good reason. Router tables are great for routing stock that's too small or too skinny to support the weight and size of a hand-held router. And router tables make all sorts of general routing operations easier and more accurate.

Luckily, making your own router table isn't all that difficult. The key is to make its top surface flat—and have it stay flat. Another goal is to make sure there's no obstruction on the tabletop that snags work. This is a common problem with router tables that rely on an insert from which the router hangs, because the insert often doesn't stay flush with the surrounding table. The result is irregular cuts and poor work. My table avoids these problems, and adds some additional and appealing features.

The router table shown in figure 2 has a ⅜ in. thick clear acrylic top, or plate, screwed to its base. You hang your router from the plate by screwing through the top and into the router's base. I make three of these plates with small, medium, and large bit holes to accommodate different size bits. Then I simply install the plate that best fits the bit I'm using.

A good fence is another important element. The fence here is sturdy, square, flat, and straight. It incorporates a pivoting design that makes it fast and accurate to align with the bit. A groove in the fence lets you install commercial featherboards for supporting work. Consider the fence expendable if necessary, and make a new one when the old one gets worn or chewed up by bits. Or make several if you need zero clearance around the bit.

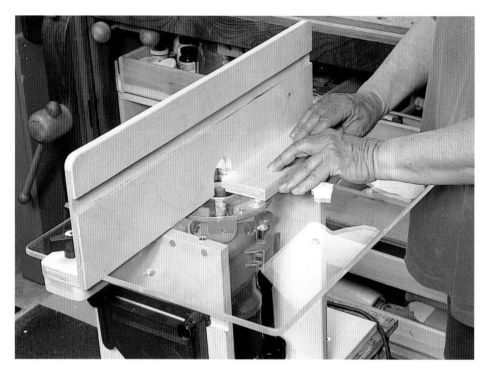

Simple but very effective. Built for precise cuts, the author's router table has a plastic top secured to a high-quality plywood base. A unique pivoting fence makes bit settings a breeze.

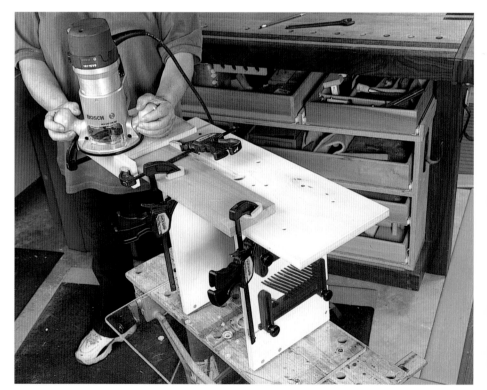

Great upside down. With its router removed, the same table becomes a mini workbench for hand-held routing by flipping it over and bolting it to a low workstand.

FIG. 2: ROUTER TABLE

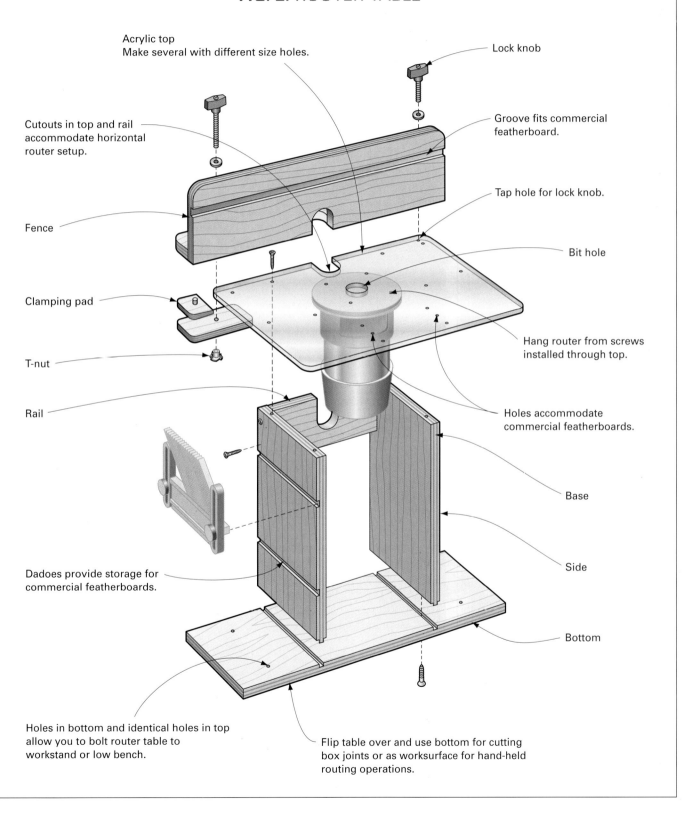

Acrylic top
Make several with different size holes.

Lock knob

Cutouts in top and rail
accommodate horizontal
router setup.

Groove fits commercial
featherboard.

Tap hole for lock knob.

Fence

Bit hole

Clamping pad

Hang router from screws
installed through top.

T-nut

Holes accommodate
commercial featherboards.

Rail

Base

Dadoes provide storage for
commercial featherboards.

Side

Bottom

Holes in bottom and identical holes in top
allow you to bolt router table to
workstand or low bench.

Flip table over and use bottom for cutting
box joints or as worksurface for hand-held
routing operations.

Refer to figure 3 for building the base. Cut all the parts to size, except for the rail, which you should keep overlong for now. Pay special attention to cutting the ends of the sides perfectly square with the edges, or the finished table will be racked.

Lay out and rout the dadoes in the bottom, making sure they're precisely parallel with each other and square to the long edges of the bottom. (See Dadoes, Grooves, and Slots, page 85.) Once you've milled the dadoes, rout the tongues on the sides to fit with a ¼ in. rabbeting bit. (See Rabbets, page 78.)

Lay out and drill four holes through the bottom for attaching the router table to a workstand or low bench. By installing T-nuts or threaded inserts in your bench, you can secure the table by slipping bolts through the holes in the bottom and into the nuts in your bench. If you have commercial featherboards, rout a pair of shallow dadoes in one of the sides for convenient storage. Then use a chamfer bit to rout an ⅛ in. chamfer on the long edges of the sides.

Once the joints are cut, dry-fit the sides into the bottom and screw the joints fast. Then, working along the bottom, carefully measure the distance between the sides and cut the rail to that length. Next, lay out and cut the U-shaped cutout in the rail, and chamfer the long bottom edges as you did the sides. Drill and countersink the sides for the screws that attach the rail.

The rail must be set back from the sides by the distance of the chamfer, or about ⅛ in., to prevent it from interfering with the operation of the horizontal router setup. In addition,

Routing horizontal. Safer cuts are possible with this horizontal setup, which aligns the bit parallel to the table. Bit height adjustment is a simple matter of loosening a lock knob on the back of the plate and pivoting the plate up or down (inset).

A unique feature of this router table is its "twin" top. While most routing takes place on the acrylic top, you can flip the whole table over and use the plywood bottom as a second "top" for routing box joints. Special holes and grooves in this second top accommodate a box joint jig for cutting box joints. (See page 46.) Best of all, the long plywood surface is a handy work platform for holding stock when routing with a hand-held router. (See bottom photo, page 38.)

Finally, an attribute I consider a must is a horizontal table setup that quickly mounts to the table for horizontal routing. This setup orients the router and its bit parallel to the tabletop, allowing you to make cuts with the work held flat on the table instead of precariously on edge. (See photos, above.)

You have the option of making all of the parts for this router table, which I think is preferable, or you can build just the top, base, and fence. If you plan on making the box joint jig (see page 38), it's wise to mill the necessary holes and the groove in the bottom piece now. If you're going to incorporate the horizontal table setup, build this first, as you'll use it to help with layout when it comes to building the router table. Another option is to buy the table in kit form or a completed version. (See www.routerlady.com.)

MAKE THE ROUTER TABLE

Start by building the base, including its plywood bottom, then make the acrylic top. Finally, make the fence.

Router Table

BITS AND TOOLS

- ⁵⁄₃₂, ³⁄₁₆, ¼, and 1 in. drill bits
- single-flute countersink bit
- 1 and 1¾ in. spade bit
- ¼-20 tap and #7 drill bit
- ¼ in. dowel center
- transfer punch, as needed
- thread-locking compound
- ¼ in. rabbet bit
- chamfer bit
- base marker
- router with offset baseplate
- drill press
- bandsaw, jigsaw, or scrollsaw

MATERIALS AND HARDWARE

- 1⅝ and 2 in. drywall screws, as needed
- 3 ea. ¼-20 T-nuts or brass threaded inserts, with appropriate drill bit
- lock knob with ¼-20 through hole, ¼-20 x 2 in. pan-head machine screw, and washer
- lock knob with ¼-20 through hole, ¼-20 x 2½ in. pan-head machine screw, and washer

CUTTING LIST

Part	Material	Qty.	Dimensions (in.)
Base bottom	Baltic birch plywood	1	¾ x 9 x 24
Base sides	Baltic birch plywood	2	¾ x 9 x 14¼
Base rail	Baltic birch plywood	1	¾ x 4 x 9½*
Top	clear acrylic	1	⅜ x 15 x 20
Fence base	Baltic birch plywood	1	¾ x 2½ x 24
Fence board	Baltic birch plywood	1	½ x 6¼ x 24
Fence brackets	Baltic birch plywood	2	¾ x 2⅜ x 4¼
Bottom pad	Baltic birch plywood	1	½ x 2½ x 5
Tapered pad	Baltic birch plywood	1	⅜ x 2 x 2½
Clamp dowel	wood dowel	1	¼ dia. x ½

* Note: Determine final length after assembling the sides to the bottom.

the top of the rail must be exactly flush with the top of the sides, or the acrylic top won't lay flat. Dry-clamp the assembly and check for square, and position both the bottom and the top of the sides on a flat surface, such as your table saw, to check for flatness. When you're satisfied, disassemble the parts, then reassemble with glue and screw the joints for the last time. Check for flatness once more, and let the assembly dry undisturbed.

MAKE THE TOP

See figure 4. Cut the acrylic top to size. (See Working with Plastic, page 36, for tips on cutting and drilling plastic.) If you're making more than one top, go ahead and cut them to size now.

Lay out and drill the bit hole and the U-shaped cutout. As you did on the bottom, drill four holes through the top for bolts that will attach the table to a low bench or workstand, or even to a dedicated shop cabinet. To repeat the precise hole pattern, align the top with the bottom and transfer the hole locations with a transfer punch. Drill and countersink the holes from the bottom side of the acrylic top.

Now set the top onto the base with its back edge flush with the rail and the two U-shaped cutouts aligned with each other. The sides should protrude about ⅛ in. Like the rail, this arrangement keeps the edge of the top from interfering with the horizontal router setup. Clamp in position, then trace the contours of the sides and the rail onto the bottom surface of the top. Use this layout to locate the six mounting screw holes. Drill ⁵⁄₃₂ in. holes, countersinking them from the top side.

Lay out and drill the pivot hole for the fence using a #7 drill bit. Use a ¼-20 tap to cut the threads in the hole. If you have a commercial featherboard, drill a series of holes through the top to attach it, using a transfer punch through a featherboard to locate the holes. Make sure to locate the featherboard so it provides support on the infeed side and directly across the bit. Countersink the holes from the bot-

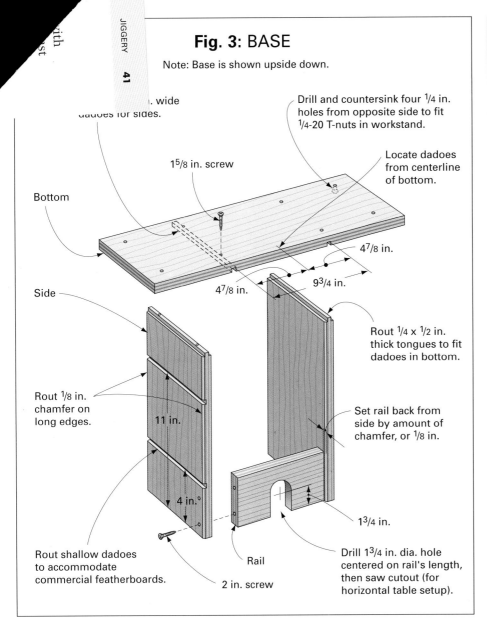

Fig. 3: BASE

Note: Base is shown upside down.

. wide
dadoes for sides.

Drill and countersink four ¹/₄ in.
holes from opposite side to fit
¹/₄-20 T-nuts in workstand.

Locate dadoes
from centerline
of bottom.

1⁵/₈ in. screw

Bottom

4⁷/₈ in.

9³/₄ in.

4⁷/₈ in.

Side

Rout ¹/₄ x ¹/₂ in.
thick tongues to fit
dadoes in bottom.

Rout ¹/₈ in.
chamfer on
long edges.

11 in.

Set rail back from
side by amount of
chamfer, or ¹/₈ in.

4 in.

1³/₄ in.

Rout shallow dadoes
to accommodate
commercial featherboards.

Rail

2 in. screw

Drill 1³/₄ in. dia. hole
centered on rail's length,
then saw cutout (for
horizontal table setup).

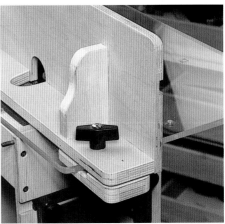

Fence features. The tall fence provides ample working room for big or small work. An integral wooden clamp pad secures the fence to the table in a jiffy.

tom. To attach the featherboard, you'll have to remove its runner.

Finally, lay out, drill, and countersink the appropriate holes through the bottom of the top for your router base, using the base marker (see page 34) to locate the holes.

CONSTRUCT THE FENCE

Refer to figure 5, and cut the parts to size. Make sure the inside corners of

the brackets are absolutely square since they help keep the fence perpendicular. The curves on the brackets aren't critical. You can saw a graceful ogee or any shape you like that marks your sense of craftsmanship.

Lay out, drill, and saw the U-shaped cutouts in the fence board and the base. Note the ³/₁₆ in. difference in the cutout locations between these two parts. If you own commercial feather-

boards, now is the time to cut the groove in the fence board that holds them. (See Dadoes, Grooves, and Slots, page 85.)

Next, lay out and drill the counterbored pivot hole at one end of the base and the counterbored clamp hole at the opposite end. I use a 1 in. spade bit to drill an ¹/₈ in. deep counterbore for a washer and a ¹/₄ in. drill bit for the through hole. Glue and clamp the base and fence board together, and add the brackets. Check the assembly for flat and square before setting it aside to dry.

Glue the clamping pads together. In the center of the tapered pad, drill a ¹/₄ in. diameter by ¹/₄ in. deep hole, and insert a metal dowel center into the hole. Align the end of the clamping pad with the end of the fence base, and press the parts together to mark the base. Drill a ¹/₄ by ¹/₄ in. hole into the base precisely where the dowel center left its mark. Sand or plane a ¹/₄ in. taper on the thinner pad, as indicated in the drawing. Then glue the wood dowel into the clamping pad, leaving ¹/₄ in. of the dowel protruding.

Fig. 4: ACRYLIC TOP

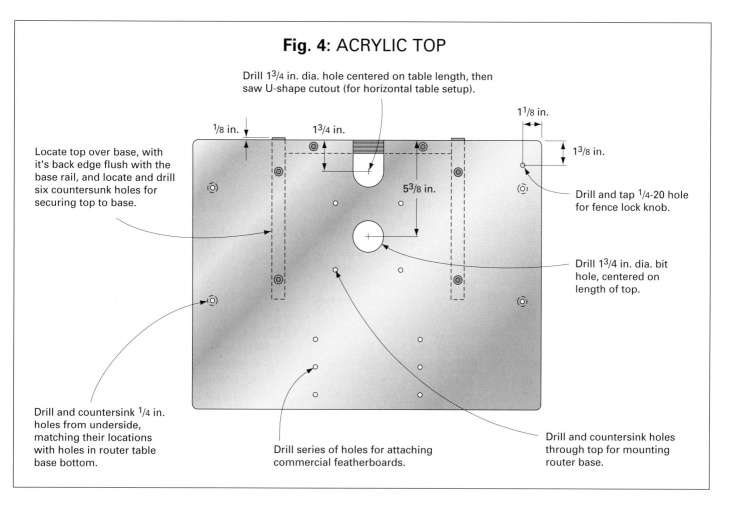

Drill 1³/₄ in. dia. hole centered on table length, then saw U-shape cutout (for horizontal table setup).

Locate top over base, with it's back edge flush with the base rail, and locate and drill six countersunk holes for securing top to base.

1/8 in.

1³/₄ in.

1¹/₈ in.

1³/₈ in.

5³/₈ in.

Drill and tap ¹/₄-20 hole for fence lock knob.

Drill 1³/4 in. dia. bit hole, centered on length of top.

Drill and countersink ¹/₄ in. holes from underside, matching their locations with holes in router table base bottom.

Drill series of holes for attaching commercial featherboards.

Drill and countersink holes through top for mounting router base.

Now realign the clamping pad with the base, and insert the dowel (no glue!) into the hole in the base. Use a transfer punch through the clamp hole in the base to mark the pad. Disassemble, drill a hole in the pad to fit a T-nut or a brass threaded insert, and insert the nut or insert from the bottom. If necessary, sand the insert flush with the top of the pad.

To make each lock knob assembly, thread the appropriate machine screw through the knob, dabbing a bit of thread-locking compound on the upper threads of the screw to hold it fast.

BUILD THE HORIZONTAL SETUP

The core of the horizontal router setup is a rigid, aluminum plate that secures your router at a perfect right angle to the router tabletop. While aluminum can be worked with regular drill bits and files, keep in mind that the plate requires a curved slot and a large-diameter hole, and most shops don't have the necessary tools for making these cuts. However, a machine shop can supply you with a plate cut to size and milled with the necessary slot and holes at minimal expense. Another option is to buy a readymade plate (see www.routerlady.com).

Note: Be sure make or buy the plate first, then use it to lay out and build the rest of the router table.

LAY OUT AND MILL THE PLATE

Refer to figure 6. Acquire the aluminum plate, making sure it's flat and cut to size. Lay out the pivot hole as shown and use a center punch to mark its location. Place the tip of a compass on the pivot hole mark and swing a 9³/₄ in. radius to draw the curved slot, stopping the curve from the bottom and top edges as indicated. Reset the compass to 4⁷/₈ in. and swing a shorter arc, then square a line 2³/₄ in. up from the bottom edge to intersect this arc. Center punch the

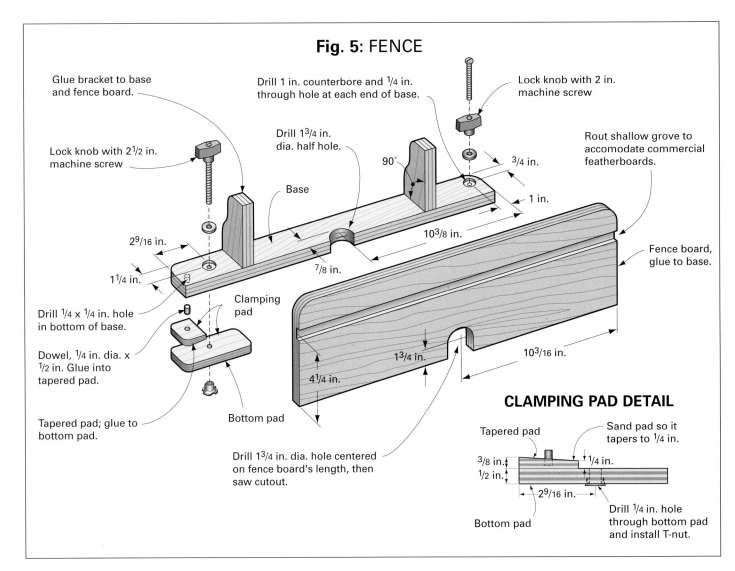

Fig. 5: FENCE

Glue bracket to base and fence board.

Lock knob with 2½ in. machine screw

Drill 1 in. counterbore and ¼ in. through hole at each end of base.

Lock knob with 2 in. machine screw

Drill 1¾ in. dia. half hole.

Base

90°

¾ in.

1 in.

Rout shallow grove to accomodate commercial featherboards.

2⁹⁄₁₆ in.

10³⁄₈ in.

Fence board, glue to base.

1¼ in.

7⁄₈ in.

Drill ¼ x ¼ in. hole in bottom of base.

Clamping pad

Dowel, ¼ in. dia. x ½ in. Glue into tapered pad.

1¾ in.

10³⁄₁₆ in.

4¼ in.

Tapered pad; glue to bottom pad.

Bottom pad

Drill 1¾ in. dia. hole centered on fence board's length, then saw cutout.

CLAMPING PAD DETAIL

Tapered pad

Sand pad so it tapers to ¼ in.

3⁄₈ in.
½ in.

¼ in.

2⁹⁄₁₆ in.

Drill ¼ in. hole through bottom pad and install T-nut.

Bottom pad

---

spot to mark the bit hole. Drill the ¼ in. pivot hole and lightly chamfer each side. Then, if necessary, have the machine shop mill the curved slot and the bit hole.

Once the slot and hole are cut, use the base marker (see page 34) to lay out the location of your router base. Make sure to orient the base so its locking mechanism is accessible and your router's handles don't interfere with the fixture's lock knobs. Drill the appropriate sized holes to mount your router, countersinking them from the working side of the plate. Then lay out, drill, and countersink the holes

for a pair of commercial feather-boards, using a transfer punch through the featherboards to mark their exact location. Soften all sharp edges with a file or 100-grit sandpaper.

HANG THE PLATE

At this point, you'll need to use the plate to help with laying out the dado locations in the router table base's plywood bottom. (See fig. 4.) To do this, center the plate on the plywood bottom with their long edges parallel with each other, and clamp. Use a transfer punch through the pivot hole in the plate to mark the bottom, and

use a pencil to trace the outlines of the curved slot. Unclamp, and mark the center of the curved slot on the bottom. Now draw a line from the pivot hole mark to the centermark of the curve, keeping the line parallel with the long edge of the bottom. Using a square on the long edge, draw a line through the pivot hole mark and another line through the curve's centermark. Each line represents the precise center of the dadoes.

Once you've made the router table base, you're ready to hang the plate, as shown in figure 6. Start by squaring lines across the base's sides, ½ in.

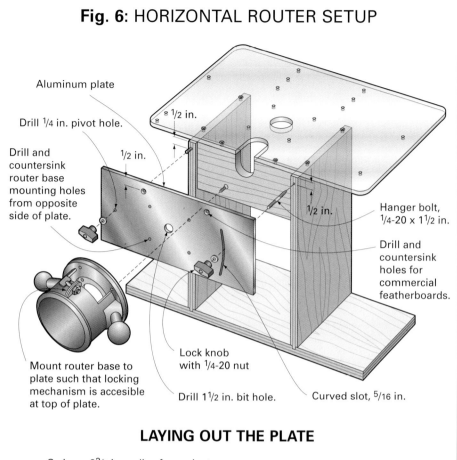

Fig. 6: HORIZONTAL ROUTER SETUP

Aluminum plate

Drill ¼ in. pivot hole.

Drill and countersink router base mounting holes from opposite side of plate.

½ in.

½ in.

½ in.

Hanger bolt, ¼-20 x 1½ in.

Drill and countersink holes for commercial featherboards.

Mount router base to plate such that locking mechanism is accessible at top of plate.

Lock knob with ¼-20 nut

Drill 1½ in. bit hole.

Curved slot, 5/16 in.

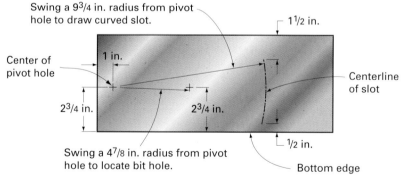

LAYING OUT THE PLATE

Swing a 9¾ in. radius from pivot hole to draw curved slot.

1½ in.

Center of pivot hole

1 in.

Centerline of slot

2¾ in.

2¾ in.

½ in.

Swing a 4⅞ in. radius from pivot hole to locate bit hole.

Bottom edge

Horizontal Setup

BITS AND TOOLS

• 5/32 and ¼ in. drill bits

• countersink bit

• center punch

• compass

• transfer punch, as needed

• base marker

• drill press

MATERIALS AND HARDWARE

• aluminum plate, ¼ x 6 x 15 in.

• 2 ea. hanger bolt with nuts, ¼-20 x 1½ in.

Sturdy setup. The author secures the table to a low workstand by driving machine screws through the table's bottom and into threaded inserts installed in the stand.

---

down from their top edges. Position and clamp the plate over these marks, aligning the marks with the plate's pivot hole and curved slot. Use a transfer punch through the plate to mark the precise hanger bolt locations on the sides. Remove the plate, and drill 3/16 in. holes into the sides on your marks. Install each hanger bolt by engaging two nuts on its machine-threaded end and wrenching the bolt into the side until ⅝ in. protrudes. Remove the nuts and, if necessary, file any sharp edges on the ends of the bolts, being careful not to destroy the threads.

Fingers and slots. This L-shaped jig rides in a groove on the router table and registers the work for cutting box joints.

Box Joint Jig

The box joint jig helps you make great box joints (see page 92) and lets you rout ¼, ⅜, or ¾ in. wide slots and fingers. The jig works equally well with my router table (see page 38) or your own router table if you modify it slightly. It consists of three parts: the sled, the stop, and the tabletop of the router table.

Note: If you plan on making my router table, mill the necessary groove and holes for the box joint jig during construction of the table, as outlined below.

MAKE THE BOX JOINT JIG

Refer to figure 7, and cut the parts to size. I use HDPE (high-density polyethylene plastic) for the runner, a dense but low-friction type of plastic, but you can substitute hard maple or oak if you like. Keep the runner slightly over width for now; you fit it more precisely later.

If you're making the router table on page 38, lay out and cut the groove and the holes as shown on the "top" side of the router table's bottom. If you're going to use the jig with your own router table, you'll have to incorporate these holes and the groove in its tabletop, or make an new top that's at least ¾ in. thick.

Lay out and rout a stopped, through slot in the center of the sub-fence piece. (See Dadoes, Grooves, and Slots, page 85.) Then lay out and rout the tongue-and-groove joint in this piece and the base. When cutting the groove, if anything make it a little "fat," but certainly not too wide. Then rout the tongue on the base to fit. Fit the joint dry and pull it together with four countersunk screws, then disassemble, add glue, and permanently

SETTING UP THE ROUTER TABLE

Secure the router table to your workstand or bench with machine screws, orienting the table as needed with the correct side up. Another option is to simply clamp the base to your worksurface. If you're routing on the acrylic top, screw your router base to the underside of the top, screw the top to the base, and install the router motor and bit into the router base.

To use the fence, thread the shorter lock knob into the pivot hole in the top, and position the clamping pad under the opposite edge. To set the fence to the bit, simply swing the fence around the pivot screw and tighten the lock knob at the opposite end. Then tighten the pivot lock knob and recheck your fence setting.

To use the horizontal router setup, mount your router base to the plate, slip the plate over the hanger bolts at the back of the router table, and secure the plate with the lock knobs. Install the router motor and bit into the base. Set the bit height by loosening both lock knobs slightly and moving the end of the plate with the curved slot up or down. Once the bit is where you want it, tighten both knobs and recheck the bit height.

One more tip: Never store your router motor in this table—or in any router table, for that matter—when not in use, or its weight can cause the top to sag.

Box Joint Jig

BITS AND TOOLS

- ³/₁₆, ¼, and 1 in. drill bits
- countersink bit
- transfer punch, as needed
- ¼-20 tap and #7 drill bit
- ¼ in. straight bit
- ¼ in. rabbet bit
- ½ and ¾ in. dado bits
- drill press
- router table

MATERIALS AND HARDWARE

- lock knob with ¼-20 insert nut and washer
- flat-head machine screw, ¼-20 x 2 in.
- steel spring pin, ⅛ dia. x 1½ in.
- # 6 x ¾ in. flat-head Phillips screws, as needed
- steel pin or wood dowel, ⅛ or ³/₁₆ dia. x 2 in.

CUTTING LIST

Part	Material	Qty.	Dimensions (in.)
Base	MDF or acrylic	1	¾ x 6 x 7
Sub-fence	MDF or acrylic	1	¾ x 6 x 5
Main fence	Baltic birch plywood or acrylic	1	⅜ x 6 x 5
Backer*	plywood	1	½ x 6 x 5
Runner	HDPE plastic	1	⁵/₁₆ x ¾ x 6⅝
Stop block	MDF or acrylic	1	¾ x 1 x 2

* Note: Make as many as you need and replace as necessary.

screw the joint fast. If necessary, use a flush-trimming bit to rout the bottom surface even.

Once you've assembled the base to the sub-fence, rout a shallow dado in the bottom, centering it side-to-side and front-to-back.

Next, align the main fence with the sub-fence and use a transfer punch through the slot in the sub-fence to mark the location for the machine screw. Separate the parts and use a #7 drill bit and a tap to drill and thread a hole in the main fence for a machine screw. Countersink the hole from the working side of the fence. Then locate and drill a hole for the spring pin, and lay out, drill, and countersink the four holes for the screws that secure the plywood backer.

Make sure to drill a ¼ in. clearance hole in the backer to allow room for the spring pin in the main fence. Then tap the pin into the main fence, and check that it protrudes at least 1 in. from the face of the fence.

Fit and install the runner to the bottom of the base, or sled, checking that it slides smoothly in the groove you cut in the router tabletop. Scrape the

edges of the runner if necessary. The runner should slide smoothly in the groove without any side-to-side play. Once the sled is moving smoothly, assemble the various fence parts and lock them together with the machine screw and lock knob. Attach a backer with the four screws.

Finally, make the stop block as shown. Drill a ¼ in. off-center hole through the stop on the drill press, and glue a steel pin or wood dowel into the hole. Label the stop as shown for the three sizes of fingers and slots.

SETTING UP THE JIG

Once you've prepped your stock (see Box Joints, page 92), simply install the sled in the groove on your router table, then use the stop block and its appropriate edge to align the jig to the bit and the size fingers and slots you wish to rout. As you use the jig to rout box joints, you'll notice the plywood backer helps to eliminate tearout on the back of the cut and protects the main fence. Expect the backer to get torn up during use, so make sure you use a fresh one for every setup.

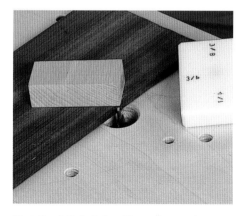

Set the bit height. Place the stock on the table, position a block on top of the work, and raise the bit to the bottom of the block.

Fig. 7: BOX JOINT JIG

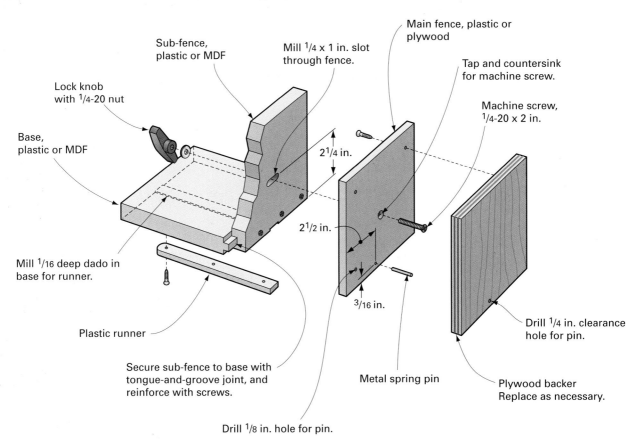

Sub-fence, plastic or MDF

Mill 1/4 x 1 in. slot through fence.

Main fence, plastic or plywood

Tap and countersink for machine screw.

Lock knob with 1/4-20 nut

Machine screw, 1/4-20 x 2 in.

Base, plastic or MDF

2 1/4 in.

Mill 1/16 deep dado in base for runner.

2 1/2 in.

3/16 in.

Drill 1/4 in. clearance hole for pin.

Plastic runner

Secure sub-fence to base with tongue-and-groove joint, and reinforce with screws.

Metal spring pin

Plywood backer Replace as necessary.

Drill 1/8 in. hole for pin.

STOP BLOCK DETAIL

ROUTER TABLE SETUP

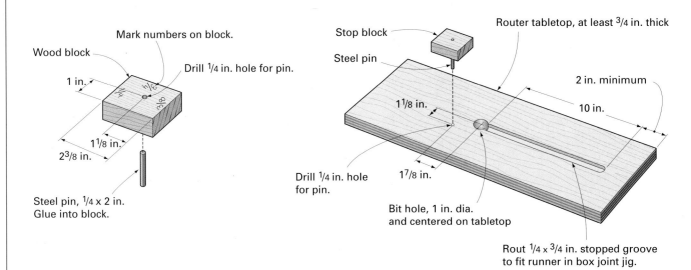

Mark numbers on block.

Wood block

Drill 1/4 in. hole for pin.

1 in.

1 1/8 in.

2 3/8 in.

Steel pin, 1/4 x 2 in. Glue into block.

Stop block

Steel pin

Router tabletop, at least 3/4 in. thick

1 1/8 in.

2 in. minimum

10 in.

Drill 1/4 in. hole for pin.

1 7/8 in.

Bit hole, 1 in. dia. and centered on tabletop

Rout 1/4 x 3/4 in. stopped groove to fit runner in box joint jig.

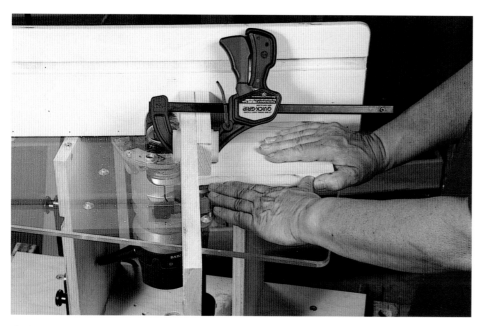

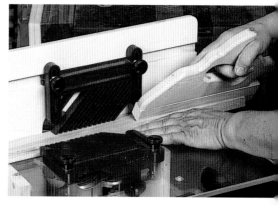

Stick and feathers. A shop-made push stick and a pair of commercial featherboards keep fingers clear of spinning cutters and provide more control for feeding the work.

Safer, cleaner cuts. This L-shaped sled lets you clamp long or wide work securely for accurate, safer routing, and backs up the work to prevent blowout.

Push Sticks, Sleds, and Featherboards

Not to be overlooked as useful jigs are push sticks and other shop-made pushing devices—vital safety items you need in many areas of the shop. Featherboards are another must-have, and you can make your own or buy commercial versions. These devices are particularly handy at the table saw and on the router table. Not only do they keep fingers and hands safe from whirling bits and blades, but they afford more control over the workpiece and often help you make cleaner, more accurate cuts.

One of my favorite push sticks is shown in figure 8. In addition to table saw work, I use this stick on the router table, especially when I'm routing narrow stock and have featherboards set up. (See top photo, right.) This stick has a lot going for it. First, its saw-handle shape is very comfortable. Also, the stick's long nose holds down stock securely to prevent kickback—unlike lots of other sticks that

simply push stock with a small heel. Make the stick from scrap plywood and solid wood, and when the sole or heel gets chewed up from use, cut it off on the bandsaw, joint the handle flat, and glue on a new part. You can repeat this procedure many times before you joint into the handle opening. The design of these sticks makes them good candidates for template routing (see page 130). Make them in batches and give them to your woodworking buddies; they'll appreciate working more safely.

The sled shown in figure 9 and in the photo, above, is very handy for supporting wide workpieces, and works particularly well when routing tenons, making cope cuts on the ends of rails, cutting lock miters, or anywhere you need to push work on the router table and back it up to prevent blowout. When the jig gets too ravaged by bits, simply make a new one.

The vertical push stick (see fig. 10 and middle photo, right) is another router table favorite, and does a won-

Control the tall stuff. By turning the L-shaped sled on end and adding a fence and handle, you can direct tall stock past the bit without tipping.

derful job of keeping your hands clear while stabilizing tall stock to keep it from tipping. The device is assembled from a modified version of my push stick and the push sled, with a thin plywood heel glued to its trailing edge.

I favor the commercial featherboards shown in the top photo, above, because they're inexpensive, easy to set up, and made from plastic, which won't harm bits and blades. Keep a pair on hand so you can place pressure on the work for safe and consistent cuts.

Fig. 8: PUSH STICK

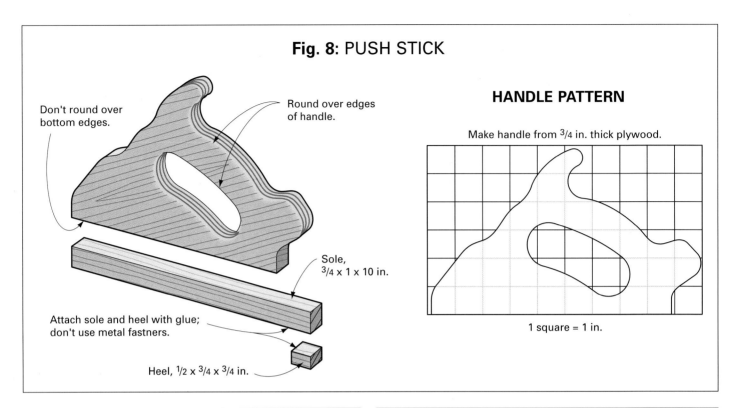

Don't round over bottom edges.

Round over edges of handle.

Sole, 3/4 x 1 x 10 in.

Attach sole and heel with glue; don't use metal fastners.

Heel, 1/2 x 3/4 x 3/4 in.

HANDLE PATTERN

Make handle from 3/4 in. thick plywood.

1 square = 1 in.

Fig. 9: PUSH SLED

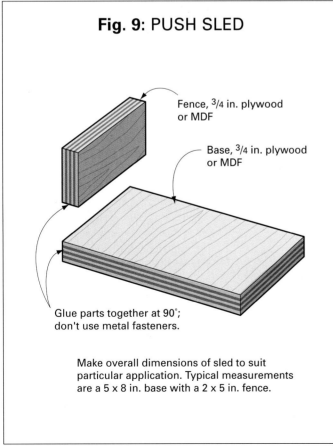

Fence, 3/4 in. plywood or MDF

Base, 3/4 in. plywood or MDF

Glue parts together at 90°; don't use metal fasteners.

Make overall dimensions of sled to suit particular application. Typical measurements are a 5 x 8 in. base with a 2 x 5 in. fence.

Fig. 10: VERTICAL PUSH STICK

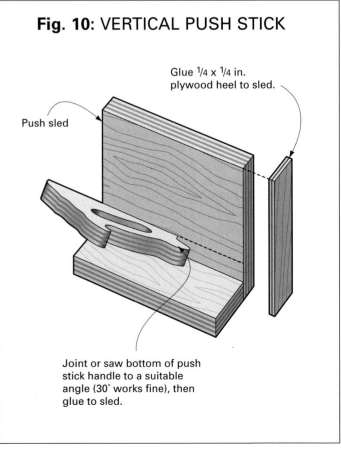

Glue 1/4 x 1/4 in. plywood heel to sled.

Push sled

Joint or saw bottom of push stick handle to a suitable angle (30° works fine), then glue to sled.

Easy bit change. Cradle your router in this home-made router motor holder for reliable bit changing.

Router Cradle

This nifty jig is a welcome third hand (or fourth, even!) for supporting the router when installing or removing bits. I designed it when I got tired of trying to squeeze router wrenches with my arthritic hands to securely tighten bits in router collets. My students discovered other benefits. The cradle arrangement allows you to use only one wrench, a much simpler approach than trying to maneuver two at a time. And the sides and bottom create a little box for neatly storing your router and its associated paraphernalia, such as wrenches, collets, and the like.

MAKE THE CRADLE

See figure 11, and cut all the parts to size, except for the bottom and sides. Leave the bottom over width and the sides over length for now.

Measure the diameter of your router motor and cap, then use a compass to lay out the curves in the motor supports, and cut them to fit. You don't have to cut the reverse curves as shown, but they look great, so indulge yourself! Chamfer or round over the supports on both faces, but not their bottom edges.

Router Cradle

BITS AND TOOLS
- ⅛ and ⁵⁄₃₂ in. drill bits
- compass
- ¼ in. roundover or chamfer bit
- bandsaw, jigsaw, or scrollsaw

MATERIALS AND HARDWARE
- brads or small finish nails, as needed
- # 8 x ½ in. screw
- fender washer
- 2 ea. 1 in. dia. ceramic magnets

CUTTING LIST

Part	Material	Qty.	Dimensions (in.)
Motor supports	plywood	2	¾ x 4¼ x 11¾
Bottom	plywood	1	¼ x * x 8¾
Sides	plywood	2	⅜ x 2 x *

* Note: Make width or length to suit length of router.

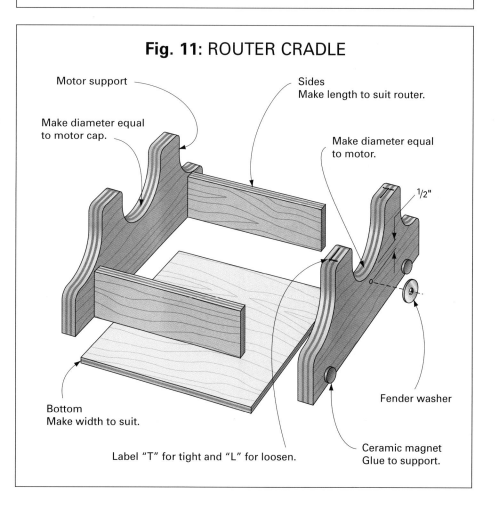

Fig. 11: ROUTER CRADLE

Motor support

Sides
Make length to suit router.

Make diameter equal to motor cap.

Make diameter equal to motor.

1/2"

Bottom
Make width to suit.

Label "T" for tight and "L" for loosen.

Fender washer

Ceramic magnet
Glue to support.

Screw the fender washer to a motor support, stand both supports upright, and lay your motor on them. Measure the distance from support to support (outside edge to outside edge) and cut the plywood bottom to fit. Measure between the supports and cut the sides to length. Round over or chamfer the top edges of the sides, then glue and brad the sides to the supports and secure the bottom. Attach the magnets with hot glue. Of course, your creative genes will require that you sand and finish the jig neatly.

For those of us who can't visualize the saying "Righty tighty, lefty loosey," mark a "T" and an "L" on the top of the motor support to remind you in which direction to turn the wrench.

Offset Baseplate

This oversized, egg-shaped baseplate consists of a plywood handle attached to a clear acrylic plate. Its purpose is to provide a large area of contact when routing the edges of wood. Without this kind of baseplate, 60 percent or more of a typical router hangs in space, depending on the diameter of the bit you're using. When this happens, it's difficult to keep the router from tipping—and ruining the cut. By using an offset baseplate, a much larger portion of the router base rides on the wood for edge work.

The jig features a saw-type handle, which is more comfortable than standard router knobs. Knobs force you to move your elbows away from your body, an awkward stance at best and a likely cause of accidents. You'll love how hand-friendly this jig is. You can buy it (see www.routerlady.com) or make it yourself. Remember, the key to using the jig when routing edges is to always keep the handle portion of the baseplate over the surface of your stock.

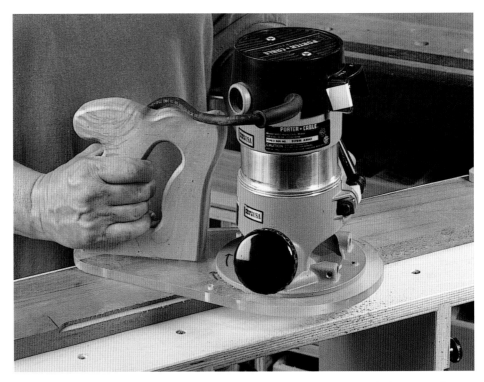

Bigger footprint. Adding an oversize baseplate to your router greatly improves its stability, especially for cuts on the edge of your work.

Offset Baseplate

BITS AND TOOLS

- $\frac{5}{32}$ in. drill bit
- $1\frac{1}{4}$ in. spade bit
- $1\frac{3}{8}$ in. Forstner bit
- compass
- center punch
- countersink bit
- $\frac{1}{4}$ in. roundover bit with bearing
- chamfer bit with bearing
- base marker
- router table
- bandsaw, jigsaw, or scrollsaw
- drill press

MATERIALS AND HARDWARE

- 2 ea. #8 x $1\frac{5}{8}$ in. drywall screws

CUTTING LIST

Part	Material	Qty.	Dimensions (in.)
Handle	Baltic birch plywood	1	1* x 6 x 6
Baseplate	clear acrylic	1	$\frac{3}{8}$ x 7 x 12$\frac{1}{2}$

* Note: If necessary, face-glue two pieces of $\frac{1}{2}$ in. plywood.

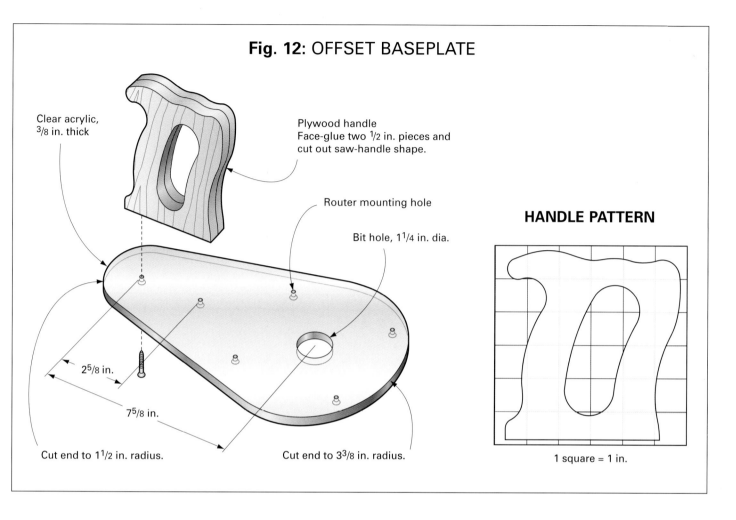

Fig. 12: OFFSET BASEPLATE

Clear acrylic, ³/₈ in. thick

Plywood handle
Face-glue two ¹/₂ in. pieces and
cut out saw-handle shape.

Router mounting hole

Bit hole, 1¹/₄ in. dia.

2⁵/₈ in.

7⁵/₈ in.

Cut end to 1¹/₂ in. radius.

Cut end to 3³/₈ in. radius.

HANDLE PATTERN

1 square = 1 in.

MAKE THE BASEPLATE

See figure 12. Cut the parts to size. (See Working with Plastic, page 36.)

Working on the unprinted side of the plastic plate, mark a centerline on the long axis to help with laying out the radii at each end. Set your compass to 1½ and 3⅜ in. respectively, and draw the arcs at each end of the plate with the point of the compass on the centerline. Then draw straight lines tangent to the arcs to outline the plate's egg shape.

Next, lay out and mark the screw holes for the handle and the bit hole as shown, then use the base marker (see page 34) to mark the mounting holes for your router. Make sure to orient the router's locking mechanism away from the handle. Drill the holes for the handle and the appropriate-sized holes for your router's mounting screws, and countersink them on the printed side of the paper. Use a spade bit to drill the bit hole, working from both sides of the plate.

Cut the baseplate to its distinct egg shape, and sand the edges smooth. Make sure to chamfer all the edges, including the bit hole.

SHAPE AND SECURE THE HANDLE

Saw a straight edge on one end of the plywood blank for the handle's bottom. Transfer the handle pattern to the plywood and cut the outside profile on the bandsaw, scrollsaw, or with a jigsaw. Use a spade bit or a 1⅜ in. Forstner bit to drill a hole at each end of the curved handle cutout to save sawing. Then use a jigsaw or scrollsaw to remove the waste between the holes. Sand the sawn edges smooth, and rout a ¼ in. roundover on all the edges except the bottom of the handle.

Remove the paper on the baseplate and fasten the handle with the two screws. Then mount your router.

Router Tracking System

Many joint-cutting procedures require the router to be guided dead straight, sometimes in reverse direction as well, such as when routing dadoes or grooves. This router tracking system (see www.routerlady.com) addresses those needs. Please, don't confuse this setup with a router edge guide. Edge guides work fine if you focus on keeping them tight against the stock's straight edge, but high rpms and centrifugal forces can often pull the router and guide away from the edge, spoiling the cut.

The router tracking system consists of a grooved baseplate that you attach to your plunge router, which in turn engages an aluminum track clamped to the workpiece. You clamp the track exactly 4 in. from the centerline of your desired cut, position the grooved baseplate over the track, and you're ready to rout. (See fig. 13.) You can buy tracks in different lengths for wide or narrow work. The great thing is, once you set up the jig, you can focus on routing and not on dealing with where the bit might accidentally wander. Setup gauges make the system easy to set up, and a variety of stops lets you make accurate stopped or repetitive cuts. There's even a separate baseplate that lets you make straight cuts with a standard circular saw.

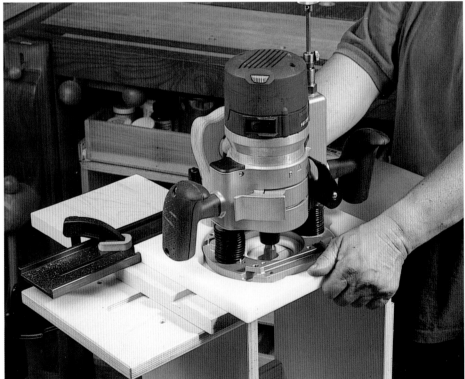

Fig. 13: SETTING UP THE TRACKING SYSTEM

Grooved baseplate rides along lip in track.

Workpiece

4 in.

Clamp track precisely 4 in. from centerline of joint.

Centerline of desired dado, groove, or slot

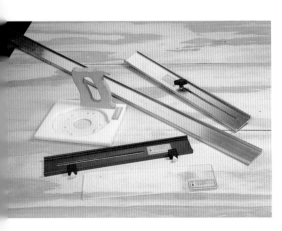

Riding a track. This commercial jig guides a router for cutting super accurate grooves and dadoes. Components include a baseplate that fits your router, work stops, and variety of tracks in different lengths (left).

Mortising Fixture

The mortising fixture holds stock in repeatable positions so mortises can be quickly and accurately routed with a hand-held plunge router. The device accommodates work up to 3¾ in. wide, such as the frame pieces for a cabinet door. The fixture features stops that limit router travel and another stop that registers the workpiece, letting you rout any desired length of mortise accurately and repeatedly on multiple workpieces. In addition, you can use the fixture for routing grooves in the edges of work.

The fixture is available commercially in kit form or as a complete version (see www.routerlady.com), or you can build your own from scratch. It consists of four main sections: the base and yoke, a fixed jaw, a moveable jaw, and a router baseplate. You'll want to visit the lumberyard, a well-stocked hardware store, your woodworking store, and a plastics company to acquire everything you need.

BUILD THE BASE

Refer to figure 15. Cut the parts to size, and saw a 1 in. radius on the top corner of each yoke end and on the two corners of the base, as shown.

Lay out and rout the through slot in the base. (See Dadoes, Grooves, and Slots, page 85.) Then use a V-groove bit to chamfer the bottom side of the slot to accommodate the head of a #12 screw.

Lay out the 1 in. hole on the yoke block with a compass, and draw a horizontal line through the center of the circle. Drill a ⁵⁄₃₂ in. hole where the line intersects each side of the circle to accommodate the two flanges on the screw nut. Drill the 1 in. hole on the drill press. Take the veneer screw

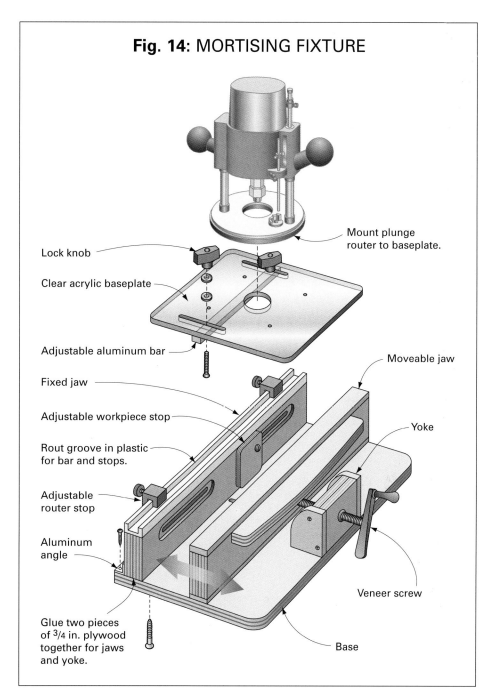

Fig. 14: MORTISING FIXTURE

Mount plunge router to baseplate.

Lock knob

Clear acrylic baseplate

Adjustable aluminum bar

Fixed jaw

Adjustable workpiece stop

Rout groove in plastic for bar and stops.

Adjustable router stop

Aluminum angle

Glue two pieces of ³⁄₄ in. plywood together for jaws and yoke.

Moveable jaw

Yoke

Veneer screw

Base

apart, separating the screw from the screw pivot and unthreading the screw nut. Hammer the nut into the hole from the back side of the yoke, aligning its flanges with the two smaller holes, and fasten with a pair of pan-head screws. Finish the yoke by gluing and screwing the yoke ends to the block.

Position the yoke on the base, centered on its length and aligned with the through slot, with its back edge flush with the edge of the base. Mark, drill, and countersink for four screws through the bottom of the base and into the yoke block and ends. Then glue and screw the yoke securely to the base. The yoke has to withstand

Mortising Fixture

BITS AND TOOLS

- $\frac{5}{32}$ in. drill bit
- 1 and 1½ in. spade bits
- compass
- ¼-20 tap and #7 drill bit
- transfer punch, as needed
- V-groove bit
- base marker
- bandsaw, jigsaw, or scrollsaw

MATERIALS AND HARDWARE

- veneer screw, ¾ dia. x 9 in.
- aluminum angle, ¾ x ¾ x 24 in.
- # 4 x ¾ in. flat-head screws, as needed
- # 6 x ½ in. flat-head screws, as needed
- # 8 x ¾ in. pan-head screws, as needed
- # 8 x 2 in. flat-head screws, as needed
- #12 x 1½ flat-head screw
- lock knob with ¼-20 through hole, ¼-20 x 2½ in. carriage bolt, and fender washer
- 2 ea. lock knobs with ¼-20 through hole, ¼-20 x 1¼ in. machine screws, standard washers, and rubber washers
- 2 ea. nylon thumbscrews, ¼-20 x ¾ in.
- aluminum angle, ⅛ x ¾ x ¾ in.
- aluminum bar, $\frac{5}{16}$ x ¾ x 12 in.

CUTTING LIST

Part	Material	Qty.	Dimensions (in.)
Base	Baltic birch plywood	1	¾ x 12 x 24
Yoke block	Baltic birch plywood	1	1½* x 3 x 4½
Yoke ends	Baltic birch plywood	2	¾ x 3 x 3
Fixed jaw	Blatic birch plywood	1	1½* x 3 x 24
Fixed jaw track	HDPE plastic	1	¾ x 1½ x 24
Workpiece stop	Baltic birch plywood	1	⅜ x 3 x 3½
Wood runner	oak or hard maple	1	¼ x ¾ x 3
Router stops	Delrin™ plastic	2	¾ x 1 x 1
Moveable jaw	Baltic birch plywood	1	1½* 3 x 24
Top wear plate	hardwood or HDPE plastic	1	½ x 1½ x 24
Bottom wear plate	hardwood or HDPE plastic	1	¼ x 1½ x 24
Stiffener	Baltic birch plywood	1	¾ x 2 x 18
Baseplate	clear acrylic	1	⅜ x 12 x 12

* Note: If necessary, face-glue two pieces of ¾ in. plywood.

the action of the veneer screw, so a good joint here is important.

CONSTRUCT THE FIXED JAW

Refer to figure 16, and cut the parts to size, except for the router stops. (More on these later.)

Lay out and rout the two rabbetted through slots in the jaw blank. (See Rabbets, page 78.) Then mill the groove in the plastic jaw track (see Dadoes, Grooves, and Slots, page 85) and screw it to the top of the jaw blank with #4 screws. The trick here is to align the groove absolutely parallel with the inside face of the jaw. Do this by placing the inside surface of the jaw blank and the edge of the jaw track down on the benchtop, and clamping them in place. Drill, countersink, and screw the parts together, then remove the clamps.

Drill and countersink the aluminum angle on both legs for #6 screws. Attach one leg of the angle to the bottom of the jaw assembly. Then position the jaw onto the base, and mark, drill, and countersink holes through the base and into the underside of the jaw. Glue and screw the jaw to the base with #8 screws. Then fasten the remaining leg of the angle to the base with #6 screws.

Next, clamp the wood runner and the workpiece stop into the slot in the jaw such that the stop is neither above the top of the jaw nor touching the base. Insert a transfer punch from the back of the jaw and mark a hole for a carriage bolt. Remove the parts and drill a ¼ in. hole through the runner and the stop. Then glue the runner to the sled. Insert the bolt through the stop and the slot in the jaw, and secure the stop with a fender washer and a lock knob.

You can use the same stops from the router tracking system (see page 54) or you can make your own adjustable router stops from Delrin™, an acetal plastic that's tough, durable, and provides low friction. If you opt to make them yourself, cut the parts to size as shown, then drill and tap a hole in each stop for a nylon thumbscrew. Use nylon because it won't dimple the plastic part of the jaw. Dimples create a "memory" that subsequent settings slide into, making new settings inaccurate.

MAKE THE MOVEABLE JAW

See figure 17. Cut the parts to size.

Glue the top and bottom wear plates to the jaw blank. The plates can be plastic, thin plywood, or solid hardwood, such as hard maple or oak. If you use wood, orient the grain with the grain of the veneered base. Don't use metal fasteners on the top plate, as you may need to rip this area of the jaw to the exact height of the fixed jaw. Once the glue has dried, flush-trim the edges of the plates even with the jaw. Remove the workpiece stop from the fixed jaw, set it aside, and clamp the moveable jaw to the fixed jaw and check that they're precisely the same height.

Drill holes through the metal flange at the corners of the screw pivot for #6 pan-head screws. Thread the veneer screw through the screw nut in the yoke block and attach the pivot with the locking screw. Now turn the veneer screw until the pivot touches the moveable jaw. Mark and drill holes, and screw the pivot to the jaw, making sure the locking screw faces up.

Position the stiffener just below the top of the moveable jaw and directly above the screw pivot, and mark an

access hole for the pivot locking screw. Drill a ½ in. hole through the stiffener at your mark, and lightly chamfer both sides. Mark, drill, and countersink six holes through the inside of the jaw for #8 screws. Then glue and screw the stiffener to the jaw. Finally, add the #12 screw through the base and into the bottom of the jaw.

MAKE AND MOUNT THE BASEPLATE

Refer to figure 18 for making the baseplate. Cut the plastic plate to size (see Working with Plastic, page 36), and cut the aluminum bar to length.

Lay out, drill, and tap two holes in each bar for ¼-20 machine screws. After drilling the holes, but before tapping them, clamp each bar to the acrylic plate and use a transfer punch through the holes to mark the center of the slots in the plate. Then finish tapping the holes.

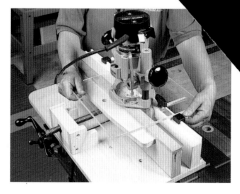

Mortises made easy. With the workpiece held securely in its jaws, this mortising fixture guides a special baseplate mounted to your router and lets you plunge-cut mortises. Setting a pair of stops determines the mortise length.

Use a square aligned with your transfer marks to lay out the slot locations on the plate. Mark the ends of the slots, then rout them with a ¼ in. bit. (See Dadoes, Grooves, and Slots, page 85.) Later, if the fit is tight, you can widen the slots slightly with a file.

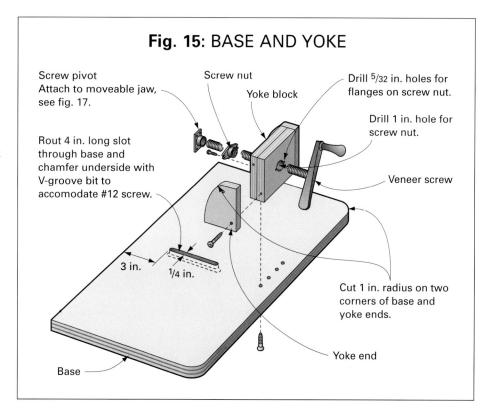

Fig. 15: BASE AND YOKE

Screw pivot
Attach to moveable jaw, see fig. 17.

Screw nut

Yoke block

Drill 5/32 in. holes for flanges on screw nut.

Drill 1 in. hole for screw nut.

Rout 4 in. long slot through base and chamfer underside with V-groove bit to accomodate #12 screw.

Veneer screw

3 in.

¼ in.

Cut 1 in. radius on two corners of base and yoke ends.

Yoke end

Base

...he bit hole. Use
...age 34) to locate
...ounting holes
...es of your
...slots. Drill the
...a 1/2 in. spade bit, then
drill and countersink the router
mounting holes.

Slide the machine screws through the
bars and through the slots in the baseplate. Place rubber washers over the
bolts and against the plastic (you can
buy rubber washers, or make them
yourself from leftover inner tube),
then add metal washers and lock
knobs. The rubber washers keep the
bar from slipping. Occasionally you'll
have to clean the sawdust from under
them to make them grab the plastic
again.

SETTING UP THE MORTISER

Insert an up-cut spiral bit into your
plunge router and fasten the router to
the baseplate. Mark a single line for
one cheek (with an "X" drawn on the
inside to remind you where to rout)
and two more lines to mark the ends
of the mortise. Place the work
between the jaws, measure the

Measure the space. Place the work into
the jig and measure the distance to the
top of the jaws.

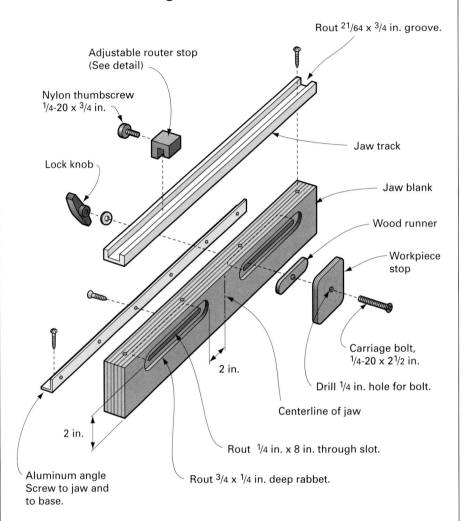

Fig. 16: FIXED JAW

Rout $21/64 \times 3/4$ in. groove.

Adjustable router stop
(See detail)

Nylon thumbscrew
$1/4$-20 x $3/4$ in.

Lock knob

Jaw track

Jaw blank

Wood runner

Workpiece
stop

2 in.

Carriage bolt,
$1/4$-20 x $2 1/2$ in.

Drill $1/4$ in. hole for bolt.

Centerline of jaw

2 in.

Rout $1/4$ in. x 8 in. through slot.

Aluminum angle
Screw to jaw and
to base.

Rout $3/4$ x $1/4$ in. deep rabbet.

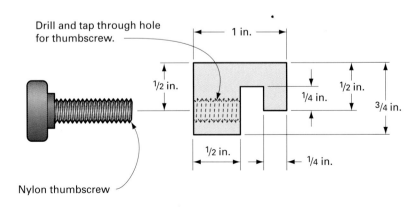

ADJUSTABLE ROUTER STOP DETAIL

Drill and tap through hole
for thumbscrew.

1 in.

$1/2$ in.

$1/2$ in.

$1/4$ in.

$3/4$ in.

$1/2$ in.

$1/4$ in.

Nylon thumbscrew

Fig. 17: MOVEABLE JAW

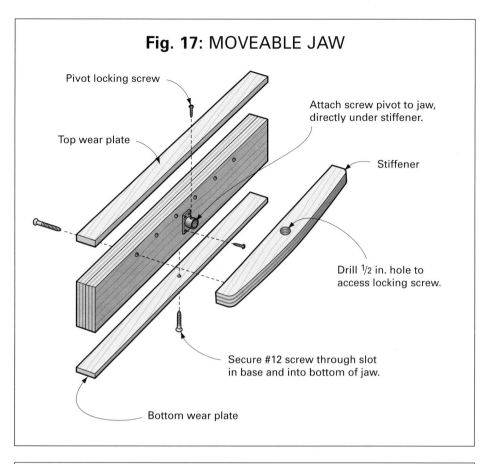

Pivot locking screw

Top wear plate

Attach screw pivot to jaw, directly under stiffener.

Stiffener

Drill ¹/₂ in. hole to access locking screw.

Secure #12 screw through slot in base and into bottom of jaw.

Bottom wear plate

Fig. 18: BASEPLATE

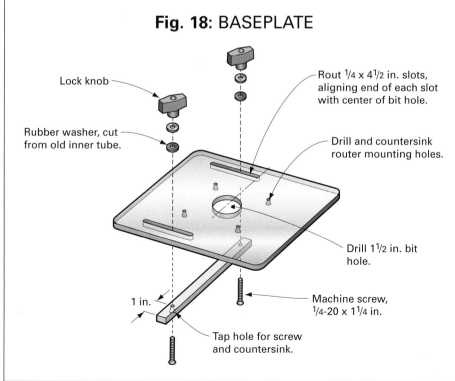

Lock knob

Rubber washer, cut from old inner tube.

Rout ¹/₄ x 4¹/₂ in. slots, aligning end of each slot with center of bit hole.

Drill and countersink router mounting holes.

Drill 1¹/₂ in. bit hole.

Machine screw, ¹/₄-20 x 1¹/₄ in.

1 in.

Tap hole for screw and countersink.

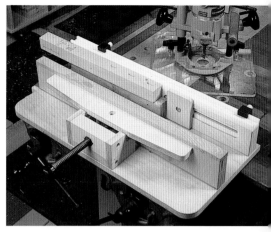

Fill the gap. Place the spacer under the workpiece to bring it flush with the top of the jaws. For multiple cuts, set the work stop against the end of the work.

remaining space to the top of the jaws, and mill a spacer slightly thinner than the workpiece and equal in thickness to the space measured. If the width and height are similar, be sure to mark the face of the spacer that faces up. Then position the work on top of the spacer, with the middle of its mortise in line with the veneer screw. Make sure the top edge of the workpiece is flush with the top of the jaws. Adjust the workpiece stop against the work for subsequent setups, and turn the screw to clamp the workpiece.

Set the baseplate bar into the groove in the fixed jaw, loosen the lock knobs, and slide the router back and forth until the leading edge of the bit touches the inside "X" of your cheek line. Tighten the knobs.

Rotate the bit 90° and slide the bar forward in the groove until the edge of the bit touches the forward end of the mortise. Lock a router stop against the leading edge of the baseplate. Then pull the router and bit back to the opposite end of the mortise and set the second stop against the near end of the baseplate.

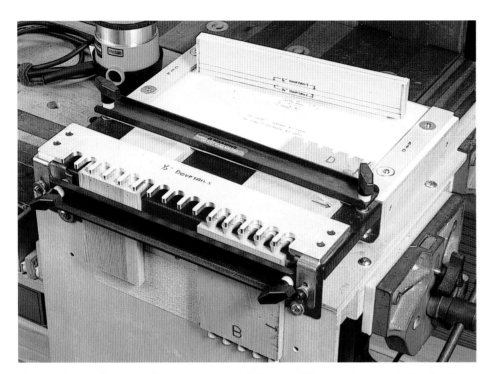

Better dovetails. Mounting your commercial dovetail jig to a shop-made jig simplifies setup and results in a better joint.

Dovetail Jig Improvements

BITS AND TOOLS
• ⅛ and ⁵⁄₃₂ in. drill bits

• transfer punch, as needed

• ⅛ in. spiral bit

MATERIALS AND HARDWARE
• 4 ea. 8-32 x ¾ in. pan-head machine screws and washers

• # 8 x 2 in. drywall screws, as needed

• 4 ea. 8-32 threaded inserts or T-nuts

• 2 ea. ¼-20 nuts

• 100-grit pressure-sensitive adhesive (PSA) sandpaper

• scrap plywood, ¼, ½ and ¾ in. thick

• scrap wood, 1 in. thick

Dovetail Jig

There are many great commercial dovetail jigs on the market that work with hand-held routers for routing dovetail joints. Some of these jigs are simple; some are more complex. Some cut a variety of dovetails, including through and half-blind dovetails; others are dedicated to one specific joint. However, all of them could stand to be a little easier to use.

The half-blind dovetail jig shown here is my personal favorite, and I use it for making half-blind dovetailed drawers. I've modified it to make it more useful, more accurate—and much easier to use. You can buy the same jig and make the exact same improvements you see here, or use my ideas as inspiration for modifying your own commercial jig.

First, a couple points about the jig I use. My jig has aluminum templates,

which are fastened independent of the clamping mechanisms that hold the workpiece. While separate aluminum templates are a little more expensive, they're far more durable than plastic and much simpler to use. By virtue of being independent of any clamping devices, you can control one thing at a time, which simplifies setup and ultimately allows greater control over the fit of the dovetails.

ADD THE IMPROVEMENTS

Refer to figure 19 to cut the necessary parts to size. Make sure to modify the dimensions if necessary to suit your particular commercial dovetail jig.

Start by measuring the overall length of your jig, and then build an L-shaped platform that's roughly 18 in. deep by 12 in. high. Make the platform 2 in. wider than the jig's length. Assemble the platform by gluing and screwing a plywood front to a ply-

Storage at back. The author included a drawer in the back of her jig for holding bits, baseplates, and other small router dovetail accessories.

Fig. 19: DOVETAIL JIG IMPROVEMENTS

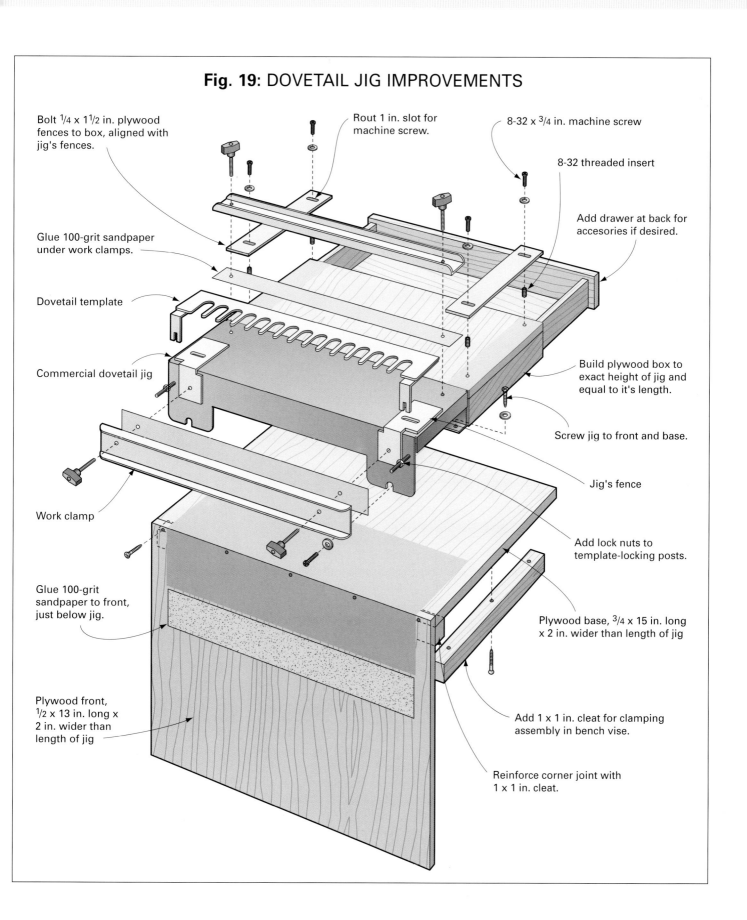

Bolt ¹/₄ x 1¹/₂ in. plywood fences to box, aligned with jig's fences.

Rout 1 in. slot for machine screw.

8-32 x ³/₄ in. machine screw

8-32 threaded insert

Glue 100-grit sandpaper under work clamps.

Add drawer at back for accesories if desired.

Dovetail template

Commercial dovetail jig

Build plywood box to exact height of jig and equal to it's length.

Screw jig to front and base.

Jig's fence

Work clamp

Add lock nuts to template-locking posts.

Glue 100-grit sandpaper to front, just below jig.

Plywood base, ³/₄ x 15 in. long x 2 in. wider than length of jig

Plywood front, ¹/₂ x 13 in. long x 2 in. wider than length of jig

Add 1 x 1 in. cleat for clamping assembly in bench vise.

Reinforce corner joint with 1 x 1 in. cleat.

More fences are better. Aligning the workpiece is easier if you add a pair of plywood fences that line up with the jig's exisiting fences.

wood base, and stiffen by attaching a wood cleat with glue and screws. Screw or bolt your dovetail jig to the platform. Measure the height of the jig on the base, and build a box to precisely that height and equal to the length of the dovetail jig. Screw the box to the base, as shown. If you want, you can build a shallow drawer and fit it into the back of the box for storing jig accessories, as shown in the bottom photo on page 60.

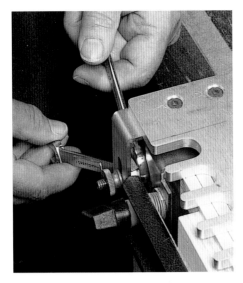

Extra nuts for accuracy. By adding a nut on each of the jig's two threaded posts, the author can reliably lock in the template setting for accurate, repeatable cuts.

Quick clamping. A cleat secured to the underside of the jig makes clamping it in the bench fast and simple.

The two plywood fences work in tandem with the jig's stock fences to help you align the work more accurately to the jig. (See top photo, left.) Rout a pair of slots in each fence, and locate them on the top of the box as shown. Use a transfer punch through the center of each slot to mark the box, install threaded inserts at your marks, and bolt the fences to the box.

I improved the arrangement that secures the jig's dovetail template setting by adding a nut (¼-20, in my case) to each template-locking post, directly in front of the hex nut on the post. (See photo, left.)

To increase the effective clamping power of the jig, apply a wide sheet of 100-grit sandpaper to the front of the platform, and add narrow strips of the same grit to the working surface of the work clamps. No more work slipping during crucial cuts!

A good dovetail jig should be held firmly to the bench, and needs to stay that way during routing. While you can use clamps to secure the assembly to your benchtop, I prefer a quicker method that works with my bench's end vise. By screwing a cleat under platform, I can quickly and conveniently place the assembly over the

vise, tighten the cleat in the vise, and confidently go about my dovetail-routing business. Bonus: there's no clamps to get in the way. (See photo, left.)

MAKE AND USE A SETUP STICK

There are three key settings for making perfect dovetails with a dovetail jig. One is adjusting the router bit depth, which is discussed in Half-Blind Dovetails (page 106.) The other two settings—positioning the jig's fences and its template—are greatly simplified if you make the setup stick shown in figure 20. You'll need to adjust the length of the stick and its markings to suit your own particular jig.

Begin by making the top horizontal stick equal to your jig's width capacity (mine is 12 in.), and cut a smaller vertical stick about 2 in. shorter. On the horizontal stick, lay out a long line equal to your jig's front-to-back template setting, or template setback. Since my jig accommodates two templates, one for ¼ in. dovetails and another for ½ in. dovetails, I lay out two sets of lines to the required setback, which in my case is $\frac{9}{32}$ in. and $\frac{19}{32}$ in. respectively. At each end of the stock, lay out a short line equal to your jig's fence setting, sometimes referred to as the edge stop distance. Again, I draw two lines—⅛ and 3⁄16 in.—that correspond to the fence settings for my two templates. Carefully read your owner's manual to find these settings. They may be called something else, but once you understand the setup you'll understand what you're looking for. Use a knife to mark the lines; pencil lines are too thick to read accurately. Once you've knifed the lines, attach the smaller vertical stick with glue and nails, centering it on the horizontal stick and keeping its top edge slightly below the surface of the marked stick.

Set up with a stick. This simple plywood jig makes setting up dovetail templates a snap and helps troubleshoot problems.

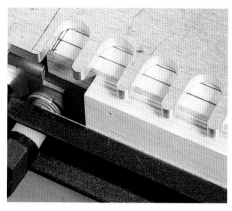

Line up the template. Move the stick under the metal template until the correct line on the stick lines up with the edge of the leftmost slot.

Set the jig's fences. With the template removed, adjust the jig's metal fences against the end of the stick.

Fig. 20: SETUP STICK

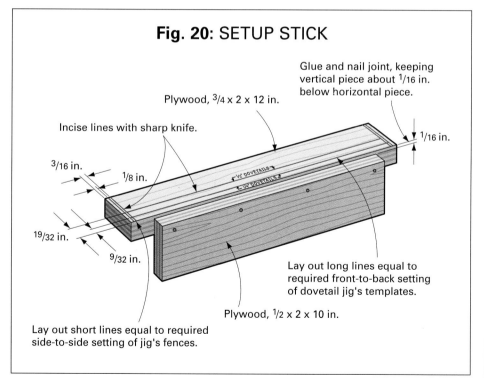

Glue and nail joint, keeping vertical piece about 1/16 in. below horizontal piece.

Plywood, 3/4 x 2 x 12 in.

Incise lines with sharp knife.

1/16 in.

3/16 in.

1/8 in.

19/32 in.

9/32 in.

Lay out long lines equal to required front-to-back setting of dovetail jig's templates.

Plywood, 1/2 x 2 x 10 in.

Lay out short lines equal to required side-to-side setting of jig's fences.

Square the plywood fences. Holding a drafting triangle against the back of the setup stick or against the workpiece, align the plywood fences with the jig's metal fences.

To position the jig's fences, start by positioning the setup stick behind the vertical work clamp and place the desired dovetail template onto the jig. Slide the stick to the left until the cor-responding line on the left end of the stick aligns with the edge of the left-most slot in the template. Tighten the clamp. (See top photo, right.) Remove the template, adjust the jig's left fence

Fig. 21: JIG MARKINGS

Draw the diagram below directly on the jig to help with marking the four parts of a drawer.

BACK
D | A
↓

LABELS ON
INSIDE FACES

LEFT SIDE D → #1 = FIRST DRAWER ← RIGHT SIDE A

C ARROWS MARK B
BOTTOM EDGE

C ↑ B
FRONT

On the left plywood fence, write "C & A"
On the right plywood fence, write "B & D"

Info where you need it. Mark the jig itself with your setup instructions so critical information is right at hand every time you make a set of dovetailed drawers.

against the end of the stick, and secure it. Repeat this procedure to set the right fence, moving the setup stick to the right side of the jig, aligning the marks on its right end with the rightmost template slot, and locking the fence, as shown in the middle right photo, previous page.

With the setup stick still clamped in the jig, use it to set the front-to-back position of the template. Place the template back on the jig, and adjust it backwards or forwards until the bottom of its slots are even with the corresponding setback line on the stick. (See top right photo, previous page.) Now turn the nut you added earlier against the jig's hex nut to lock it into position.

Before putting the setup stick aside, place a large drafting triangle against the stick's back edge and against each of the jig's fences to square the plywood fences and align them with the jig's fences. (See bottom right photo, previous page.) Keep in mind that the plywood fences are a guide to help position the workpiece in the jig. They shouldn't interfere with the jig's primary fences, which must make full contact with the work for successful dovetails.

Mark the Setup Info on the Jig

The last step is to mark some pertinent information right on your dovetail jig assembly. Using a permanent marker, draw a diagram in the center

of the top platform that depicts marking your drawer stock, as shown in figure 21. Draw corresponding letter designations on the left and right plywood fences to indicate which end of each drawer part goes on the left or right side of the jig. If you follow your labeling system, you can't screw up and rout the wrong end of a drawer part.

Finally, in a clear area, jot down these reminders for correcting loose or tight-fitting joints: "Too loose? Increase bit depth." "Too tight? Decrease bit depth."

Special Holding Systems

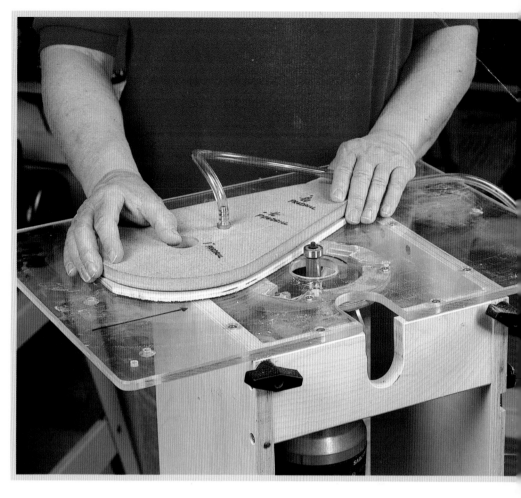

The side-cutting action of router bits combined with their high rpms makes holding workpieces safely an important aspect of router work. While this issue is greatest for hand-held routing, milling small pieces safely and accurately on the router table can also present a challenge. Luckily, there are three proven holding techniques that let you deal with this problem successfully. The first and most obvious means of gripping your work is to use standard woodworking clamps. (See The Router Toolbox, page 21.) The big advantage of common clamps is that we usually have suitable ones available in our shops. But a distinct disadvantage is that they often get in the way, forcing you to rout in stops and starts as you move a clamp and reposition it to clear it from the oncoming path of a bit. The result is burning and inconsistent cuts. To overcome this problem and address some other clamping concerns, the following two holding techniques take over where normal clamps leave off.

The Secret of Hot Glue

Hot glue, and the accompanying squeeze gun that heats and distributes it, is one of the secrets to holding stuff in my shop. This thermoplastic (heat sensitive) glue has some appealing attributes for router work. It grabs super quick, allowing you to position parts accurately without slippage or misalignment. And you can easily release stuck parts once the routing job is done. In addition, the glue won't leave residue in the pores of your work, which ensures you don't compromise your finish techniques down the road. Once you've invested in the gun that dispenses the glue, the glue sticks themselves are inexpensive.

One of my favorite tricks is to use hot glue for holding a workpiece to a sacrificial platform or scrap piece for more practical and safer routing. This technique works really well for small work, where hands and fingers are at risk. By sticking the workpiece to a larger piece, you can safely maneuver the assembly past the bit.

There are two approaches you can use. The first is to make a stepped platform, which consists of a bottom and a raised platform attached to it. The workpiece sits on the bottom, and you make the platform to the same thickness as the stock you're routing. By having both parts flush with each other, you can now attach guiding jigs to the assembly for more accurate routing. (See top left photo, page 66.) Although practically any material will work for stepped platforms, I favor melamine-coated particleboard (MCP) for the bottom because the glue is easy to remove from its slick surface once the job is done, readying it for the next use.

Glue keeps it together. To rout a groove in a plywood part, the author holds it in a stepped jig. Dots of hot glue under the part keep it tight to the jig while cutting.

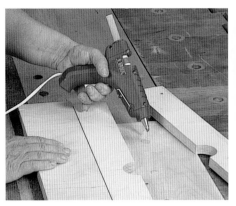

Not too much. Be sparing with your glue, so you can unclamp the work once the routing is done. Dots about the size of a pea hold tenaciously but allow you to release the work without damage.

The second approach is to glue extensions, or handles, directly to small work. Handles can be made from any material on hand, such as leftover scrap parts or, one of my favorites, wood dowels. (See photo, below.)

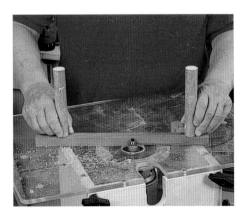

Dowels will do it. By hot-gluing a couple of dowels directly to small work you'll keep hands clear of cutters and gain more control.

The question always comes up about how much glue to use. In general, it's best to use dots of glue about 3/16 in. in diameter, spaced about 5 to 6 in. apart. (See top photo, right.) When you separate the pieces, the glue spot shouldn't have spread any larger than about 1/2 in. in diameter. Anything more just makes more work. Once you've dabbed on the glue dots, immediately press the parts together. The glue is very tacky and dries as it cools, so the bond is almost instant.

Once the routing job is done, I use two simple tools—an old butcher's knife and a sharp scraper—to separate the assembly and remove remnant adhesive. (See The Router Toolbox, page 21.) Use the butcher knife as a wedge by slipping it into the seam between the workpiece and the platform or scrap piece, and gently lever with the knife to pop the two pieces apart. If necessary, you

can use the edge of the knife to help cut through the glue spots. Once the pieces are separated, scrape away the old glue with the scraper.

Using a Vacuum Clamping System

The strongest, quickest, and most convenient clamping system I know is provided by vacuum. By using atmospheric pressure, you can clamp parts quickly and without fuss—and just as easily unclamp them. The system is easy to make yourself, and consists of two main components: a vacuum plate, which holds the work, and a source of vacuum connected to the plate via an air hose.

PICK YOUR VACUUM SOURCE

There are two sources of vacuum you can consider. The first is a compressor and a venturi valve, through which compressed air blows. The problem with this setup is that the venturi requires the compressor to run continuously to hold clamping pressure, and most compressors would soon burn out running in this manner.

A better and more lasting choice is an electric vacuum pump and motor fitted with the necessary airline accessories. (See fig. 1.) There are three kinds of pumps: diaphragm, rotary vane, and piston. A diaphragm pump is the smallest and most compact, and works very well to clamp parts for routing. A rotary-vane pump is also quite small and works equally well for router clamping, as well as other operations such as veneer clamping. In addition, a rotary pump is reasonably priced, relatively easy to find, and you can fit the pump to an air tank for situations where you need to hold parts for an extended period. A piston pump is very expensive, and practically impossible to repair when it needs attention. I would avoid it. Both diaphragm and rotary-vane pumps are easy and inexpensive to repair and maintain.

You can find an inexpensive used pump from surplus equipment catalogs and stores. Be sure you acquire a vacuum gauge (it measures in inches of mercury—not pounds-per-square inch, or psi) before you go pump shopping. Test the pump in the store

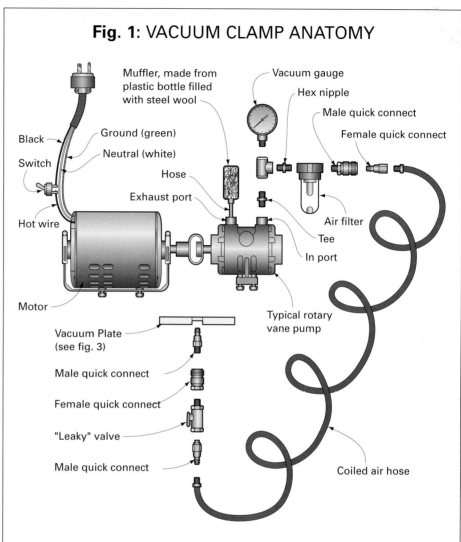

Fig. 1: VACUUM CLAMP ANATOMY

No clamps in the way. Using a vacuum plate to hold your work keeps the working surface free of clamps and other obstructions for easy routing.

to see that it measures at least 24 in. of mercury. More is better, but even NASA has trouble building those! Also, look for a pump that has an in port and an out, or exhaust, port with at least ¼ in. pipe threads so airflow won't be restricted. Reducers can be used in larger ports.

Once you've located the pump, you'll need to connect it with the correct air-hose fittings, as shown in figure 1. Study the drawing to understand how the air circulates: it's just opposite of how we usually think of moving air. From an auto-supply store or

discount import store (and some hardware stores), buy a coiled air hose (without the swivel fittings—they leak), a small inline air filter, and the necessary male and female air hose fittings.

The out port of the pump will require a muffler. There are vacuum pump mufflers available, and a used pump may already have one, but most don't. I made my own muffler from a discarded plastic vitamin bottle stuffed with steel wool. Connect the muffler to the exhaust port with a length of hose from the port and into

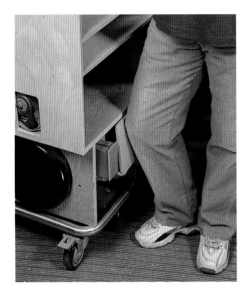

A knee is better than hands. The author uses her knee to push a plywood paddle when turning on and off her pump, keeping her hands free for more important tasks.

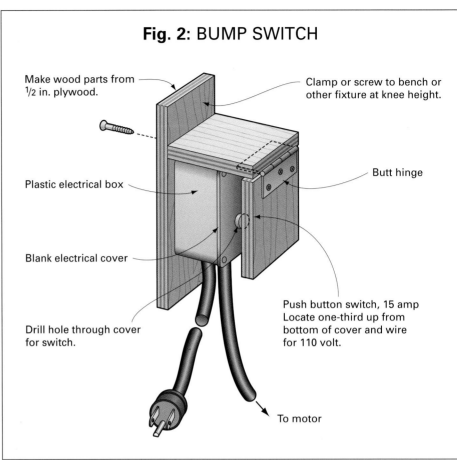

Fig. 2: BUMP SWITCH

Make wood parts from ¹/₂ in. plywood.

Clamp or screw to bench or other fixture at knee height.

Plastic electrical box

Butt hinge

Blank electrical cover

Push button switch, 15 amp Locate one-third up from bottom of cover and wire for 110 volt.

Drill hole through cover for switch.

To motor

the bottle's cap. Drill a series of holes in the bottom of the bottle to allow air to escape. The steel wool does a great job of muffling the sound.

You'll find that many used pumps don't have an on/off switch. A simple toggle switch mounted in an electrical box will work. Make sure the switch is rated for 15 amps and wired for 110 volt. For added convenience, I made a "bump" switch by hinging a shop-made wooden paddle over a heavy-duty push button switch, as shown in figure 2. Clamp or screw the switch in range of your knee. While both hands are busy getting ready to rout, you simply bump the paddle to turn on the pump. The clamping action is nearly instantaneous. Bump the paddle again to turn it off. (See photo, above.)

USE A VARIETY OF VACUUM PLATES

The heart of the vacuum system is the vacuum plate which holds the

workpiece. A closed loop of gasket material adhered to the plate creates a chamber in which the vacuum can create pressure to hold the work. (See fig. 3.)

It's best to make different size plates for different routing jobs. Plates must be "leakproof," so it's important to use a non-porous material. I've found that painted MDF is inexpensive and works well, but MCP will work if you apply a coat or two of shellac or paint on any exposed edges, such as the vacuum hole or any sawn edges. Drill a hole in the plate for the hose fitting. Then use either self-adhesive, closed-cell insulation tape or specialized vacuum tape (available from the companies that supply vacuum clamping systems).

Arrange the tape in a closed loop so it surrounds the vacuum hole and creates a chamber. Make the chamber as large as is practical, ideally about 8 in. square, which will provide almost 100 psi of holding power. (See bottom left photo, opposite page.) Keep in mind that chambers can be too big. If you find that the workpiece distorts when it's clamped to the plate, make the chamber smaller. For really small parts, I make a vacuum "wand," which is particularly useful for router table operations. (See middle right photo, opposite page.) Experiment with chamber layouts to see what works best for you. To make it easy to clamp my plates, I often screw a wood cleat under them and grip them in my bench vise.

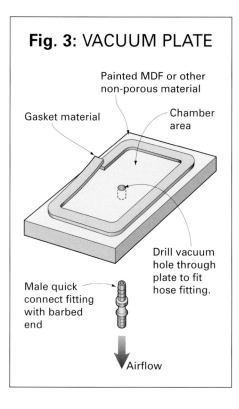

Fig. 3: VACUUM PLATE

Painted MDF or other non-porous material

Gasket material

Chamber area

Drill vacuum hole through plate to fit hose fitting.

Male quick connect fitting with barbed end

Airflow

Removing your work from the vacuum plate requires that the vacuum seal be broken. If simply turning off the pump breaks the seal, it's a clear sign your plate is leaking, so be sure to correct the seal or clamp failure can result. A good seal should be impossible to separate by hand. To break the seal, I use a "leaky" valve, as shown in figure 1.

To make the valve, buy a plastic ball valve and drill an ⅛ in. hole just slightly past center on the workpiece side of the valve. Be sure to turn the valve halfway open before drilling, and drill carefully, retracting the bit as soon as you break through the valve body so you don't damage the ball and render the valve useless. Connect the leaky valve to your air line. To break the seal, simple turn the valve off and the vacuum is instantly collapsed. (See bottom photo, below.)

Keep in mind that your vacuum clamping system can be upgraded for veneer clamping with the addition of one-way valves and a vacuum bag, so don't hesitate to add this valuable system to your shop as soon as you can.

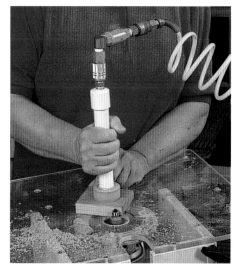

Stuck from above. For holding small stuff, make a smaller plate and connect it to a handle made from PVC pipe.

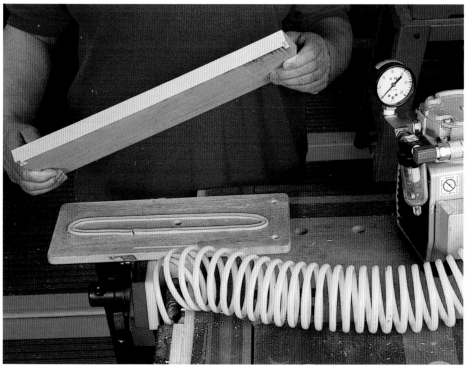

Clamp it to a plate. A closed loop of gasket material surrounds a hole, through which the vacuum draws air. Simply place the stock on the plate, turn on the pump, and you're ready to rout.

Quick work release. Instead of disconnecting the hose fitting, simply turn the valve to break the vacuum seal and release the workpiece.

Basic Router Techniques

subtract the amount to be removed, and then measure that amount from the end of the board. Aside from being awkward, this adds a complicated math operation that encourages mistakes.

However, sometimes you're forced to measure the waste, such as when setting up a cutter to a specific depth or length in relation to a guide or fence—a common task in router work. In cases like this, remember to measure the thickness of the stock first so you can determine how much the bit needs to remove and the amount of material that will be left after routing. At this point, your measurement must be quite exact—measuring for dovetails is a good example—and your best bet is to use dial calipers for accuracy. (See The Router Toolbox, page 21.)

Marking is another key aspect for cutting good joints. You'll find many references to marking stock in the book so that router operations will occur where you intend them. This is important, because with the price of today's lumber we can't afford cutting mistakes. The most important mark you can make is a *reference edge*. This is the first mark you make, often on the long edge or the end of a board. Once you've designated a particular edge with your mark, you reference all subsequent marking or cutting sequences from this master mark. I use the letter "R" for my reference mark, but you can write any symbol you like.

There are several essential router techniques that make cutting joints a whole lot easier, more accurate, and much safer. If you practice the following tips your router joinery will become more effective and more enjoyable.

Measuring and Marking Stock

The first step towards good joinery is stock preparation: milling wood to the proper thickness, ripping it to width, and cutting it to length. If you take your time during the milling process and pay attention to the particular characteristics of the wood you're sizing, you'll discover important information that will help you set up your routing operations more accurately.

Proper measuring technique goes hand-in-hand with stock preparation. There's an old adage that says, "Measure the work, not the waste." For example, when marking a board to length, mark the length you want and make a cut at that mark. You don't first measure the entire board,

In line with the fence. A small rule is handy for aligning a bit bearing with the fence. While holding the rule against the fence, pivot the fence until the bearing comes in contact with the rule.

Be consistent when marking from piece to piece, so reference edges are complementary from one part of the project to another. For example, if you're building a bookcase with shelves dadoed into the sides, designate the bottom end of each case side as the reference edge, and lay out your dadoes referencing these edges. Then lay the long sides edge to edge to confirm that the shelves will be parallel with each other and perpendicular to front of the case. By using reference marks on your work, you'll make your joints more accurately and with a lot fewer mistakes.

Hand-Held or Router Table?

Once you've milled your stock to dimension, you now face the choice between using a hand-held router or the router table to cut your joints. So how do you choose which one to use? First, remember that the router table is the best choice for routing narrow or small stock. It's risky and often downright dangerous to use a hand-held router for this type of work, because the workpiece itself

doesn't offer enough support to stabilize the router's baseplate.

On the other hand, it's better to use a hand-held router for really big stuff. The best approach is to clamp your stock to a worksurface and take multiple passes to achieve the final cut (see Taking Incremental Cuts, page 75). With this approach, you're moving a relatively lightweight router rather than muscling a big chunk of wood across a table, which will quickly tire you and often results in inconsistent cuts.

Using a Router Table Fence

When you're cutting joints on the router table, you'll quickly come to appreciate using a fence. Once you learn how to set one up correctly, your joint cutting will become much more accurate. Remember that one of the nice things about using a fence is that you can choose practically any type of bit, which increases your joint-cutting repertoire. However, keep in mind that routing with a fence limits you to straight cuts only.

Setting the fence to the bit accurately is one of the keys to good fence technique. I've simplified this routine with the fence shown in the book (see Router Table, page 38) by designing one that pivots at one end. Often, the simplest approach is to eyeball the desired distance from the bit and simply pivot the fence into position, then tighten the lock knob.

Other times you'll need to align the fence flush with a bearing when working with piloted bits. The trick is to place the edge of a small rule against the fence at the level of the bearing, then pivot the fence until the rule touches the bearing. (See top photo, left.)

When you need to dial in the fence to a specific measurement, you can use a bit gauge and a bit of simple math. For example, let's say you want to make an odd-size rabbet and your rabbet bit set doesn't have the correct diameter bearing for the desired rabbet width. Start by choosing a straight bit whose diameter is larger than the rabbet width. Now calculate the distance needed from the outside edge of the bit to the fence and set the bit gauge to that amount. Rotate the router bit so the gauge touches the corner of one of its cutting edges, and pivot the fence until it contact the gauge, as shown in the photo, below. Lock the fence and you're done.

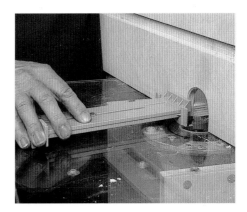

Easy bit setup. With a bit gauge set to the desired width of cut, set the fence by pivoting it until the bit's cutting edge contacts the gauge.

Making a Zero-Clearance Fence

Some cutters, such as the lock miter bit (see page 118), yield better results with less tearout when you provide "zero clearance," or the smallest possible gap between the bit and the fence. In addition, cutting with a zero-clearance fence is generally safer for any type of cut, since offcuts and even the workpiece itself can't get

Bit makes the fence. Use the bit you'll be routing with to create a zero-clearance fence by clamping a piece of plywood to the fence and rotating the assembly into the spinning bit.

wedged or pulled into the gap between the bit and fence.

To create a zero-clearance fence, simply install your existing fence on the table and then clamp a piece of ½ in. plywood against the face of the fence. Raise the bit to the desired height, turn on the router, and slowly pivot the fence into the spinning cutter, as shown in the photo, above. Adjust the fence until the bit is completely buried in the plywood, but make sure you don't rout through the fence's base. Unclamp the temporary fence and reverse its face so the torn side is now against the table fence and reclamp. Now you can reset the fence for your specific cut.

Routing Without a Fence

You'll want to remove the fence when it comes to routing irregular shaped parts. This setup requires a bit with a bearing since the wood must reference against something to yield a consistent cut. Keep in mind

that any shaped or curved edges whose inside radii are bigger than the diameter of the cutter can be routed. Smaller radii will need smaller-diameter bearings.

When working with a bearing-guided bit, it's important to begin the cut safely. For years woodworkers have advocated using a starting pin, onto which you place the work and then

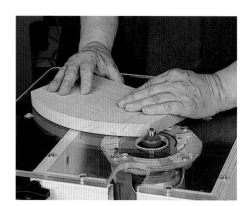

Heel starts the cut. You can safely start an un-fenced cut by planting the heel of your left hand on the table and then pivoting the work into the cutter.

pivot it into the cutter to commence routing. The problem with this approach is that once the cut has begun and you no longer need the pin, it's in the way. A simpler and better method is to use the heel of your left hand as the starting pin. The technique is easy once you practice it a few times. Plant the heel of your hand on the table, place the work against your hand, and pivot the work into the cutter with your opposite hand and onto the bearing, using the skiing technique (see page 75). Once the workpiece makes contact with the bearing, you can pick up you hand and continue routing. The process of starting the cut and then routing along the edge should happen in one smooth, continuous motion. (See bottom photo, left.)

When routing around the shape of the piece, plan to have your hands on opposite sides of the bit at all times as a safety measure and for better control. Even if you rout off the end of the work, your hand will still be around another corner before it can encounter the bit.

Setting Bit Height and Depth

One of the keys to accurate joints is setting the bit precisely to the right depth or height. The sequence for setting the bit differs between fixed-base and plunge routers, and each tool requires a specific approach.

When setting the bit depth on a fixed-base router, there are two tools I use to get the bit set to exactly the right height. When I need a specific measurement I use a commercial bit gauge (see page 22). This gauge has positive settings divided into 32nd's of an inch, which lets you dial in very precise settings. Once you've set the desired bit height on the gauge,

Fig. 1: SETTING THE BIT WITH A PLUNGE BASE

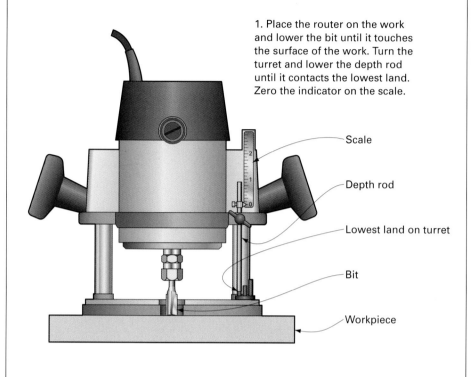

1. Place the router on the work and lower the bit until it touches the surface of the work. Turn the turret and lower the depth rod until it contacts the lowest land. Zero the indicator on the scale.

— Scale

— Depth rod

— Lowest land on turret

— Bit

— Workpiece

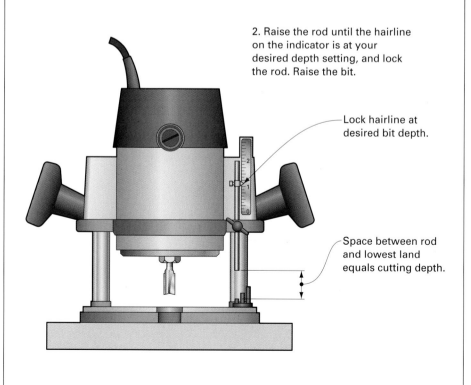

2. Raise the rod until the hairline on the indicator is at your desired depth setting, and lock the rod. Raise the bit.

— Lock hairline at desired bit depth.

— Space between rod and lowest land equals cutting depth.

Two hands free. Using a bit gauge to set the bit depth leaves your hands free for adjusting and locking in the setting.

place the gauge on the router's baseplate, where it will stand up by itself. This frees up both hands so you can move the bit up or down in the router and then tighten the base to lock in the setting. (See photo, above.)

My second favorite bit setting tool is a small block of hardwood, cut to ¾ x 1 x 2 in., or any dimensions that suit the particular work you're doing. You can use the block to gauge all sorts of bit setups. For example, when you need to determine how much of a bead you might want with a beading bit, place the block on the router's baseplate and next to the bit before you make the cut to get direct visual feedback on just how big the bead will be. Or when you're trying to set up a roundover bit so it will cut flush with the work, place the block on the router again and use your finger to feel the corner of the bit where it rests against the block. If it feels flush, your cut will be flush. Another good example is when setting up a bit for routing a chamfer. Simply place the block against the

Visual feedback. To help set the bit depth, place a block of hardwood next to the cutting edge of the bit to show how much material the bit will cut.

chamfer bit to see precisely how wide the facet of the chamfer will be, as shown in the photo, above.

Setting the bit depth on a plunge router takes a little more effort than when using a fixed-base router because plunge routers have different bit-setting mechanisms, as shown in figure 1. Follow the steps shown in the drawing to dial in your setting exactly where you need it. Once you've set the depth, you're ready to rout. Turn on the router and plunge the bit until the depth rod touches the land, then feed the router along the cut. Once you've made the cut, raise the bit clear of the stock before turning off the router, then wait until the bit stops spinning before you move the router off the stock. If you need to make incremental cuts (see opposite page), set up the depth of cut as described above, then turn the turret until the highest land fits under the depth rod. Make a pass, then turn the turret again to the next highest land. Keep routing and repositioning the turret in this manner until you've reached the lowest land.

Making Safe and Accurate Cuts

We all know how important safety is when it comes to routing. In addition, routing in a safe manner results in increased accuracy because it affords you more control over the process, which results in fewer mistakes and better cuts. The following information should help you approach the art of routing joints in a controlled and secure manner.

SPEED AND FEED

It's important that you understand feed and speed when it comes to routing joints. Speed refers to the rotational speed of the router's spindle. This is a fixed quantity (which can be altered on routers with variable-speed motors) and it's determined by the router, not you. Feed is two things. It refers to the direction you move the router and the bit past the work, and also the rate at which that pass is made. You and your technique determine the correct feed.

Moving the router in a specific direction is discussed in detail below (see Conventional or Climb Cut?, opposite page). Both this technique and the feed rate will impact how cleanly you cut, as well as whether or not you experience burning. For example, moving the router too slowly past certain woods can produce excessive friction from the bit and burn the wood. Conversely, moving too fast results in tearout or inconsistent cuts. Different materials will require different kinds of feed. The best way to learn the right feed is to practice on every specific operation. Luckily, every joint setup requires you to make a practice cut, which is your opportunity to help you to learn the correct feed for any given situation.

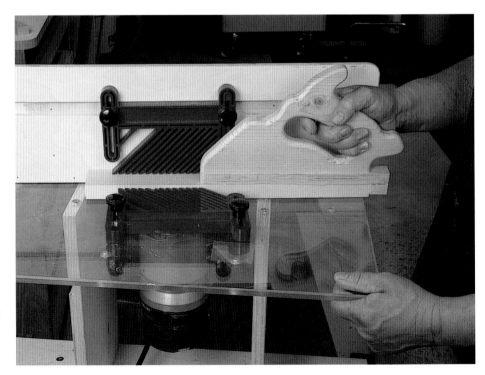

Save your fingers. A pair of commercial featherboards attached to both the fence and the table keeps your hands clear of the cut and affords more control.

TAKING INCREMENTAL CUTS

Incremental cutting means that only a portion of a profile or cut is made with each pass until the final cut is achieved. This is an important safety issue, because taking too big a bite in one pass can throw a workpiece or unexpectedly pull your hands into the cut. And taking incremental cuts results in a much smoother finish.

Adjusting the cutter up through the table or down through the base is one method. The other approach is to creep up on the final depth of cut by moving the fence a bit at a time. Typically, you should make your cuts in increments of ⅛ in., sometimes less. Let your work be your guide. The more material you have to remove, the smaller your increment should be. For example, the routed bevel on a raised panel offers a very long profile, and cuts in increments of 1/16 in. or less are needed for a smooth, safe finish.

USING FEATHERBOARDS

When routing narrow stock on the router table, featherboards are finger savers. In addition, they afford more control and result in smoother, more cleanly cut surfaces. If you mill a shallow dado into a tall router table fence (see Router Table, page 38), you can position a commercial feather-board on the fence to help place pressure on the work directly over the cutter. It's wise to install a second featherboard to the table itself to provide lateral pressure against the stock. (See bottom photo, oppostite page.)

CONVENTIONAL OR CLIMB CUT?

Feeding work into the cutter is a conventional cut, while feeding into the backside of the bit is known as a *climb cut*. In most cases, a conven-

Know your rotation. Arrows marked on fences, tables, and routers let you know which direction the cutter is spinning, which helps you feed your work in the right direction.

tional cut is the appropriate choice. But when the grain is unpredictable or particularly curly and prone to tearing, your final pass should be a climb cut. Be aware that climb cuts can be dangerous because the feed direction is the same as the rotation of the cutter. This situation tends to pull the workpiece faster than you want it to go. Caught unaware, you can have your hands unintentionally dragged into the cutter in router table operations, or you can be thrown off balance when routing with a hand-held router. So study the cut, and if you choose to climb cut, make sure you take a very light pass.

Knowing when the router is cutting conventionally or making a climb cut can often confuse us. A good trick that helps verify which way the cut is going to go is to mark your router with arrows indicating the rotation of the cutter. Do this on the base and

on the motor. Also mark the rotation on the router tabletop and on the horizontal plate (if your router table has one). In addition, mark the feed direction on the router tabletop and the horizontal plate. (See photo, above.) These little arrows are easy to draw and will remind you to rout in your chosen direction—no matter which operation you're using.

SKIING INTO THE CUT

"Skiing" into the cut eliminates burning and unintentionally routing around corners. I call it skiing because it resembles the lifting and landing action of the popular wintertime sport. The basic technique can be used with a hand-held router or on the router table. (See figure 2.) Begin a cut by starting about 1 in. in from the end of the work. Using a slanting movement, steer the router (if you're in a hand-held situation) or move the

Fig. 2: HOW TO SKI INTO THE CUT

1. Start cut about 1 in. from end, moving workpiece (or bit) at an angle into the bit.

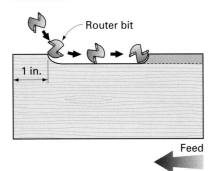

Router bit

1 in.

Feed

2. Finish the uncut end by reversing the feed direction, again approaching the work at an angle.

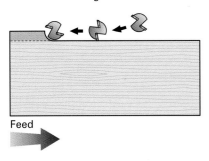

Feed

workpiece (if you're working on the router table) so the cutter approaches the work at an angle and then makes full contact with its edge. Keep the router (or the workpiece, depending on your situation) moving at all times, and continue to move it until you reach the end of the board. This approach prevents burning.

Now go back to the first 1 in. of uncut material and, as before, ski into the cut, but this time move in the opposite direction, or climb cut, and rout to the end. This method leaves reliably crisp corners.

ROUTING REALLY SMALL PIECES

Routing small parts presents a real safety hazard, and requires you to take an alternative approach to holding your work. When a piece is smaller than your hand, the easiest and safest method is to use hot glue to hold it to a larger piece of scrap, such as a leftover piece of the project you're working on or a piece of plywood. (See The Secret of Hot Glue, page 65.) This trick keeps your hands a safe distance from the bit. And there's a bonus: The glue is easy to pop off so you can quickly reapply more glue and reposition your stock for another cut.

Safe Routing Habits

There are a few key safety routines that I follow whenever I rout in my shop. Once you become familiar with them, you and your work will be safer and you'll have more control over the cut.

- Always unplug the router when changing bits or making adjustments.

- Make sure the bit is clear of the wood before turning the router on.

- Never hold the router in the air while turning it on or off.

- Check that the base makes firm contact with the work or jig before bringing the spinning bit into play.

- Plan the cutting sequence so your body movement is comfortable, with your weight well within your center of balance. If it doesn't feel good, don't do it.

- Change whatever you need until you're comfortable, be it your body stance, your clothing and gear, or the particular setup.

- In the middle of a routing job, but during a point when you're not routing, stand the router on its head on your bench, out of the way. Both the bit and you will be safe until you're ready to make the next cut.

- Unplug the router if you're going to be away from your work for awhile. It's too easy to forget that it's plugged in.

ROUTER FLIGHT CHECK

The "router flight check" is similar to the flight check a pilot makes before taking off in an airplane. A pilot's check covers all the important things. It's always done in the same order, and it's committed to memory. Most important, it's done every time before taking off. In the same way, the checklist below should be done every time you're about to turn on your router, and should begin with the router unplugged. To help me memorize the sequence, I have a mantra: tight, right, tight, set, off, clear, on. Here's what it means:

- Is the bit **tight** in the collet?

- Is the bit at the **right** height?

- Is the base-tightening mechanism **tight**?

- On a variable-speed router, is the speed **set** correctly?

- Is the switch **off**?

- Will the pass be **clear**, no clamps in the way, cord won't get caught somewhere, etc.?

- Put safety gear **on**.

When you've gone through the list and checked everything out, you can safely plug in the router. Make sure the bit is clear of the stock, turn on the machine, and proceed.

SECTION 2:
The Joints

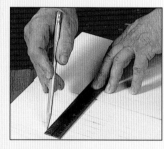

Rabbets

THROUGH RABBET

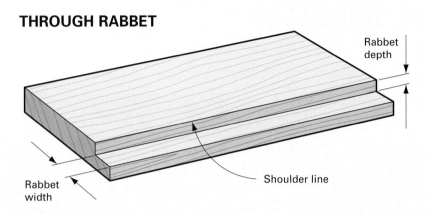

Rabbet
depth

Shoulder line

Rabbet
width

STOPPED RABBET

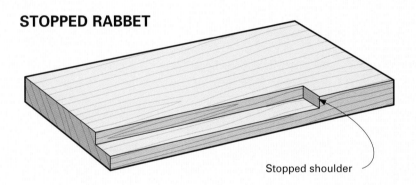

Stopped shoulder

APPLICATIONS

Rabbets are commonly used to let in a back panel in a cabinet, a technique which hides the edge of the panel from the public when viewed from the side of the cabinet. This is particularly useful if your back panels are made from plywood, as the rabbet conceals the raw plywood edges. In addition, the shoulder of a rabbet helps resist racking and strengthens the joint.

Another use for rabbets is to reduce the thickness of a panel or shelf so it can be inserted into a dado or groove. For example, drawer backs are often fitted into rabbets cut into drawer sides, permitting quick and easy drawer construction.

You can mill rabbets on both faces of the work to create stub tenons or tongues. (As a bonus, by making

A rabbet is a notch cut into the edge of wood, and it's one of the simplest joints in woodworking. In fact, rabbets are really one-half of a joint, since a mating member always makes the connection. Rabbets can be milled into either end grain or long grain, or along straight or curved edges. Either a hand-held router or the router table can be used to make these joints.

Stock Preparation

In general, since you size a rabbet to fit the part that it mates, it's best to cut your stock to final length, width, and thickness.

Routing Rabbets

Choose from the following five setups for your particular application, and be sure to practice them all.

IRREGULAR SMALL STOCK

The router table is the ideal platform for routing rabbets in small multiple passes, you can even mill long tenons on long stock.) One example of using rabbets is with table buttons, which have a tongue that engages a groove in a table frame for securing a tabletop. You'll find buttons used on the Small Table project in this book (see page 148).

WHAT'S NOT COVERED

I've omitted the use of template guides for cutting rabbets because they require confusing math to establish the correct offset, and all too often the non-concentricity of the guide to the base results in undulating rabbet widths, complicating the assembly process.

Another setup you won't find is the use of router edge guides. While it's certainly possible to use edge guides to make rabbets along straight edges, I don't recommend the practice. This

operation calls for more than half of the router's base to hang out in thin air without the stock's support, risking tipping of the router and unwanted stock removal. If you do decide to try your hand at rabbeting with an edge guide, I suggest you equip your router with an offset baseplate for more support.

WHAT YOU NEED TO KNOW

• the thickness of the material you're fitting into the rabbet

• the width of the rabbet your material is fastening into or the width of the groove or dado receiving a panel or shelf

• whether the rabbet will be cut into a straight or curved edge

• the shape of the stock, whether it's straight, curved, large, small, long grain or end grain

JIGS

• push sled (page 49)

• shoulder gauge (see fig. 1)

• offset baseplate (page 52)

• router tracking system (page 54)

• router table and fence

BITS AND TOOLS

• rabbeting bit set

• spiral, straight, or mortising bits

• bit gauge

• calculator

• hot glue gun

and irregularly shaped workpieces, such as curved box sides or wooden handles.

1. Using a rabbet bit set, choose a bearing that provides the width of your desired rabbet and, with the router unplugged, install it in the router.

2. Install the router in the router table and adjust the bit height equal to the desired depth of the rabbet. (See Setting Bit Height and Depth, page 72, and photo, right.) If your rabbet is going to be more than ¼ in. deep (which is uncommon), plan to

make the cut in increments, not in one pass.

3. Place the stock on the table and make a dry run (with the router unplugged and the switch turned to the "off" position) to assure yourself of the cutting sequence. (Review Routing Without a Fence, page 72.)

One safety note: Is the piece smaller than your hand? If so, review Routing Really Small Pieces (page 76) and secure the work to a larger scrap block.

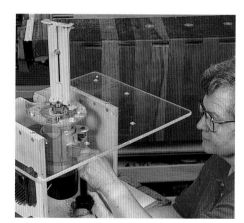

Set the height. The author adjusts a bit gauge to the desired depth of the rabbet, then raises the bit until it touches the gauge.

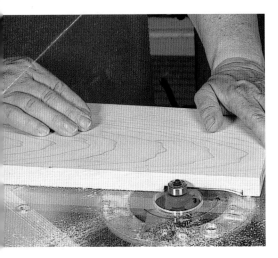

Bearing determines width. Ride the work against the bit's bearing to rout the rabbet to the correct width.

4. Perform the router flight check (see page 76) and plug in the router. Using the heel of your left hand, rotate the stock into the spinning bit and onto the bearing. Move the work from right to left as you face the bit to rout the rabbet along the edge. (See photo, above.)

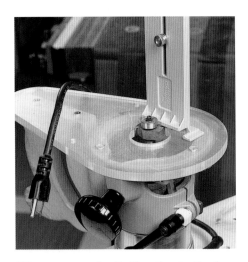

Bit gauge again. Setting the depth of cut is identical to router table work by setting a bit gauge to the rabbet depth, and using the gauge to adjust the amount the bit protrudes form the baseplate.

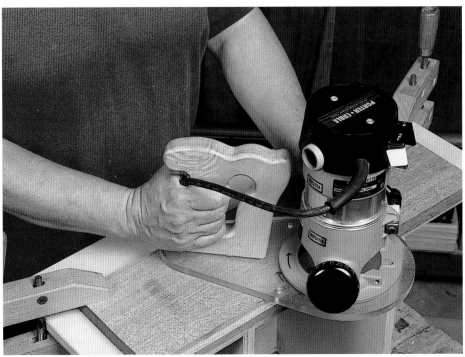

From right to left. Rout against the cutter rotation by orienting the cut away from you and moving the router from your right to your left.

LONG GRAIN IN LARGE STOCK

Large work is best tackled with a hand-held router equipped with an offset baseplate.

1. Select a bearing for the rabbet bit set for your desired rabbet width and, with the router unplugged, install it in the router. Then attach the offset baseplate to the router.

2. Set the bit height equal to the desired depth of the rabbet. (See photo, left.) If you're routing a rabbet deeper than ¼ in., plan on taking incremental cuts by adjusting the bit a little deeper with each pass.

3. Secure the stock to the bench with clamps or with a vacuum setup. (See Special Holding Systems, page 65.)

4. Position the router on the stock, with the bit's bearing against the edge, and make a dry run to make

sure power cords and clamps are out of the way.

5. Carry out the router flight check, and plug in the router. Start the router with the bit and bearing off the work, then rout the rabbet by moving the router from right to left with the cut facing away from you (See photo, above.)

LONG GRAIN IN SMALL STOCK

Using a fence on the router table is a smart approach when routing long-grain rabbets in small stock.

1. Install a spiral bit in your router's collet, and secure the router in the router table. Another option is to use a rabbet bit set, but make sure the bearing doesn't protrude or interfere with the fence when guiding the stock. For the best cut, choose a bit whose diameter is at least twice the width of the rabbet. For example, a

Keep it tight. Use a pair of feather-boards to maintain pressure against the work and hold it snug against the fence and table.

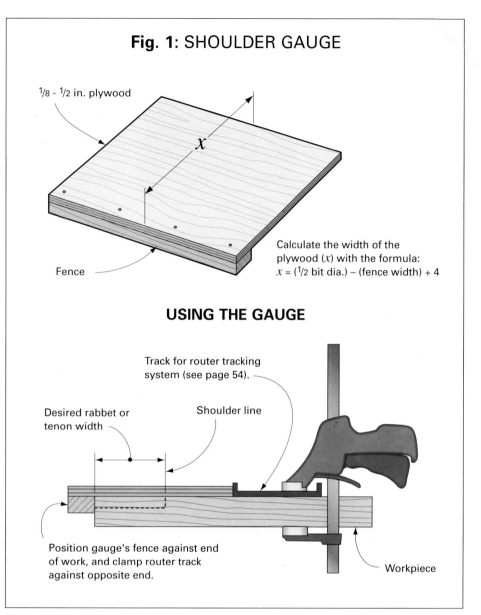

Fig. 1: SHOULDER GAUGE

⅛ - ½ in. plywood

x

Fence

Calculate the width of the plywood (x) with the formula:
$x = (½$ bit dia.$) - ($fence width$) + 4$

USING THE GAUGE

Track for router tracking system (see page 54).

Desired rabbet or tenon width

Shoulder line

Position gauge's fence against end of work, and clamp router track against opposite end.

Workpiece

⅜-in.-wide rabbet should be made with a ¾ in. bit. Smaller diameter bits risk tearing out the grain.

2. With the router unplugged, adjust the bit height to the desired rabbet depth and use a bit gauge to help set the fence for the desired width of the rabbet.

3. Attach a pair of featherboards to the fence and table, using the stock to align the featherboards so they place pressure against the work. (See photo, above.)

4. Perform the router flight check and plug in the router. Rout the rabbet, feeding the stock at an even pace past the bit.

END GRAIN IN SHORT STOCK

Just like when you're working with long-grain rabbets in small stock, it makes sense to use a fence on the router table when routing end-grain rabbets. The addition of a push sled makes this cut safe and predictable.

1. Install a spiral, straight, or rabbet bit set in your router motor, and secure the router in the router table.

If you use a rabbet set, make sure the bearing won't interfere with the fence.

2. With the router unplugged, set the bit height to your desired rabbet depth.

3. Use a bit gauge to set the fence for the desired width of the rabbet.

4. Complete the router flight check and plug in the router. Rout the rab-bet by guiding the work with the sled, moving the stock from right to left as you face the fence. (See top left photo, page 82.)

END GRAIN IN LONG STOCK

Long stock is cumbersome and dangerous to rout on the router table, especially when routing end-grain rabbets on the narrow end of a board. The most reliable method is to use a hand-held router guided by a router tracking system. A shop-made

Sled makes it safe. Use a push sled to guide wide work when routing a rabbet on the end grain of a board.

shoulder gauge lets you quickly and accurately position the system's fence, as shown in figure 1.

Note that the following procedure works equally well to mill tenons on the ends of long stock. All you do is repeat the cutting sequence on both sides of the stock to form the tenon. To determine how much material to take off each side of the board, start with your desired tenon thickness, subtract the thickness of the stock, and divide by two. Remember that this method works for tenons up to about 2 in. Longer tenons—which, thankfully, are unusual in general woodworking—require a different methodology, such as using the table saw or bandsaw.

1. Draw the shoulder line of the desired rabbet (or tenon) onto the stock, measuring its width (or the tenon's length) from the end of the stock.

2. Clamp the stock to your bench with 12 in. or so beyond the edge of the bench.

3. Use the shoulder gauge to position and fasten the router tracking system's track onto the workpiece. (See top left photo, page 84.)

(Continued on page 84.)

Look for the line. A clear sight of the stop line through the router base is essential for stopping a rabbet by hand.

Stopping the Rabbet

Stopped rabbets are handy for all sorts of furniture work, especially when you want to conceal the end of a part, such as a rabbetted box top or the top of a cabinet's back panel. There are two approaches to cutting stopped rabbets: You can use a hand-held router, or you can make the cut on the router table.

WITH A HAND-HELD ROUTER

This method employs some hand and eye coordination, but it's fool-proof and simple once you understand the principles involved. It works particularly well with long or heavy stock.

1. Mark a shoulder line on the stock where you want the rabbet to stop.

2. Peering through the center hole of the router's base, rout in an even feed speed right up to the line, then immediately reverse direction and pull the router and the bit back and away from the shoulder. Don't stop against the shoulder line, or the wood will burn. If you didn't quite reach the line with the first pass, repeat the procedure by moving the bit deliberately to the line, then retreating as before. (See photo, above.)

ON THE ROUTER TABLE

This technique requires more layout and takes a little more practice than the hand-held method, but once you get the knack of it, it's very accurate. Use this method for small to medium-sized parts.

1. Mark a shoulder line on the stock for the stopped rabbet. Using a small square, transfer the line over the edge and onto the opposite face. If you want to stop the rabbet at both ends, repeat the layout at the opposite end of the board. On the non-rabbeting side, mark the left line (as the board faces you) with an "L" and the right line with an "R."

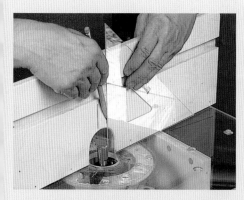

Square up your lines. Use a large drafting triangle placed against the cutting edges of the bit to establish stop lines on the fence.

2. Move the fence so it straddles the center of the bit. Raise the bit well above the table and place a drafting triangle against the fence and just touching the left edge of the bit (router off and unplugged, please). Mark a line on the fence. Use the same procedure to mark a second line to the right of the bit, as shown in the photo, above. These two marks outline the edges of the bit, and will tell you exactly where the bit stops cutting.

3. Lower the bit below the table and lay the workpiece on the router table, with the face to be rabbetted down on the tabletop and the edge to be rabbetted against the fence. Align the "R" on the

Watch your marks. Pivot the work into the cutter, and push it along the fence until the line on the stock meets the line on the fence.

stock with the line on the right side of the bit. It may be necessary to use a small block (see page 31) to assist in matching the lines. Without moving the board, draw a third line on the left end of the fence, following the left end of the stock. Use a drafting triangle to extend the line above the stock. Mark this line as "1." It's the first line you'll rout to. (See bottom photo, left.)

4. Repeat the previous step, this time aligning the "L" line on the stock with the line on the left side of the bit, then marking a line on the right end of the fence at the right end of the stock. Extend that line above the stock as before, and mark this line as "2."

5. Adjust the bit height for the rabbet depth and set the fence for the rabbet width.

6. Perform the router flight check, and review Skiing into the Cut (see page 75). Rout the rabbet by skiing into the cut near the left end of the stock (but between the lettered lines) and pushing the board from right to left as you face the fence. (See top photo, middle.) As soon as the line on the board meets the line on the fence, pivot the near end away from the fence. Don't dwell, or the bit will burn the wood.

7. To stop the rabbet at the opposite end, repeat the previous step. Note that this will be a climb cut, so be sure to review Conventional or Climb Cut? (see page 75). As before, ski into the cut, again starting near the left end of the stock (into the already milled rabbet), then push the work from left to right (as you face the fence). Pivot the work away from the fence as soon as the line on the stock meets the line on the fence.

The finished stopped rabbets will have rounded ends, which you can clean up with a few deft cuts from a chisel. (See photo, left.)

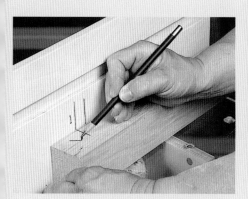

Make your marks. A "1" and the letter "L" tell you where to stop the rabbet on the far end of the board.

Square the ends. Use a sharp chisel to square up the rounded ends left by the bit.

Gauge, then track. With the shoulder gauge clamped against the end of the workpiece, clamp the router track against the gauge.

4. Install a bit in your router, using a spiral or mortising bit that's greater than the intended width of the rabbet. (You won't have this option when making really wide tongues or tenons, so use the biggest bit you have.)

5. Install the tracking system's baseplate to your router. For now, keep the bit clear of the bottom of the baseplate, but nearly flush with it, until called to set the bit depth. Position the router assembly over the rail on the fence and double-check the alignment of the baseplate to the fence.

6. Make a practice run with the router riding along the tracking system, checking that the perimeter of

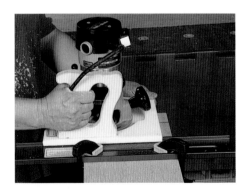

A simple push. Once the track is clamped to the work, simply push the router away from you to rout the rabbet.

Routing tenons. After cutting the shoulder with the router riding on the track, take multiple passes by disengaging the router and cutting freehand to the end of the tenon.

the bit just touches the shoulder line and that the power cord doesn't snag on something.

7. Set the bit to the depth of the rabbet.

8. Do the router flight check and plug in the router. Rout the rabbet by pushing the router away from you, as shown in the photo, left.

The technique is identical when routing a tongue or tenon that's longer than your bit's diameter, by making the first pass with the router engaged in the fence as described above. Then, to lengthen the tenon, lift the baseplate off the fence after the first pass and make multiple passes to the end of the stock, as shown in the photo, above.

Practice Projects

If you've practiced all of the rabbets described here, my heartiest congratulations! Rabbets are usually combined with other joints in woodworking, but you are well on your way to making something useful. To get you going, there are three projects that involve rabbets: Small Bookcase (page 144), Small Table (page 148), and Router Bit Cabinet (page 150). These projects also require other joints, but go ahead and check them out now to see how rabbets are commonly used in furniture.

Dadoes, Grooves, and Slots

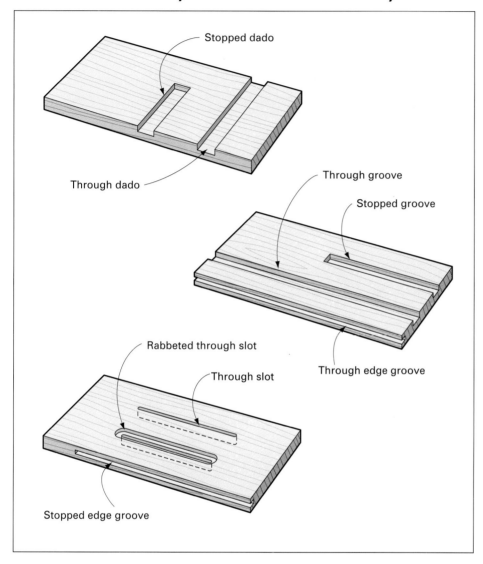

Stopped dado

Through dado

Through groove

Stopped groove

Rabbeted through slot

Through slot

Through edge groove

Stopped edge groove

Stock Preparation

DADOES

One trick to getting really crisp through-dado ends is to leave the stock ¼ in. over final width, make your cuts, and then rip ⅛ in. off each edge. This extra step removes any blowout you may experience during routing. Stopped dadoes, however, require the stock to be cut to final size before routing.

GROOVES

In general, cut the stock to final size, since you'll need to accurately locate and lay out the groove from the finished reference edge.

SLOTS

When routing slots with the grain in narrow work, leave the stock oversize in width, then rip it to final size after cutting the slots. Keep in mind that, with all slots, you should work with one finished reference edge from which to lay out and cut the slot. Always keep that edge against the fence or jig, and never cut it away. If you're making identical slots in multiple pieces, consider routing all the slots in one blank, then sawing the blank into individual parts of final size.

Routing Dadoes, Grooves, and Slots

One of the following procedures should fit your project's particular joinery needs. Try them all on practice stock, and then pick a real project to use them on.

Dadoes and grooves are flat-bottomed channels with straight, square sides milled into the broad face of your stock. Dadoes are defined as going *across* the grain; grooves are oriented *with* the grain. Slots can be oriented with or across the grain, go all the way through the stock, and are typically stopped at either end. Like rabbets, all three types of joints join with another part to complete the connection. In most cases, dadoes, grooves, and slots are milled dead straight, either using a hand-held router or on the router table, depending on the application.

APPLICATIONS

Dadoes and grooves are used to receive shelves, partitions, and frames. The shoulders on these joints mechanically lock the member inserted into them. Shelf standards, hinges, and other hardware also require a dado or groove to set them flush with the wood's surface.

A *through dado* is commonly used in cabinetmaking when a face frame will cover the front edge of the case sides and hide the joint. A *stopped dado* is appropriate for open shelving, where you don't want to see the shoulders and the bottom of the joint at the shelf-to-case side connection.

Like a through dado, a *through groove* exits the edges of the stock. One application is in web frames and frames for dust panels in the interior of fine furniture. Here, the panel as well as the frame's tongues or tenons fill the grooves. You'll see this application on the bottoms of many chests of drawers. Pull the bottom drawer out of yours; you may see a web frame there.

A *stopped groove* is useful for framework, such as in a frame-and-panel door where you stop the groove for the panel to leave room for other joinery at the corners, such as biscuits or mortise-and-tenon. Other examples are the panel on the back of a cabinet that slides into a stopped groove, either at the top or bottom of the case, or a box with a sliding lid that stops in one direction.

Slots are frequently often used in jig making, a wonderful coincidence for this book! A *standard slot* is cut through the face of the stock, and allows other parts to pass through, such as a screw or bolt. This arrangement allows the bolt to slide along the slot. To keep the bolt's head recessed below or flush with the surface of the work, you'll need to create a *rabbeted slot*. A variation is to chamfer the slot, such as for a flat-head screw. (See Mortising Fixture, page 55, for examples of both standard and rabbeted slots.)

WHAT'S NOT COVERED

Grooves made with a commercial router edge guide are not covered here, since I feel there's a risk of routing off your intended path with these devices. Milling a groove in the edge of stock while holding the work precariously on its edge on the router table is also not covered. It's far safer—both for you and your work—to rout the stock either with a mortising fixture or using a horizontal router table setup.

WHAT YOU NEED TO KNOW

Dadoes

- the centerline of the dado
- the dado's width
- the dado's depth
- is the dado stopped, or not?

Grooves

- the groove's shoulder locations relative to the edge of the stock
- the groove's width
- the groove's depth
- is the groove stopped, or not?

Slots

- the location of the centerline of the slot
- the slot's width
- the stock's thickness
- the depth and width of the rabbet

JIGS

- angled dado gauges (see fig. 1)
- stepped platform (page 65)
- vacuum-clamping jig (page 66)
- router tracking system (page 54)
- mortising fixture (page 55)
- router table with fence and horizontal table setup (page 38)

BITS AND TOOLS

- spiral, straight, or mortising bit; diameter equal to width of dado, groove, slot, or rabbet
- bit gauge
- calculator
- push stick
- featherboards
- plunge base

Dadoes

Try your hand at milling through and stopped dadoes, including angled dadoes.

THROUGH DADO

Through dadoes are best handled with a hand-held router and a router tracking system. For angled dadoes, use a pair of angled dado gauges (see fig. 1) to help with laying out the joint.

1. Review Measuring and Marking Stock (see page 70) and label the reference edge. Calculate the centerline of the dado by taking into account where you want the shoulders of the dado to fall on the work. Divide the diameter of the bit by two, and add that to the distance of the shoulder

nearest the reference edge of the stock. Draw a mark to indicate the centerline.

2. Usually you'll want a dado that's square to the edge of the stock. Use a square aligned with your mark to draw a line across the stock perpendicular to its edge. Furniture has two mirror-image case sides, so it's more accurate to position the two sides together, with their reference edges touching, and draw the line across both at once. This technique insures the dadoes are exactly opposite each other when you assemble the case, and keeps shelves and partitions correctly spaced. (See photo, right.)

If you want to rout a dado that angles from the edge of the stock (in other words, anything other than 90°), it's best to use a pair of angled dado gauges to establish the angled centerlines on the case sides. Start by laying out the centerline as described in step 1. Laying out angled dadoes can be tricky. Take your time, being careful to use the correct gauge for each side. (See bottom photo, right.) After laying out mirror-image centerlines on the sides, stand them

Two at a time. Align the ends and the back edges of the case pieces, and square your dado locations across both sides.

upright and side by side, orienting them as they'll go in the cabinet to check that you've drawn the complementary angles correctly.

3. Equip your plunge router with the router tracking system's baseplate. Fasten the stock to the bench with regular clamps (or see Special

Holding Systems, page 65) and clamp the router track to the stock at the correct distance from the centerline. Check the distance with the ruler. It must be 4 in. from your line to anywhere along the track.

4. Select the bit, install it in the router, and set the bit depth.

Fig. 1: ANGLED DADO GAUGES

Use the two gauges for laying out angled dadoes, one for the "right" side, and a mirror-image gauge for the "left" side.

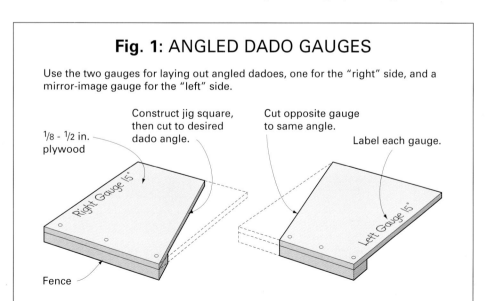

1/8 - 1/2 in. plywood

Construct jig square, then cut to desired dado angle.

Cut opposite gauge to same angle.

Label each gauge.

Right Gauge 15°

Left Gauge 15°

Fence

Gauge the angles. For angled dadoes, use an angled dado gauge to mark the centerlines on each case piece.

5. Perform the router flight check (see page 76) and engage the baseplate in the track, with the bit raised clear of the wood. Turn on the router, plunge the bit, and mill the dado.

STOPPED DADO

Like through dadoes, the setup for cutting a stopped dado involves using a hand-held router and a router tracking system, except you use a stop attached to the track to stop the router at the desired spot.

1. Lay out the dado centerline and set up the router tracking system as when routing a through dado (see page 86).

2. Draw a perpendicular line across the dado's centerline at the spot where you want the dado to stop. Install the bit in the plunge router, engage the router in the track, and lower the bit until it almost, but not quite, grazes the surface of the work. Slide the router along the track until

Stopping the cut. A stop block secured to the tracking system's track stops the dado at the correct location.

Clean Cuts Across the Grain

When you're cutting joints in plywood (and in a few super-brittle hardwoods), you have to be extra careful. The veneer on all plywood is so thin that cutting across the grain can result in severe splintering. The secret is to score across the grain with a sharp craft knife precisely along the cutline before sawing or routing. Use a straightedge to guide the knife as you slice. This initial prep work allows the wood fibers to separate cleanly during the cut.

Slice the shoulders. Use a straightedge and a craft knife to establish the shoulder lines before you rout or saw the joint.

the bit touches the stop line. Be sure to rotate the bit so its outermost corner touches the line. Without moving the router, fasten a stop on the track so it contacts the baseplate.

3. Set the bit depth and perform the router flight check, turn on the router, and push it until it contacts the stop. (See bottom photo, left.) Don't stop the router when it contacts the stop, or you'll burn the wood. Simply touch the stop, and immediately back up the router slightly. Turn the router off, wait for the bit to spin to a halt, and lift the router off the track.

Grooves

Practice routing through and stopped grooves on the face or edge of the work.

THROUGH GROOVE IN WIDE STOCK

The setup and routing procedures for this joint are almost identical as when routing a through dado (see page 86) using a hand-held router and the router tracking system. The

only difference is you rout the groove in the direction of the grain, not across it.

THROUGH GROOVE IN NARROW STOCK

Narrow stock is best cut on the router table against the fence, where you have more control of the cutting action.

1. Chuck the bit in the router and install the router in the router table. Place the fence on the table, then raise the bit slightly above the table.

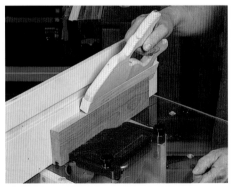

Small grooving. Routing narrow stock is accurate and safe if you use a featherboard to keep the stock against the fence and a push stick to guide the work.

Determine where the groove's shoulders fall relative to the edge of the stock, and adjust a bit gauge to the shoulder line that's closer to the fence. Then use the gauge to set the fence.

2. Set the bit height to the depth of the groove. Install a featherboard on the table, orienting it so you can push the stock from right to left as you face the fence.

3. Perform the router flight check, turn on the router, and guide the stock along the fence with a push stick, as shown in the bottom right photo, opposite page.

STOPPED GROOVE IN WIDE STOCK

Use a hand-held router and a router tracking system equipped with stops for milling a stopped groove. The setup is similar to routing a stopped dado (see opposite page). The only difference is you orient the stock so you cut the joint with the grain, not across it.

STOPPED GROOVE IN NARROW STOCK

Stopping a groove in narrow stock presents some unique problems. Avoid the router table, because featherboards prevent you from lifting the stock up once you've stopped the cut. In addition, your stock is often too long for accurately setting up stops on the router table's fence. The answer is to use a hand-held router and the router tracking system, while safely holding the workpiece by sticking it to a larger board with hot glue or by using a vacuum-clamping arrangement. (See page Special Holding Systems, page 65.) The following shows my preferred method of using a vacuum to hold the work.

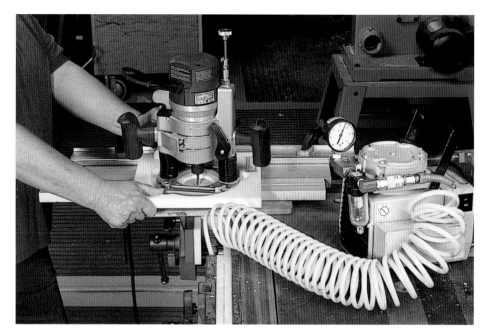

Hold it with vacuum. For stopped grooves in small stock, clamp the workpiece to a vacuum plate and use the router tracking system.

1. Lay out the stopped groove in the same manner as when laying out a stopped dado (see opposite page), making sure to orient the groove with the grain of the work.

2. Secure the work to a vacuum plate.

3. Set up the router tracking system using the same setup as when making a stopped dado.

4. Set the bit depth, and make your router flight check. Turn on the router, push it until it contacts the stop, and immediately pull it back to prevent burning the end of the groove. (See photo, above.)

THROUGH OR STOPPED EDGE GROOVE

Through or stopped grooves cut in narrow edges can be tricky to rout while balancing the stock on edge on the router table. I don't recommend this approach. For narrow work

(stock 3¾ in. wide or less), the best method is to use a hand-held router and the mortising fixture. Stock wider than this, or longer than the length of the mortising jig, should be cut laying flat and using a horizontal table setup on the router table.

IN THE MORTISING FIXTURE

Review Mortising Fixture (see page 55), secure the jig to your bench, and equip your plunge router with the fixture's baseplate and the appropriate spiral bit.

1. Lay out the groove, and clamp the work into the mortising fixture. If you want to stop the groove, lay out and mark these areas now, and attach stops to the jig. Clamp the work into the fixture.

2. Place the router onto the fixture, set the bit depth, and align the bit with the layout on your stock.

3. With the bit retracted, make your router flight check. Power up the

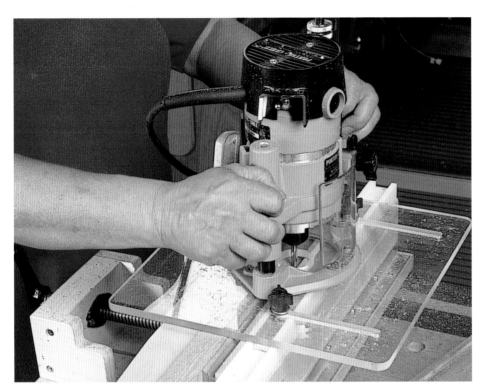

Grooving on the mortiser. Clamp the work in the mortiser and use stop blocks or stop the router by eye to rout a stopped groove.

router, plunge the bit, then push the router along the fixture to rout the groove. (See photo, above.) If you're routing a stopped groove, stop when the router contacts the stop or stop to a marked line by eye, then instantly pull back the router to avoid any burning. If the groove is deep, make the cut in successively deeper passes.

ON THE HORIZONTAL TABLE SETUP

Review the Horizontal Table Setup (see page 38) and set up the fixture on the router table.

1. Lay out the groove on your stock. If you're stopping the groove, lay out and mark these areas now.

2. Install a spiral bit in the router, and set the bit depth. Adjust the metal plate, which becomes your fence, to set the bit height.

3. If you're routing a through groove, secure a featherboard to the fence and another to the tabletop, positioning them to accommodate the thickness and width of the stock. For a stopped groove, clamp a stop block at each end of the table at the desired stopping distances.

4. Perform the router flight check and turn on the router. For a through groove, use a push stick to guide the work over the bit. If you're cutting a stopped groove, use hot glue to adhere the push stick to the stock. Place the left end of the work against the left stop (as you face the fence), and pivot the work into the bit. (See bottom photo, left.) Once the stock makes full contact with the fence, move the work from left to right with a push stick until its end makes contact with the second stop, as shown in the bottom photo, middle. Immediately pull the work back slightly and, keeping the end against the fence, pivot the workpiece away from the bit. (See photo, below.)

Start from the left. With one end against a stop, pivot the work into the bit using a push stick glued to the stock.

Move from left to right. Push the stock along the fence until it contacts the second stop block.

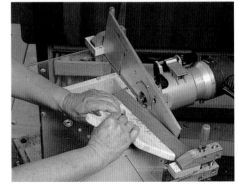

Pivot safely away. Once the work contacts the stop block, immediately pivot it away from the bit to prevent burning.

Stick it to a jig. Use hot glue to temporarily hold the work to a stepped platform.

Slots

Try routing a standard slot or its variation, a rabbeted slot.

STANDARD SLOT

Use a hand-held router and the router tracking system set up with stops. With wide stock, use the same setup as when routing stopped dadoes (see page 88) but make sure to mount the setup on a scrap board so you don't rout through the work and into your workbench. For narrow stock, you use the same track setup, but stick the work to a platform with hot glue. (See Special Holding Systems, page 65.)

1. Secure the work to a platform with hot glue, as shown in the photo, above.

2. Lay out the slot and its stopped ends using the same technique as when laying out a stopped dado.

3. Set up the router tracking system using the same setup as when making a stopped dado. Make sure to use two stops on the track, setting them at either end of the slot layout.

4. Set the bit depth slightly deeper than the thickness of the stock, and adjust the plunge router's turret to cut the slot in two or more passes. Carry out the router flight check, and turn on the router. Plunge-cut the slot in successive passes, pushing the router from stop to stop with each pass. Keep routing until you reach the lowest setting on the router turret and are through the stock. (See photo, right.)

5. Pop the stock off the platform and scrape away any glue residue.

RABBETED SLOT

Use the same setup as when routing a standard slot (see above), routing the slot with a hand-held router and the router tracking system and stops.

1. Rout a slot in the work by following the layout and cutting procedures described in routing a standard slot. Once you've routed the slot, don't alter the track setup or remove the stock from the platform.

2. Unplug the router, and switch bits to one with a larger diameter equal to the desired rabbet width.

3. Engage the router and baseplate in the track, and set the bit depth to the desired depth of the rabbet. Make your router flight check, turn on the router, and rout the rabbet by pushing the router from stop to stop. (See photo, right.)

4. Separate the stock from the platform and scrape away any excess glue.

Practice Projects

You've practiced all the dadoes, grooves, and slots. Good for you! You're ready to combine these joints

Routing through. With the router riding the router tracking system's track, rout the through slot by plunging through the work and slightly into the jig below.

with others found in the book to make a useful woodworking project. Projects that feature dadoes, grooves, and slots are Totebox (page 142), Small Bookcase (page 144), Small Table (page 148), Router Bit Cabinet (page 150), Frame-and-Panel Door (page 153), and Dovetailed Drawer (page 155).

Bigger bit; same setup. Without changing the slot-cutting setup, rout the rabbet using a larger diameter bit.

Box Joint

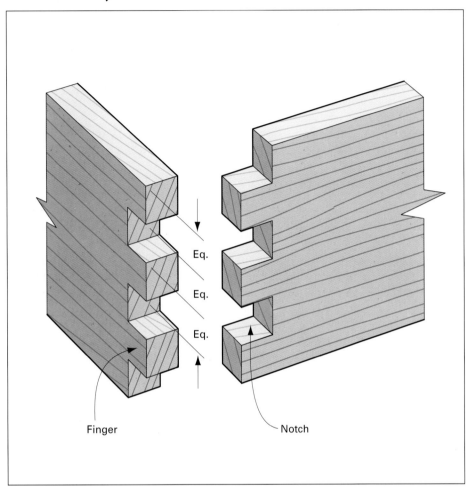

Eq.

Eq.

Eq.

Finger

Notch

APPLICATIONS

As the name implies, box joints are used in box making. When I was young, it was common to see wooden cigar boxes made with this joint. Box joints also make very acceptable corner joints for drawers, which are essentially boxes themselves.

The completed joint displays square corners that consist of long grain and end grain in an attractive, alternating pattern. The fingers are usually evenly spaced, but varied spacing is possible for special effects. You can even round over the completed joint for a softer appearance if you wish. For a mechanical lock, you can pin the joint vertically with a wood dowel or metal rod. Or try combining these two approaches by rounding the corners and pinning the fingers. If you assemble the joint without glue, you'll create a wooden hinge which can be used for fitting table leaves to tabletops, or anywhere you

The box joint, also known as a finger joint, is comprised of identically sized "fingers" on the end of one piece that fit into matching sockets cut into the end of an adjoining piece. It's an exceptionally strong joint because it provides about three times the glue surface of a butt joint.

Stock Preparation

The width of the stock must equal a multiple of the bit's diameter. For example, a 2½-in.-high box can have ¼ or ½ in. fingers, but not ⅜ in. Simply divide the desired height by the bit diameter, rounding off any divisions to a whole number, and cut your stock to that width.

The length of the two sides and two ends must equal the finished dimensions of the box, because the fingers interlock. The cut ends must be precisely 90°, so set your crosscut saw carefully.

need an extension. For example, I used the box joint as a hinge for building a flip-up extension for my workbench.

WHAT'S NOT COVERED

Variable-spaced sockets and fingers are not discussed, because they're a horse of another color in their execution and require different marking, jigs, and procedures. However, once you have more routing experience under your belt, feel free to tackle this more challenging aspect of the joint.

WHAT YOU NEED TO KNOW

• thickness of the stock

• size of the intended box (height, width, and length)

• lay out the joint so you start and end with whole fingers or sockets

• width of box sides must equal a multiple of the bit diameter

• all errors are accumulative, so make your setup precise!

JIGS

• box joint jig (see page 46)
• router table

BITS AND TOOLS

• spiral bit equal in diameter to the size fingers desired
• feeler gauge
• dial calipers
• calculator
• small hardwood block (see page 31)

Note: Spiral bits are best, because they cut the end grain fibers crisply. For ¾ in. box joints, try a ¾ in. diameter mortising bit rather than a standard straight bit. A bit with a negative shear angle is best for clean cuts.

2. Set the bit height equal to the thickness of your practice stock by laying the stock next to the bit and raising the bit until it's level with the top of the stock. Since sharp bits can draw blood, use a small hardwood block rather than your finger to determine when the bit and the stock are flush.

3. Make and install a fresh backer board for the box joint jig. Install the jig into the groove in the router table, and move it adjacent to the bit.

4. Once the jig is set up correctly, your box finger width should equal the diameter of the bit. To get this setting, place the stock on end on the table with one edge against the pin. Now loosen the jig's main fence and shift it until the spacing is correct. (See photo, below.) Lock the fence.

5. Insert the jig's stop block into the hole in the router table and orient it so the number on the block that corresponds to your bit diameter points toward the bit. (See bottom left photo, page 94.)

Marking the Stock

Number each piece in the order it goes around the box, such as front end, right side, back end, and left side. Also, letter each corner in the same order, and indicate the top edge of each piece. Place all your marks on the outside faces. Make sure to choose which pieces will start with a finger or a socket, and mark them accordingly. I like to mark an "X" where all the sockets will go to remind me where wood needs to be removed.

For a nice touch and a mark of fine craftsmanship, it's worth matching the grain in a continuous pattern all the way around the box. Practice this by marking the pieces in the correct order.

Setting Up and Making Test Cuts

1. Set up the router table so the bottom faces up for box joint-making. Mount a router base in the table, install the bit in the motor, and position the motor in the base.

Set the finger width. Hold the stock against the pin and eyeball the location of the cutting edge of the bit.

Box Joint Math

Below is a handy formula for successfully setting up the box joint jig and the cut. As you can see, it comes full circle. Write down the formula near your work station and refer to it every time you make a fresh batch of joints.

- bit diameter = stock thickness

- stock thickness = finger width

- finger width = socket width

- socket width = bit diameter

6. Perform the router flight check (see page 76) and rout a series of fingers across the entire end of one practice piece. The procedure is to hold or clamp the stock to the jig with its end down on the router table and its outside surface facing the bit. For the first cut, locate the edge of the stock against the fence pin. Now push the assembly forward and over the bit until it contacts the stop block, and then slide the assembly back until it clears the bit.

For each remaining finger, move the stock over so the freshly cut edge of the finger contacts the fence's pin, and repeat. (See photo, right.)

7. Using calipers, measure the width of a notch and a finger. The notch should equal the diameter of the bit, and the finger must equal the notch. Adjust the jig as necessary. (See Making the Joint Fit, opposite page.)

8. After making any adjustments, perform the router flight check again and rout two separate pieces of practice stock. Rout the fingers in the first piece, as described above. With the first piece still on the jig and its last finger contacting the fence pin, place the edge of the second piece against the first piece and clamp or hold it in position. Then push the assembly forward as before to rout the first notch, as shown in the middle left photo, opposite page. To rout the remaining notches, remove the first piece and repeat the cutting sequence on the second piece by indexing the stock against the metal pin for each cut.

9. When the two practice pieces fit together perfectly, you're ready to rout the project's stock.

Pin registers the cut. Index the previously cut notch against the pin to rout each successive notch.

Routing a Box Joint

1. Install a fresh backer board on the box joint jig. Arrange all your parts so your marks (and the outside surfaces) face up. Remember that you're routing one half of a corner joint at a time, so it's important that you stack the pieces in the lettered order of the corners.

2. Perform the router flight check and rout the fingers or notches in the first corner. Then, in successive

Block stops the cut. Insert the stop block into the hole in the table, orienting the number on the block equal to the bit diameter towards the workpiece.

Dealing with Tearout

Tearout can be a problem when making box joints, especially if your bit is dull or dirty. To overcome this, always use a fresh backer board on your box joint jig and place your stock with its outside surface facing out, or towards the bit. The backer will virtually eliminate all tearout on the back side where the danger is greatest. Any small tearout on the outside, or show surface, can be dealt with after assembly with a little judicious sanding.

Make a clean cut. Use a fresh backer board behind the workpiece to avoid tearout at the back of the cut.

Making the Joint Fit

When setting up and making test cuts with the box joint jig, it's not uncommon for fingers to be either too loose or so tight that you can't fit the joint. To adjust the fit, measure the fingers and notches with a dial caliper. They should match each other. Once you've measured the amount of error, select a feeler gauge whose thickness equals that amount and perform one of the following adjustments.

If the finger is too skinny, place the feeler gauge against the metal pin and then clamp a scrap block to the table such that it contacts the gauge. (See photo, right.) Without disturbing the setup, carefully remove the gauge, loosen the fence, and slide it over until the pin touches the block. Tighten the fence, remove the block, and you're good to go.

If the finger is too fat, position a scrap block against the pin and clamp it to the table. Loosen the fence, insert the feeler gauge against the block, and then slide the fence so the pin contacts the gauge. Lock the fence, remove the block and the gauge, and rout.

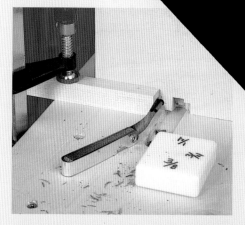

Fatter fingers. Use a feeler gauge and a scrap block clamped to the table to adjust the fence and pin for fine-tuing the fit.

Notch the adjoining board. Begin the cut on the second piece by holding the completed first board against the pin and registering the second board against the first.

order, rout all the box parts including the last corner, which mates with the first corner you routed.

3. Assemble each corner joint by intersecting the fingers. (See photo, right.) Check that the ends match each other, as well as the sides. If they don't go together correctly, check your marking system or the order of the stack.

Practice Project

Wow, once you've got it, you've got it! You can do a whole run of boxes and stash them for gifts. Or be the woodworking hero in your family and make a box for everyone. The practice project that features box joints is the Totebox (page 142), another fine gift idea.

Check the fit. A properly cut joint reveals fingers that mesh together without gaps, and with top and bottom edges flush with each other.

...es and Tenons

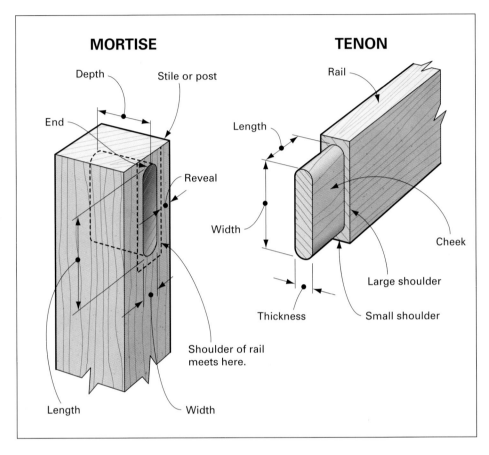

MORTISE

- Depth
- Stile or post
- End
- Reveal
- Width
- Shoulder of rail meets here.
- Length
- Width

TENON

- Rail
- Length
- Width
- Cheek
- Large shoulder
- Thickness
- Small shoulder

The mortise-and-tenon joint is arguably the strongest joint in woodworking. It's been around for thousands of years and is the mark of fine craftsmanship. The joint consists of a tenon milled on the end of a rail that's inserted into a hole, or mortise, cut into the adjoining piece, usually a post or stile.

Standard Mortise

The standard mortise is a hole milled into the long grain of the face or edge of a piece of wood. Typically, a tenon cut on the end of another piece is inserted into the mortise to provide an exceptionally strong union of end grain to long grain. The procedures below describe milling mortises in a table leg, but you can use the same techniques for cutting other mortises, such as for door frames.

Stock Preparation

1. Choose the leg stock from wood with no knots and relatively straight grain. Mill the stock straight and square, except for round stock. (See Mortising Non-Square Stock, page 98.)

2. Mill a spacer for the mortising fixture.

3. Mark the surface of the spacer on which the leg rests, as shown in the photo, right.

Spaced out. Insert a scrap block into the jig of the correct thickness and width to bring the workpiece level with the jig's jaws.

STANDARD MORTISE

APPLICATIONS

Mortises and tenons have been used to frame huge buildings as well as join small, delicate pieces of furniture—and many wooden things in between! The most common type of mortise today is a standard mortise used for joining door and table frames, where rails, aprons, or stretchers join door stiles or table legs.

WHAT'S NOT COVERED

The common mortise has a flat bottom, two parallel cheeks, and two ends. A mortise can also have no bottom, called a through mortise. In addition, a mortise can have an open end, known as a bridle joint. And one end of the mortise can be altered to accept a haunch, or step, cut in the tenon. All these mortise variations are created in the same way as the standard mortise covered here by simply altering the depth of the cut or by milling the mortise all the way through the stock.

WHAT YOU NEED TO KNOW

- length, depth, and width of the mortise
- thickness of tenon stock
- dimensions of the leg
- reveal (the distance the leg is set back from the apron or stretcher)
- shoulder depth of tenon

JIGS

- mortising fixture (see page 55)
- spacer for mortising fixture, milled to accommodate stock

BITS AND TOOLS

- ⅜ x 3 in. up-cutting spiral bit
- calculator
- bit gauge (see page 22)
- plunge router

End marks tell the story. With the grain arranged so the inside of the tree faces in, mark each leg so you can keep track of adjoining mortises.

Position your mortise marks. Make sure the adjoining mortise points toward the moveable jaw when inserting the stock into the jig.

Marking the Stock

1. Study the end grain of the legs and arrange them so the center of the tree faces the inside of the table. Then mark and number the top end of each leg for each mortise location. (See top photo, right.) This marking system orients each face to be mortised relative to an adjacent face as well as to neighboring legs. Best of all, it prevents you from accidentally routing a mortise in the wrong place!

2. Once you've marked the legs, match the mortise numbers to the aprons. This allows you to sequence the grain of the aprons around the table in a continuous pattern.

3. Lay out and mark the width and length of two mortises on one leg only, drawing one cheek line and both ends of each mortise. Make sure to mark an "X" on the inside of the cheek line. Although you'll be milling eight mortises in four legs, the router baseplate on the mortising fixture can be set to this one leg for all your mortises.

Setting Up the Cut

1. Set up the mortising fixture with your plunge router and install a spiral bit. Position the spacer for the leg stock so the stock sits flush with the top of the fixture's jaws.

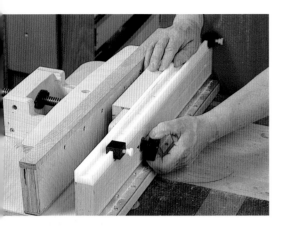

Stop the workpiece. Line up the area to be mortised in the stock with the center of the jig's screw, and lock the stop against the stock.

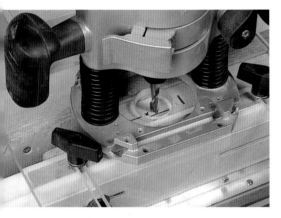

Locate the cheeks. With the bit as close as possible to the surface of the work, line up the edge of the bit with the cheek line and lock the bar to the baseplate.

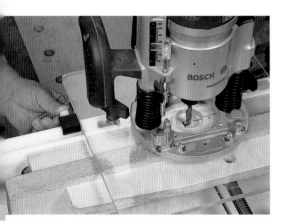

Find the ends. Line up the bit with the end of the mortise and lock the end stop to the fence.

2. Place the marked leg into the fixture with the surface to be mortised facing up and the adjoining mortise oriented towards the moveable jaw. (See middle right photo, previous page.)

3. Line up the center of the mortise with the screw clamp, then slide the workpiece stop to the end of the leg and tighten it, as shown in the photo, left. Clamp the work between the fences by tightening the moveable jaw.

4. Set the router on the jig and lower the bit until it touches the stock. Turn the bit until one of the cutting edges points toward the cheek line, loosen

the bar on the baseplate, and slide the router sideways until the corner of the bit touches the "X" side of the cheek line. Align the baseplate parallel to the bar by eye and tighten the lock knobs. (See middle photo, left.)

5. Rotate the bit so the cutting edge points towards the end of the mortise, and move the router until the bit aligns with the end mark. Without moving the router, position a router stop against the baseplate and lock it into the fixed jaw. (See bottom photo, left.) Repeat the procedure to set the opposing stop, sliding the router to the opposite end and fastening a second stop at that end of the jaw.

Mortising Non-Square Stock

Add blocks to a leg. Plywood squares attached to either end of a shaped leg allow you to register the part accurately in the jig.

If your design calls for milling mortises in stock that's not square, you may need to alter your mortising sequence or devise an alternative method for holding your work, depending on the shape of the stock you're working. For example, if you plan on tapering the stock, such as for tapered table legs, then it's wise to do the tapering *after* the mortises are milled. This leaves you with square stock for mortising so the milling process is much easier and more accurate.

If you want round or otherwise shaped legs, turn them on the lathe or mill them first. Once you've shaped the work, make two plywood squares that equal the major diameter of the leg and screw them to each end of the leg, centered on the leg's axis. Now you have square references for cutting mortises that are precisely 90° apart and perpendicular to the stock.

Mortise Math

Here are simple formulas for calculating critical mortise dimensions.

$$\text{tenon shoulder depth} = \frac{(\text{tenon stock thickness} - \text{tenon thickness})}{2}$$

cheek line = reveal + shoulder depth

one mortise end = shoulder depth

opposite mortise end = shoulder depth + tenon width

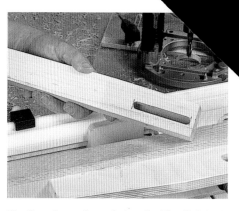

Perfect length and depth. The finished mortise falls between the end lines and is cut to a precise depth.

6. Set the depth stop of your plunge base to equal the depth of the mortise, and turn the turret so the highest possible land is under the depth rod. (See Setting Bit Height and Depth, page 72.)

7. Slide the router back and forth between the two stops to make sure you and your router are ready. Check that the cord isn't going to catch on something, the stops are in the right places and securely tightened, and the path of the bit will cut what and where you want it to. Make any adjustments if necessary.

Routing a Mortise

1. Carry out the router flight check (see page 76). Plunge the bit into the wood until the depth rod touches the first turret land. Slide the router back and forth between the end stops. (See center photo, right.) Raise the bit above the work. You may feel safer turning off the router before the next step.

2. Reset the turret to the next lower land and repeat the plunge cut as before. If you feel comfortable leaving the router on during this step, be very careful that your fingers do not get near the spinning bit! Personally, I prefer to turn the router off.

All you do is push. Once the jig is set up, rout the mortise by simply sliding the baseplate back and forth between the two stops.

3. Repeat the plunge cuts until the depth rod contacts the lowest land and the final mortise depth is reached. Then remove the router, loosen the clamping screw, and remove the leg. (See top photo, right.)

4. Rout a single mortise in each of the remaining three legs by simply inserting the leg into the fixture

against the workpiece stop and tightening the clamp. Watch the orienting marks.

5. To mill the adjacent mortise in each of the four legs, you'll need to readjust the router stops and the workpiece stop. Repeat the setup instructions, using the marked-up leg and adjusting the workpiece stop so it registers the uncut mortise layout, then follow the step-by-step routing instructions as before. (See photo, below.) Congratulations! Every mortise is now on the correct face of each leg.

A completed leg. The adjacent mortises line up with each other, and are ready to receive tenons.

...SE

...andy for
...g applica-
tions, including doors and cases,
lids and panels, and box tops.

WHAT YOU NEED TO KNOW

Have the hinges on hand; the jig
you'll make is specific to the
hinge.

JIGS

• hinge jig (see fig. 1)

BITS AND TOOLS

• ½ in. hinge bit (page 23)
• fixed-base router with offset
  baseplate

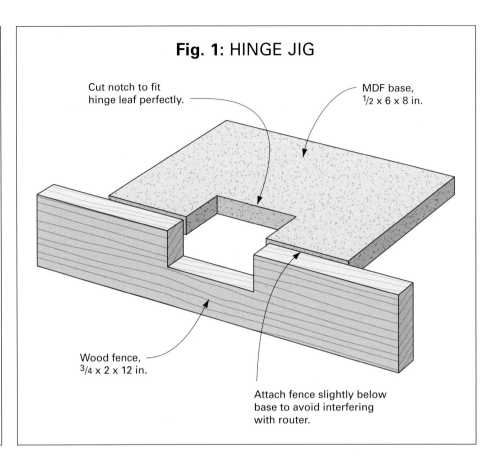

Fig. 1: HINGE JIG

Cut notch to fit
hinge leaf perfectly.

MDF base,
½ x 6 x 8 in.

Wood fence,
3/4 x 2 x 12 in.

Attach fence slightly below
base to avoid interfering
with router.

Hinge Mortise

Adding doors to your furniture projects broadens your woodworking
skills and expands the variety of
projects you can build. Those doors
will need hinges, and the hinge
leaves require cutting a shallow mortise. You can cut these mortises by
hand with a chisel, but routing them
with a jig is often more accurate and
can save time, especially when you
have multiple hinges to install.
Other hardware, such as locksets,
also requires shallow mortises, and a
variation of the jig shown here will
work. You'll love this procedure!

Stock Preparation

It's best to build the cabinet and door
first. If you're hinging inset doors,
remove the back from the cabinet.

Marking the Stock

Line up the edge of the door with the
cabinet, clamp the door in place, and
position your hinges. Use a pencil or
a knife to mark the hinge locations
both door and cabinet by following
the leaf of each hinge. Make sure to
mark an "X" on the side of the line
to be mortised. Now deepen each
mark by placing a square on the
scored line and retracing it with a
sharp knife. (See photo, right.)

Knife your lines. With the door
clamped to the case, use a small square
to incise lines across the case and the
back of the door.

Set the bit depth. Place the hinge jig on the baseplate, set an open hinge on the jig, and adjust the bit level with the leaf.

Setting Up the Cut

1. Install the hinge bit, set the router on its head, and install the offset baseplate. Place the hinge jig upside down on the baseplate, and adjust the bit until it's slightly above the jig.

2. Open the hinge and carefully place one leaf on the jig and next to the bit. Adjust the bit until it's perfectly flush with the leaf, and set the hinge aside. (See photo, above.)

3. Position the jig with its inner edge against the marked line, inserting the tip of the knife into the line and sliding the jig against the blade to register it accurately. Clamp the jig

Knife locates the jig. Stick the knife into your previously cut line, slide the jig up to the blade, and clamp the jig in place.

in place. Check that the "X" is visible through the opening in the jig. (See bottom photo, left.)

Routing a Hinge Mortise

1. Carry out the router flight check, place the router on the jig with the bit clear of the work, and turn on the router.

Rout the mortise. Keep the majority of the baseplate over the jig and let the bit's bearing follow the contours of the jig to rout the hinge mortise.

2. Bring the bit's bearing in contact with the edge of the jig and ride the bit around the opening in a clockwise fashion, as shown in the photo, above. Then move the router back and forth to remove any uncut fibers, leaving a perfectly clean bottom to the mortise. Move the bit sideways out of the mortise with the baseplate still on the jig, and turn the router off. This prevents you from accidentally dinging the jig and having to start over.

3. Without moving the jig, place the back of a sharp chisel against the edge of the jig and pare down to square the mortise corners. (See top photo, right.) Chisel the end grain first, cut the long grain, and then pare across the bottom to remove the waste.

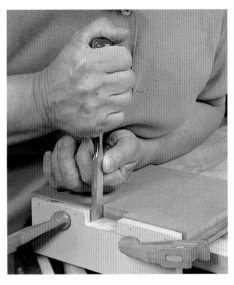

Carve the corners. Use the jig to guide your chisel for cleaning up the rounded corners.

Fit the hinge leaf into the mortise. (See photo, below.) If the leaf doesn't fit or isn't flush with the workpiece, make any necessary adjustments to the jig or to the bit depth setting.

4. Remove the clamps and re-clamp the jig for the next hinge mortise. Repeat the preceding steps for all the mortises.

A perfect fit. Try the leaf in the mortise to see that it fits along the shoulders and is flush with the work.

Tenons

This is the adjoining half of a mortise-and-tenon joint. Tenons are created by removing wood from the opposite faces on the end of a board, as well as sometimes removing stock from the opposite edges to create shoulders. In most cases, it's best to cut the tenon after milling the mortise, so you can fine-tune the fit. Below is the sequence for milling a tenon in apron stock to fit the leg mortise you routed earlier.

TENONS

APPLICATIONS

The most common application is milling tenons on rails, aprons, and stretchers when connecting these parts to door frames or table legs. Other uses include tenons cut in the ends of shelves, web frames, and dust panels for fitting into case sides.

WHAT'S NOT COVERED

Through-tenons, loose tenons, and haunched tenons are not covered as they're simply variations of the basic tenon that has a shoulder milled on all four edges. After mastering the setup here, variations can and should be practiced. Different setups may have to be considered. That's the fun of learning and growing as a woodworker.

The setup shown here works best with aprons up to 36 in. long.

Cutting tenons in longer stock works better with a different setup, as shown in Rabbets (see page 78).

WHAT YOU NEED TO KNOW

- depth, length, and width of the mortise
- shoulder depth of the tenon
- final thickness of the aprons
- final width of the aprons
- distance between the legs

BITS AND TOOLS

- ⅜ x 3 in. up-cutting spiral bit
- machinist's dial calipers
- bit gauge (page 22)
- a few playing cards

JIGS

- push sled (page 50)
- router table with horizontal table setup (page 38)

Stock Preparation

1. Surface all the stock, plus one practice board, to final thickness and width.

2. Calculate the overall length of the apron by adding two mortise depths plus the distance between the legs, or the shoulder-to-shoulder length. Crosscut the stock to this length, making sure the ends are precisely 90°. Note: If your design calls for decorative apron cuts, mill the tenons first so you're working with square stock, then make any curved cuts after completing the tenons.

Marking the Stock

Consider having the grain of the apron stock run continuously around the frame. To do this, cut your aprons from a single length, and mark each piece in successive order. It's a nice touch for a custom look.

Setting Up the Jig

1. Secure the router base to the horizontal table setup on the router table, and tighten both the lock knobs on the horizontal plate.

2. Install the router bit and the motor in the base. Loosen the lock knob slightly, pivot the plate up until the bit is above the table, and lock the plate.

3. Set the tenon length by adjusting the bit gauge to the depth of your mortise, then placing it against the plate and adjusting the bit until it touches the gauge. Lock the depth on the router. (See photo, below.)

Bit length equals tenon length. Use a bit gauge to set the depth of the bit, which determines the length of the tenon.

Tenon Math

Here are simple formulas for determining critical tenon dimensions.

overall apron length = (2 × mortise depth) + distance between legs

tenon length = mortise depth

tenon width = mortise length

tenon thickness = mortise width

Shoulder first. Hold the stock on edge and use a push sled to rout the first shoulder.

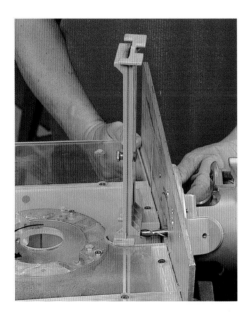

Bit height is the shoulder depth. Reset the gauge and adjust the height of the bit, which equals the depth of the tenon shoulder.

4. Reset the gauge to the shoulder depth, loosen the lock knob slightly, and pivot the plate until the bit touches the gauge. Tighten the knob. (See photo, above.)

Note: Since you're removing wood from each side of the stock to form the tenon, any error in height adjustment for the shoulder depth is doubled. If you are ever so slightly high, your tenon will be too thin. You're best approach is to be a little "fat" and sneak up on the right height, taking successive cuts and readjusting the bit height accordingly.

Routing a Tenon

1. Complete the router flight check, and place the practice stock on edge with its end against the plate and its face against the push sled. Turn on the router and push the stock and sled against the fence and into the bit, using a smooth motion and an even feed rate. (See top photo, right.) As soon as the shoulder is fully milled, pull the stock and the sled away from thc platc and bit. It's not necessary to push the sled all the way through.

2. Rotate the stock 90° and repeat the cutting sequence to rout one cheek, as shown in the photo, right.

3. Turn the board 90° again and onto its second edge, and repeat to rout the opposite shoulder.

4. Rotate the stock 90° once more and rout the second cheek, again repeating the same routing sequence. (See photo, right.)

5. Once you've routed the cheeks, round the corners of the tenon with a chisel by slicing down each square corner and paring it into a round corner. Then place the back of the chisel on the shoulder and "walk" it around the corner to remove the waste. The rounded tenon should closely match the rounded ends of the mortise, as shown in the bottom photos, page 104.

Then the face. Rotate the stock 90° and mill the first cheek.

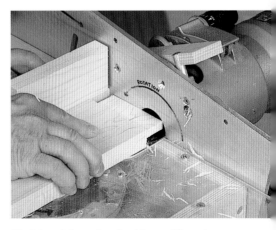

Finish with a cheek. After milling the second shoulder, complete the tenon by routing the opposite cheek.

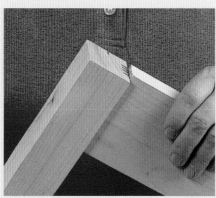

Dropped below. The poor fit here is due to a tenon whose shoulder has been cut too deeply.

Poking above. A shoulder that's cut too shallow results in the apron rising above the surface of the leg.

Just right. Tight-fitting shoulders and flush edges are the hallmarks of a properly cut joint.

Testing the Fit

It's important that a tenon fits securely in its mortise, or the joint is likely to fail. The best test is to push the tenon into the mortise by hand. If the tenon slips smoothly into the mortise without hammering, and there's no wriggle in any direction when the tenon is fully inserted, you've achieved the perfect fit. Make sure to push the tenon back and forth along the length of the mortise to test the width. Again, it shouldn't move.

Another key to a good fit is to check that adjoining surfaces are flush with each other. For example, if the apron is below the edge of the leg when the parts are joined, then the top edge of the tenon is too far away from the edge of the apron stock. In effect, the shoulder has been cut too deep, as shown in the top photo, left. Conversely, if the apron is above the leg, the tenon is too near the edge of the stock, or its shoulder is too shallow. (See photo, above.)

Make sure to measure the length of the tenon and compare that with the depth of the mortise. It must not be longer than the mortise is deep. In fact, ideally it's slightly shorter. (See Leave Room for Glue, opposite page). If the shoulders of the apron don't make intimate contact with the face of the leg, the tenon is too long. A well-fitted tenon should sit nice and tight, as shown in the photo, above.

The final step is to test the fit of the tenon to your mortise. (See Testing the Fit, above.)

Practice Project

Toast yourself! You've milled standard mortises and hinge mortises, plus routed and fitted tenons. You're ready to use the mortise-and-tenon joint to build the Small Table (page 148), or try your hand at routing hinge mortises for the Frame-and-Panel Door for the Router Bit Cabinet (page 153). Of course, the door will swing perfectly.

Rounded to fit. Chisel the square edges to round so the tenon fits the round ends of the mortise.

Leave Room for Glue

It's good practice to make your tenons slightly shorter than the depth of your mortises. The reason for this is to leave some room for glue. If you size a tenon to the full depth of the mortise, the glue can hydraulically push the tenon out of the joint during assembly. Making your tenon a little short also ensures that its shoulders meet tightly against the adjoining piece before the tenon bottoms out. One approach is to simply crosscut 1/16 in. off the end of each tenon to provide this clearance. Whenever possible, I prefer using the no-math procedure for its simplicity. Or you can consider the following technique: To get the tenons slightly shorter but the distance between the legs exactly right, reduce the overall length of the board by 1/8 in., then mill each tenon 1/16 in. shorter than the depth of the mortise.

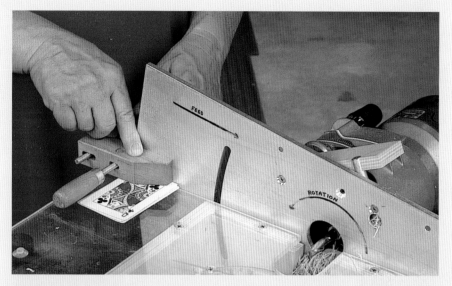

Cards raise the bit. Use a few playing cards to help with raising the bit up by a predetermined amount.

Adjusting The Fit

When cutting a tenon on your practice board, there are five situations you're likely to run into that will prevent a good fit. Perform the following adjustments to your router setup depending on the specific situation at hand.

If the tenon is too thin, the shoulder depth setting is too high. Cut off the tenon to start anew, then loosen the lock knob on the plate and reduce the height of the bit very slightly.

If the tenon is too thick, the shoulder depth setting is too low. Measure the tenon thickness with machinist's dial calipers. Also measure the width of the mortise. Now subtract the two, divide the result by 10, and round to the nearest whole number. Count out the number of playing cards that represent that number, plus one more card. Clean off the router tabletop and clamp a small handscrew to the horizontal plate such that the clamp lays flat on the table. Loosen the lock knob,

pivot the plate up, and position the cards under the clamp, as shown in the photo, above. Tighten the knob.

If the edge of the apron is lower than the leg when dry-assembled, consider crosscutting a little off the top end of the legs. Make sure to replace any marks you may have on the tops of the legs. Another option is to reduce the width of the tenon on its upper edge on the bandsaw or with a handsaw.

If the apron is higher than the leg when dry-assembled, consider ripping the excess from the top edge of the apron. If you have marks on this edge, replace them. If this option isn't acceptable, reduce the width of the tenon on its lower edge on the bandsaw or with a handsaw.

If the tenon is too long, crosscut the excess from the end of the tenon. Don't adjust the length of the tenon stock and don't adjust the router bit depth, since both approaches will alter the distance between the legs.

A gap is good. Leave a small gap between the bottom of the mortise and the end of the tenon to ease assembly and allow room for excess glue.

Dovetails

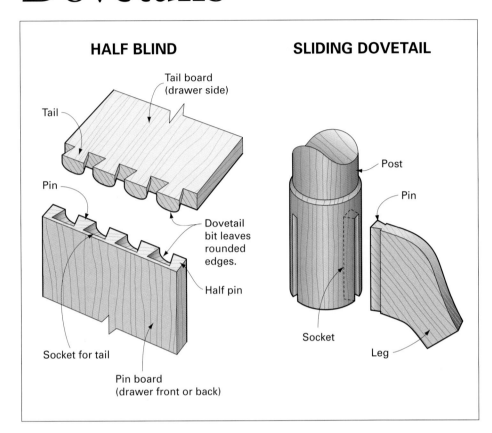

HALF BLIND

Tail board
(drawer side)

Tail

Pin

Dovetail
bit leaves
rounded
edges.

Half pin

Socket for tail

Pin board
(drawer front or back)

SLIDING DOVETAIL

Post

Pin

Socket

Leg

Dovetails have a rich history spanning centuries. The joint precedes reliable glues and inexpensive fasteners and requires no hardware, since the wedged-shaped pins and tails create a mechanical lock that allows for expansion and contraction of solid wood. Originally sawn and chopped by hand, dovetails have traditionally required great skill to make successfully. Today, everyone can make this strong joint with a router accurately and quickly. However, while routing dovetails can be fast and predictable, careful setup is very important.

Dovetails are seen in three variations: through dovetails, half-blind dovetails, and sliding dovetails. Each type requires its own jig, and there are many commercial models to choose from, including templates to make your own jig. You can often pick up a used jig, typically for half-blind dovetails. Just keep in mind that the user manual is often missing from these older jigs.

Half-Blind Dovetails

The half-blind dovetail joint consists of pins and tails that intertwine with each other, much like lacing the fingers of both hands together in prayer. Since the parts are flared, or shaped to an incline, the joint locks mechanically in one plane. There are numerous inexpensive commercial half-blind dovetail jigs that help you cut the joint, but they have confounded woodworkers for decades. I use a popular jig that I modified to help take the frustration out of using these kinds of jigs (see page 60). You may not have the same brand, but you can make many of the modifications to upgrade yours and use the setups and executions similar to those described here.

Unlike through and sliding dovetails where you rout the pins and tails (or sockets) separately, you'll make an entire corner joint at one time, consisting of an end (pins) and a side (tails). This is an advantage, since you're guaranteed the best fit by keeping these two parts together during the milling process. Since the most common application is a drawer, all references are for a drawer box, which is really just a box without a lid!

Stock Preparation

The thickness of your stock is critical when routing dovetails. Prepare all stock, including practice material, at the same time. Poplar and Baltic birch plywood, both in ½ in. thickness, are often used for drawer sides. For smaller boxes, ¼ in. stock works fine. Whatever your choice, drawer

Pins and Tails Terminology

When it comes to making dove-tailed drawers, the terms used to describe parts can be confusing. Here's a crash course on dovetail terminology.

- A *drawer side* consists of a tail board, into which you rout sockets for pins, leaving a series of tails.

- A *drawer end* (drawer front or drawer back) consists of a pin board, into which you rout sockets for tails, leaving a series of pins.

- Looking at the face of the stock, the tails look like a bird's tail and the pins look straight.

HALF-BLIND DOVETAILS

APPLICATIONS

It's wise to decide which dovetail you are likely to utilize and then learn all of its idiosyncrasies. Having said this, the most common joint is the half-blind dovetail, typically used in corner joints for drawers. Through dovetails are best for large corner joints, such as case pieces like chests of drawers, blanket chests, or even firewood boxes. The sliding dovetail is great for case parts, such as dividers that keep chests of drawers together, and for table legs held firmly to posts, commonly seen in pedestal-style tables. One variation is the French dovetail, a sliding dovetail that joins drawer fronts to sides.

WHAT'S NOT COVERED

Through dovetails are not included, as the setup and execution relies on the specific jig being used. However, if you own a dovetail jig that handles both half-blind and through joints, once you learn to rout half-blind dovetails you'll be well on your way towards making through dovetails. Tapered sliding dovetails are also excluded, as they require tricky jig setups and are best practiced once you've mastered the basic sliding dovetail joint.

WHAT YOU NEED TO KNOW

- drawer opening
- the perfect half-pin width
- drawer stock width
- length of ends and sides

JIGS

- half-blind dovetail jig (page 60)
- setup stick (page 62)
- right-angled spacer, made from the same thickness stock as the sides and ends

BITS AND TOOLS

- ½ in. dovetail bit (14°, or the angle specified for your jig)
- template guide bushing specified for your jig
- machinists' dial calipers

side stock must be the same thickness or the joint will not fit.

Calculating the right dimensions is key to good stock preparation, and it begins with choosing the width of your drawer stock. First, measure the height of the drawer opening in the case, which determines the maximum drawer height, or the width of your drawer stock. This width must be less than the opening, and your choice of whether you use commercial metal drawer slides or wooden runners (or web frames) will determine the correct width. (See Drawer Height Math, page 109.) Of course, you'll want to consider what the drawer is going to store, and make sure there's enough height inside the drawer to accommodate these items. Remember to subtract the thickness of the drawer bottom and any extra material below the bottom to calculate the useable interior space.

Knowing the maximum drawer height that will fit in the case is one part of the equation. The other key aspect is the "perfect" width that will work with your dovetail jig. With half-blind dovetails, the joint always starts and ends with a half pin. Therefore, only certain widths of stock will work in your jig, as shown in figure 1. For ½ in. dovetails, the perfect widths are multiples of ⅞ in. For ¼ in. dovetails, the multiple is ⁷⁄₁₆ in.

Once you've determined the width of your stock, you can calculate the length of the ends and sides. Remember, these parts create the width and length of your drawer, respectively. (See Drawer Length Math, page 109.) Be sure to crosscut the ends of your stock at a perfect 90° angle. Forgo this, and the drawer will rock on two corners, or won't go together at all. And keep paired ends and paired sides to exactly the same length, which you can do by registering the parts against a stop when crosscutting.

Fig. 1: DETERMINING STOCK WIDTH

Attach a copy of this drawing to your dovetail jig for reference.

FOR ½ IN. DOVETAILS

Increase width of stock in increments of $7/8$ in.   Finger template

$1^3/8$ $2^1/4$ $3^1/8$ 4 $4^7/8$ $5^3/4$ $6^5/8$ $7^1/8$ $8^3/8$ $9^1/4$ $10^1/8$ 11 $11^7/8$ $12^3/4$

Start your measurement at the second finger to allow for a half pin at each end of stock.

FOR ¼ IN. DOVETAILS

Increase width of stock in increments of $7/16$ in.

$1^5/16$ $2^3/16$ $3^1/16$ $3^{15}/16$ $4^{13}/16$ $5^{11}/16$ $6^9/16$ $7^7/16$ $8^5/16$ $9^3/16$ $10^1/16$ $10^{15}/16$ $11^{13}/16$

$7/8$ | $1^3/4$ | $2^5/8$ | $3^1/2$ | $4^3/8$ | $5^1/4$ | $6^1/8$ | 7 | $7^7/8$ | $8^3/4$ | $9^5/8$ | $10^1/2$ | $11^3/8$ | $12^3/4$

Keep parts tight and flush. Use a small straightedge to check that the end of the drawer side is flush with the top surface of the drawer end.

Marking the Stock

Mark the stock as described under Dovetail Jig, page 60. If you are making more than one drawer at a time, number individual drawers so corners that are milled together will mate correctly during assembly.

Setting Up the Jig

1. Use a setup stick to position the jig's fences and template for the stock you'll be routing.

2. Using the same thickness stock as the drawer parts, nail together a right-angled spacer to help prevent the work clamps from bending. Insert the spacer under the clamps at the far left of the jig, as shown in the photo, left.

Clamp the appropriate side piece to the front of the jig and against the front right fence, with its end about ¼ in. above the top of the jig. Then clamp the mating end piece to the top of the jig and against the top right fence, with its end butted tight against the side piece. Now loosen the front clamp and raise the side piece flush with the top surface of the end piece. Tighten the clamp, and use a small straightedge to

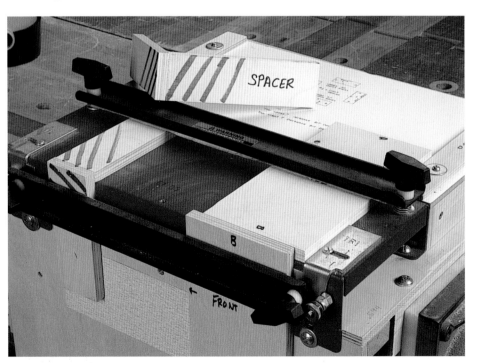

Spacer prevents twist. Position a shop-made spacer at the opposite end of the work to keep the work clamps from bending and losing their grip.

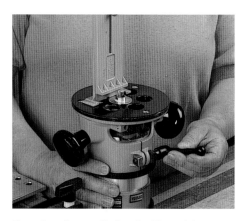

Set the dovetail depth. Use a bit gauge to set the depth of the dovetail bit. Adjust the gauge by taking into account the thickness of your jig's template so the bit cuts ½ in. deep in your stock.

check that the two pieces are flush and tight against each other. (See top right photo, opposite page.)

Remember, all drawer parts should be oriented with their outside surfaces against the jig. If your marking system is accurate, your layout marks (made on the inside surfaces) should always face out and bottom edges are always against the jig's fences. Ends are always on top of the jig and sides are always clamped to the front.

3. Fasten the jig's template to the top of the jig.

4. Install the template guide bushing in your router's baseplate and chuck the dovetail bit in the collet. Set the router bit depth to ½ in., making sure to take into account the thickness of your jig's template. (See photo, above.)

Routing Half-Blind Dovetails

1. Perform the router flight check (see page 76). Place the router on the left side of the top board with

Drawer Height Math

The following formulas allow you to calculate the maximum width of your drawer stock to accommodate the specific drawer hardware you plan to use.

For a drawer hung with commercial slides:
side or end width = case opening − 1 in. slide allowance

For a drawer operating on wood runners:
side or end width = case opening − ¹⁄₁₆ in. clearance

Drawer Length Math

The following formulas will help in determining the lengths of your drawer parts.

1. To find the length of your ends (front and back pieces), use one of the following formulas.
   For commercial drawer slides:
   end length = width of drawer opening − drawer slide allowance

   For inset drawers with wooden runners:
   end length = width of drawer opening − ¹⁄₁₆ in.

2. To find the length of the sides, use one of the following formulas.
   For a full overlay drawer with false front:
   side length = depth of drawer opening − ½ in.

   For a half overlay drawer with false front:
   side length = depth of drawer opening − (.5 × thickness of false front) − ½ in.

   For a flush, or inset, drawer:
   side length = depth of drawer opening − length of drawer stop system − ½ in.

the bit clear of the wood and, holding the router with both hands, rotate the base until one hand is over the stock and one hand is off. Turn on the router and make a light pass from left to right, making a shallow scoring cut all the way across the stock. The guide bushing should just touch the fingers of the template. (See photo, right.)

2. After the scoring cut, move the router to the right side of each finger and push it in and out of the finger, moving the router from right to left and always keeping the guide

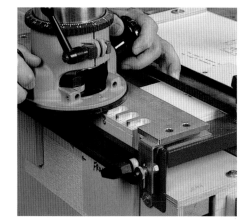

Score it first. For the cleanest cut, make an initial light pass across the stock to reduce tearout at the shoulder.

Rout both parts at once. Push the router in and out of the fingers of the template, cutting both pins and tails at the same time.

Making Dovetails Fit

There are six problems that can result in a poor-fitting joint, as shown in the list below. Four have to do with the adjustment of the jig itself, and two have to do with the depth of the router bit. For the procedures necessary for adjusting the jig, see Dovetail Jig (page 60). For router bit depth adjustments, see Adjusting the Depth of Cut, opposite page.

1. **Edges of adjoining pieces are uneven:** Reset fences to create half pins at ends
2. **Tails are proud of pin board:** Move finger template further away from front of jig
3. **Pins are proud of tail board:** Move finger template closer to front of jig
4. **Pins and tails at uneven depths:** Adjust template parallel with front edge of work
5. **Fit is too tight:** Adjust router bit up for a shallower cut
6. **Fit is too loose:** Adjust router bit depth for a deeper cut

bushing against the template. (See photo, above.) When you've finished the last finger, go back through each one, this time from left to right. When finished, pull the bushing and bit away from the template and turn the router off, but *don't lift the router* or you'll spoil the joint. When the bit stops spinning, set the router aside.

3. Look carefully at the milled joint and the template fingers. If everything looks symmetrical and cleanly cut, loosen the clamps and remove the stock. Test the fit by fitting the tails into the pins. (See photo, right.) If you see gaps or unevenness in the joint, make any necessary adjustments to your setup now. (See Making Dovetails Fit, above, right.)

4. Still working on the right side of the jig, clamp the correct side piece to the front of the jig and clamp the corresponding end piece to the top. Repeat the routing procedure to mill this second corner joint.

5. With the two "right" corners routed, slide the right-angled spacer to the right and clamp the appropriate side piece to the front of the jig, this time positioning it on the left side of the jig and aligned with the left fence. Do the same for the corresponding end piece by clamping it to the top of the jig, again on the left side. Rout the joint as before.

6. Finish up by clamping the remaining side and end pieces to the left side of the jig and routing the pins and tails as before.

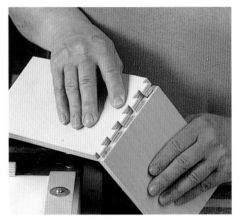

Test the fit. Assemble the tails into the pin board, and check that the joint is tight and without gaps. Make any corrections to your setup now before going further.

Practice Project

Congratulations on your tenacity and on the well-fitted dovetails you've done! You win an "Atta-boy" or a "You go, girl"—your choice. Now go make the Dovetailed Drawer (page 155) that fits inside the Router Bit Cabinet.

Adjusting the Depth of Cut

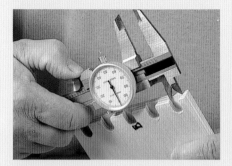 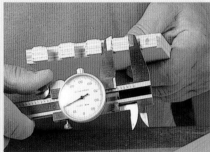

Compare the difference. Use a dial caliper to read the width of both the tail socket (left) and the tail (right) and note any difference between the two.

If your dovetails are too tight (and impossible to assemble!) or if they're loose and rattle like loose teeth, your bit is set at the incorrect depth and you'll need to reset it to make the joint fit correctly. First, determine whether the bit is cutting too deep or too shallow, as described in Making Dovetails Fit, opposite page. Then use the machinist's dial calipers to take a comparative reading of both the width of the tail socket and the width of the tail itself, and note the amount of error. (See photos, above.) Unplug the router, and use your calipers again to measure the existing bit depth. Use one of the following procedures to make the fix, depending on the type of correction needed.

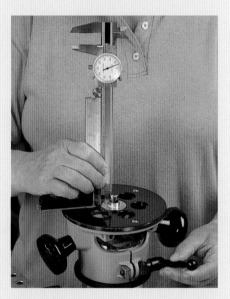

Reset the bit. Steady the caliper with a small square while you adjust the bit to the correct depth.

If the bit is too deep, subtract the amount of error from the existing bit depth, and reset the caliper to that measurement. Use the caliper to help with adjusting the bit to the corrected depth. (See photo, above.)

If the bit is too shallow, add the amount of error to the existing bit depth and reset the caliper to that measurement. As before, use the new setting on the caliper to adjust the bit to the correct depth.

Sliding Dovetail

A sliding dovetail is made up of two parts, a flared pin and a matching flared, or wedged-shaped, socket. The pin and socket mate together for an exceedingly strong joint that locks mechanically. When properly constructed, the joint stays together with little or no glue.

The joint is cut in two parts using the same dovetail bit. The size of the bit determines the width of the dovetail socket you'll cut, and you use the same bit to cut the pin. The following procedure utilizes a ½ in. bit with a 14° angle to make a leg-to-post joint, but you can choose larger bits for larger work, or bits with different

---

SLIDING DOVETAIL

WHAT YOU NEED TO KNOW

- diameter of dovetail bit
- width of dovetail socket

JIGS

- mortising fixture (page 55)
- spacer for mortising fixture, milled to accommodate stock
- two equilateral plywood triangles (for three-legged post) or two plywood squares (for four-legged post)
- push block made from wide scrap
- router table with horizontal setup (page 39)

BITS AND TOOLS

- spiral bit, diameter equal to or smaller than the narrowest diameter of dovetail bit
- ½ in. x 14° dovetail bit
- 30°/60°/90° drafting triangle

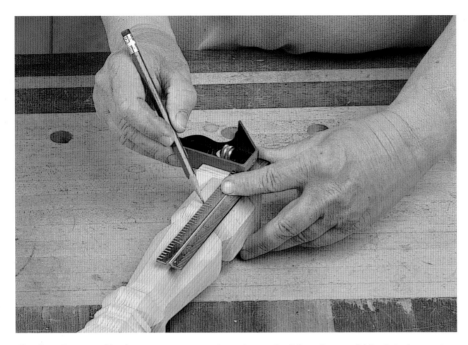

Socket layout. Register a square against the end of the plywood block to lay out the centerline for each socket.

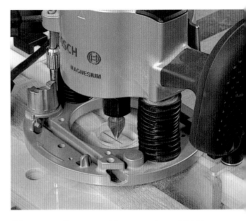

Line up the cut. Use a pointed bit to help position the baseplate so the cut is centered on the socket centerline.

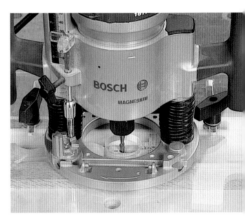

Straight cut first. Remove most of the waste with a spiral bit, routing through the plywood block and stopping when the baseplate contacts the router stop.

Dovetail next. Switch to a dovetail bit and repeat the routing procedure to mill all the dovetail sockets.

angles. You cut the socket in the mortising fixture, then mill the pin on the router table.

The same ½ in. bit shown here works great for joining ½ in. thick drawer sides to a drawer front, sometimes referred to as a French dovetail. To make this joint, follow the directions for routing a stopped dado (see page 88). The difference is that first you rout out most of the waste with a spiral bit whose diameter is less than or equal to the narrowest part of the dovetail. Then follow up with the dovetail bit. The router tracking system (see page 54) excels at this because you can back out of the cut under power without changing the geometry of the dovetail.

Stock Preparation

Shape the post first and cut it to finished length before cutting the joints.

Marking the Post Stock

Fasten plywood triangles or squares at either end of the post so it rests flat, depending on whether you're making a three- or four-legged pedestal. Either way, don't make the blocks any larger than they need to be. For three legs, mark a socket centerline along each facet of the post that's referenced to a point on the triangle. For four legs, lay out a socket centerline on each face using a square referenced against the center of the plywood square, as shown in the photo, above. Using the square again, mark the end of each socket.

Routing the Socket

1. If necessary, make a spacer to fit the post. Insert the post and spacer into the mortising fixture, with the center of the socket aligned with the veneer screw. Side the work stop against the post and lock it in place.

2. Install any pointed bit in your plunge router (a V-groove bit works well) and mount the router onto the baseplate of the mortising fixture. Adjust the baseplate so the point of the bit aligns with your socket centerline and tighten the plate. (See top right photo, opposite page.) Remove the bit and replace it with a spiral bit whose diameter equals the narrowest part of the dovetail bit.

3. Slide the baseplate until the bit touches the socket end mark and lock a router stop to the fixture's fence. Set the bit depth to slightly less than the final depth of the dovetail socket.

4. Carry out the router flight check, and start the cut by pushing the spinning bit through the plywood block and into the stock. Rout to the stop. (See middle right photo, opposite page.) Back out of the cut, and turn off the router. Rotate the post to the remaining mortise positions and repeat the routing procedure to mill all the straight slots.

5. Without adjusting the setup, replace the spiral bit with a dovetail bit, setting its depth to the desired final socket depth. Repeat the routing procedure as before to mill all the sockets in the post. (See bottom right photo, opposite page.)

Routing the Pin

1. Measure the depth of the socket you just routed with dial calipers, and install a dovetail bit in the horizontal router table setup. Extend the bit to the exact measured depth of the socket.

2. Subtract the width of the dovetail bit from the thickness of the leg stock, divide by two, and set the bit height to that amount, or slightly

less. The idea is to sneak up on the fit in increments. Perform the router flight check, and make a first pass run by pushing the stock with a piece of wide scrap the same thickness as the stock. If the ends of your leg stock are cut at a specific miter angle (a common practice with pedestal legs), make sure to cut a complementary angle on the scrap block to fully support the cut. (See photo, right.) Check the depth of the pin to the socket and adjust the bit depth as necessary.

3. Flip the stock and the push block over, and rout the opposite face. (See middle photo, right.) Now check to see that the widest part of the pin fits the widest part of the dovetail socket. If necessary, use the playing card trick you learned when making tenons (see Adjusting the Fit, page 105) to adjust the fence to sneak up on the fit.

4. Rout each leg and fit it in turn to its mating socket. I always number and mark each leg and socket, which is valuable information come glue-up time. The completed joint should slip together with hand pressure alone. (See bottom photo, right.)

Practice Project

Make a tabletop for a pedestal base, then go ahead and cut the leg-to-post sliding dovetail joint. There are no specific plans for this particular project in the book, but by now I know you can figure it out. You are getting soooo good!

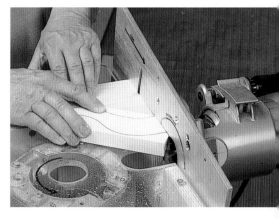

One half of a pin. Rout the first face of the leg stock using an angled push block to steer the work safely past the bit.

Rout the other side. Flip the work over and complete the pin by milling the opposite face.

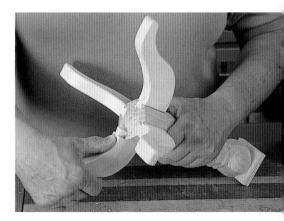

A nice fit. The finished joint can be assembled by hand and is very strong thanks to its wedge-shaped connection.

Special Joints with Special Bits

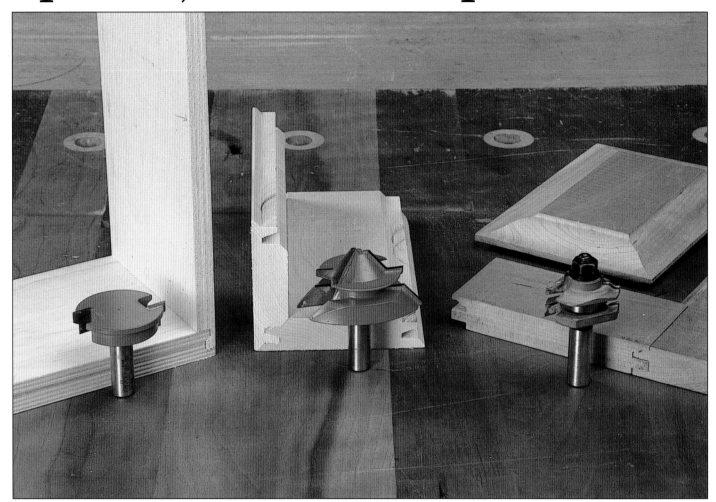

There are many special joints that require specific router bits. Three of the most useful joints are included here: the drawer joint, the lock miter, and the cope and stick. The drawer-joint bit is used to make boxes or drawers quickly and easily. The lock-miter bit is also a good choice for joining boxes, and makes assembly and glue-up easy when two hands are all you can bring to the job. The cope-and-stick bit is used for building door frames for holding glass or wood panels. As a bonus, I'll demonstrate how to use a raised-panel bit for making panels to fit those frames.

DRAWER LOCK

APPLICATIONS

The drawer lock bit is used to make 90° corners for boxes and drawers. Drawer ends (fronts and backs) must be at least ¾ in. thick; sides can be thinner if desired.

WHAT YOU NEED TO KNOW

- use bit in router table only, and at maximum 18,000 rpm
- overall drawer dimensions
- drawer front style (inset or overlay)

JIGS

- vertical push stick (page 49)
- push sled (page 49)
- router table and tall fence, both with large holes (page 38)

BITS AND TOOLS

- drawer lock bit
- dial calipers
- bit gauge (page 22)
- router with variable speed

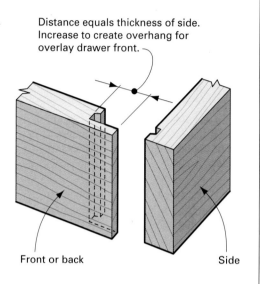

Distance equals thickness of side. Increase to create overhang for overlay drawer front.

Front or back   Side

Drawer Lock

This bit produces slightly angular edges in the mating parts that interlock with each other when the joint is assembled. The result is a corner joint with great strength. Since you only need a single bit height setting to rout both parts, the drawer lock bit offers a quick and easy routing operation for making perfectly fitting corner joints.

Stock Preparation

Mill the sides ½ in. shorter than the overall length of the drawer, and cut the back to the overall drawer width. The desired style of the front (inset or overlay) dictates the length of the stock. To find the length for an inset front, subtract ⅛ in. from the width of the drawer opening. For an overlay drawer front, add twice the amount of overlay desired to the width of the opening.

Have some practice stock on hand to test your router's rpm settings so you can achieve the best cut in addition to getting the setup exactly right. You'll also need some extra stock for the drawer front to get its length precisely right. It's best to leave these pieces overlong to start.

One tip: I like to rip my stock about ¼ in. wider than its final width. This way, I can rip ⅛ in. off each edge after cutting the joint to remove any possible blowout.

Marking the Stock

Mark the inside faces of the ends and sides, as these are the surfaces that will contact either the router table or its fence. Mark the top edge of each piece, and make sure to label the back and the front. If you're making more than one drawer, go ahead and number individual drawers so you don't mix up the parts.

Setting Up the Bit

1. Install the bit in a variable-speed motor in the router table with the tall fence, and set the speed to 18,000 rpm or lower. Make sure the hole in your table and your fence is large enough to accommodate the bit's diameter. (See photo, below.)

Keep it clear. With large bits, such as the drawer lock shown here, make sure the holes in the router fence and the baseplate are large enough to clear the bit's cutting edges.

Set the depth. When setting up to cut the ends, use a bit gauge to adjust the depth of the bit equal to the thickness of the sides.

2. For ½ in. stock, use a bit gauge to adjust the bit to ³¹⁄₆₄ in.—a tad under ½ in.— above the table.

3. For routing end pieces (fronts and backs), use a bit gauge to set the fence so the lead cutting edge of the bit protrudes from the fence equal to the thickness of the side stock, plus any desired overlap. (See photo, above.)

4. For routing sides, use a routed end and measure the depth of its groove with dial calipers, as shown in the photo, below. Adjust the bit gauge to that distance, then use the gauge to

Cut, then measure. Measure the groove depth on an end piece with calipers, then use a bit gauge set to this measurement to adjust the fence for cutting the sides.

set the fence. Remember, you won't need to alter the bit height when switching from ends to sides.

Routing a Drawer Lock Joint

1. You'll rout the ends first. Perform the router flight check (see page 76) and rout the end of one practice piece using a push sled and orienting the inside surface down on the table. (See photo, right.)

2. Now set up for routing the sides and rout a practice side, this time using a vertical push stick and registering the inside surface against the fence. (See top left photo, opposite page.)

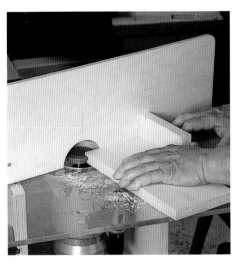

The end comes first. Rout the end pieces using a push sled and feeding the work past the bit in one continuous, smooth motion.

Making the Joint Fit

Here's what to watch for when setting up for cutting the drawer lock joint. As the drawing shows, in two cases an ill-fitting joint is due to the bit being set too high or too low. The two other poor fits are the result of a fence that's set either too close to the bit or too far away. Dry-fit your test pieces to see which fix you need to make, then make sure to unplug the router before making any adjustments to the bit height or fence.

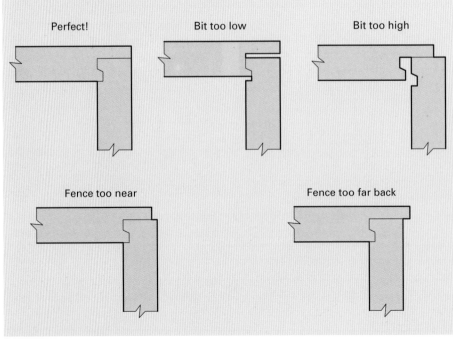

Then the sides. Stand the side stock upright and with its inside surface against the fence, and use a vertical push stick to move the work past the bit.

3. Once you've cut the side, insert it into the end piece. Check that the two pieces are fully engaged, and that the end is flush with the out-side face of the side. (See photo, below.) If not, make any necessary adjustments to either the fence or the bit. (See Making the Joint Fit, opposite page.)

4. When you're satisfied with the fit, execute the router flight check again, and rout each end of the back ends inside face down, using a push sled.

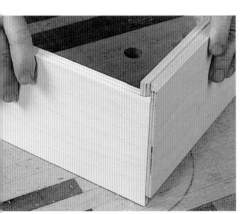

Check the fit. A properly cut joint won't have any gaps and the end will be flush with the outside surface of the side piece.

Overlapping front. Reset the fence to expose more of the bit for routing drawer fronts that overhang drawer sides.

If you're making a box, as opposed to a drawer, run the front ends the same way as the back ends.

5. Rout each end of the sides with the inside face against the fence, again using a vertical push stick.

6. If you're making drawers, reset the fence for the front to accommo-date any overhang. The formula is the thickness of one side plus the desired overhang at one end. Carry out the router flight check and rout one end of the front. (See photo, above.) Measure the overlap, as shown in the right photo, above. Adjust the fence if the overlap is not what you intended.

7. Now dry-assemble the back piece with the two sides and measure the outside distance between the sides. Add the correct overlap to this meas-urement, then crosscut the unrouted end of your drawer front to that length. Perform the router flight check again and rout the remaining end of the front.

8. As a final check, clamp all four parts of the assembly together and measure the width of the box from side to side, at the front, and again at the back. (See middle photo, right.)

Measure the overlap. Use a small rule to check the amount that the front will overlap the side, and adjust the fence as necessary.

The distance must be the same to create a square drawer. If necessary, adjust the length of the front to square up the box.

Assemble and test for square. Dry-fit the box and use a tape to measure the side-to-side distance at the front and the back.

Practice Project

It's time to make something practical with your new skill. Try replacing the dovetail joints on the Dovetailed Drawer (page 155) with the drawer lock joint.

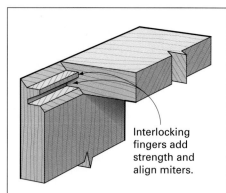

Interlocking fingers add strength and align miters.

LOCK MITER

APPLICATIONS

Consider using the 45° lock miter to make mitered boxes, hollow beams, large panel glue-ups, frames, face frames, mitered frames, or any place that a splined joint works.

WHAT'S NOT COVERED

The 22½° lock miter is not covered because a similar setup methodology is used to cut the joint. Make future setup gauges for this one, too, after you get the perfect fit.

WHAT YOU NEED TO KNOW

Note: This bit is restricted to router table use with a speed limit of 16,000 rpm. Be open to run it even slower. Different species of wood or the use of plywood will determine the best speed at which to run your router.

JIGS

• push stick (page 49)
• vertical push stick (page 49)
• router table and tall fence, both with large holes (page 38)

BITS AND TOOLS

• lock miter bit
• dial calipers
• router with variable speed

Lock Miter

The lock miter bit can be used to make edge-to-edge glue joints, but it really shines when it comes to making miter joints. It has the advantage of interlocking fingers that add strength and easy alignment during assembly, which is particularly handy when gluing up slippery miters. Keep in mind that the bit really isn't designed for end-grain cuts, where you'll get lot of tear out. It's best to reserve this joint for long-grain corners.

Typical 45° lock miter bits are available in two sizes related to stock thickness ranges. Since these bits are large and moderately expensive, it's wise to choose the smallest bit that will do the job for you. At least one manufacturer has a 22½° version for making octagonal joints, and the setup consists of two separate bits for the male and female halves of the joint.

Stock Preparation

The most important operation is to rip each practice workpiece to exactly the same width. Rectangular boxes must have sides and ends of equal length. Surface all the stock and plenty of practice stock to exactly the

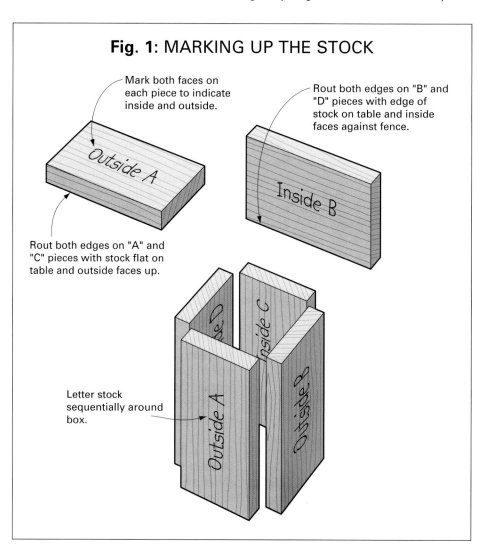

Fig. 1: MARKING UP THE STOCK

Mark both faces on each piece to indicate inside and outside.

Rout both edges on "B" and "D" pieces with edge of stock on table and inside faces against fence.

Outside A

Inside B

Rout both edges on "A" and "C" pieces with stock flat on table and outside faces up.

Letter stock sequentially around box.

Inside D

Inside C

Outside A

Outside B

same thickness. You'll get less blowout of the fragile outside corner if you choose relatively straight grained stock.

Marking the Stock

Lay out the pieces as if you opened one corner and unrolled the assembly. That means all the inside faces are up and all the tops and bottoms are aligned with one another. Letter and mark the inside faces, as shown in figure 1. Now turn the pieces over and mark the outside faces. Number the edges on the faces (far enough away from the edge so you don't rout them off!) to determine which edges are routed face down and which edges are routed on edge, so assembly goes as planned.

Setting Up the Bit

Each lock miter bit has a point that aligns with the middle of the edge of your stock, both vertically and horizontally. (See fig. 2.) I call that the

"sweet spot" because when you find it and set the fence to register this spot, the bit will cut correctly, which is sweet indeed! Part of setting up the bit includes finding this sweet

area. You can study a full-size drawing in a bit catalog to help you get some reference points. Once you find the spot, I suggest you make a reference gauge from a test piece to set

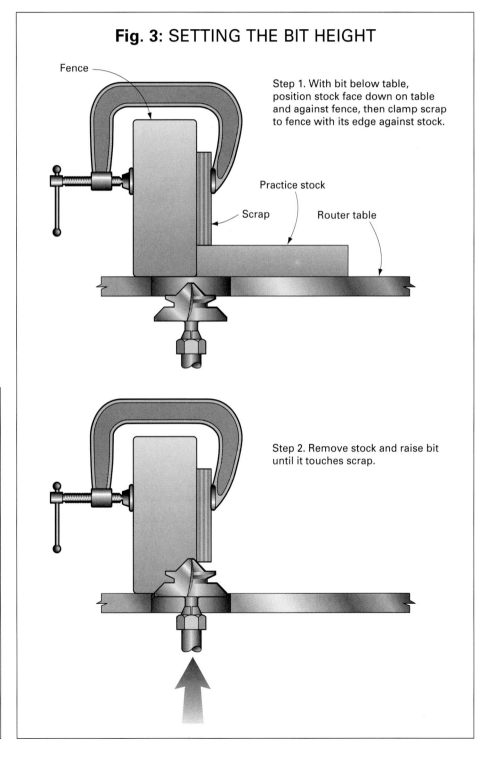

Fig. 3: SETTING THE BIT HEIGHT

Fence

Step 1. With bit below table, position stock face down on table and against fence, then clamp scrap to fence with its edge against stock.

Practice stock

Scrap

Router table

Step 2. Remove stock and raise bit until it touches scrap.

Fig. 2: SETTING THE FENCE TO THE BIT

The distance from the point on the bit to the fence equals $1/2$ flat plus $1/2$ thickness of workpiece.

Fence

Measure from this point on bit to fence.

Router table

"Flat"

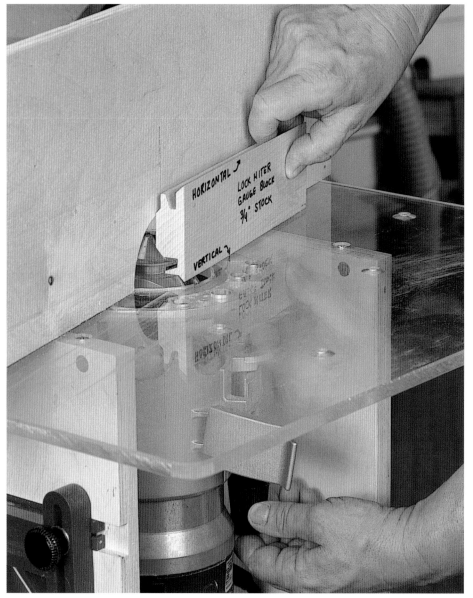

Gauge the bit and fence. Use a previously cut joint to set the bit height and its distance from the fence.

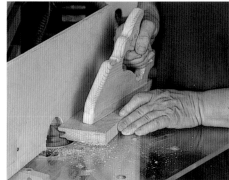

Keep it steady. Use a push stick to move the work safely past the bit, and feed the piece in an even rate to avoid burning.

the table and placing a piece of the practice stock face down on the table and against the fence. Next, position the edge of a piece of thin scrap on top of the stock and clamp it to the fence. Move the stock aside. Now raise the bit until its cutting edge contacts the scrap. Remove the scrap and the stock.

4. Execute the router flight check and rout an edge on two practice pieces, using a push stick. (See photo, above.) Fit the two pieces together and check with your finger that their surfaces are dead flush. (See photo, below.) If the setup looks good, you've just cut an edge-to-edge joint. And it's a necessary step for setting up to cut the miter joint.

the bit height and fence for your specific stock thickness. Store the gauge with your bit so you'll have a close starting place for future setups.

1. Install the bit in a variable-speed motor in the router table with the fence, and set the speed at 16,000 rpm or lower.

2. Set the fence to the bit. As shown in figure 2, you can measure the flat with a dial caliper. Once you've cut the joint a few times, you can use a previously cut setup gauge to set the fence as well as the bit height. (See photo, above.)

3. The best method of setting the correct bit height is described in figure 3. Start by lowering the bit below

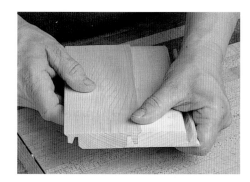

Flat test. After making the cut in two pieces, fit them together and check that their surfaces are flush with each other.

Routing a Lock Miter Joint

1. Carry out the router flight check and rout the pieces marked "A" and "C" with the inside faces down on the table, just as you did the test sample when setting up the bit. Make sure to rout both edges on each piece, and use a push stick for safety.

2. Rout both "B" and "D" pieces by standing each piece on edge with its inside face against the fence. This time, use a vertical push stick, and again rout both edges. (See photo, right.) Dry-fit the joint. If you're not happy with the fit, you'll have to make an adjustment to either the bit height or the fence setting. (See Making the Joint Fit, below.)

Stand it up. When constructing the miter joint, stand the adjoining piece on edge and make the cut with the bit and fence at the same setting.

Making the Joint Fit

Setting up the lock miter bit correctly on the router table is crucial to achieving a properly fitting joint. Once you've cut some sample pieces, test-fit the joint. If you're not satisfied with the fit, refer to the drawing below to see what the problem is. The fault will lie either with an incorrect bit height or fence setting. Once you've determined the problem, unplug the router and then make the necessary adjustments to the bit or the fence.

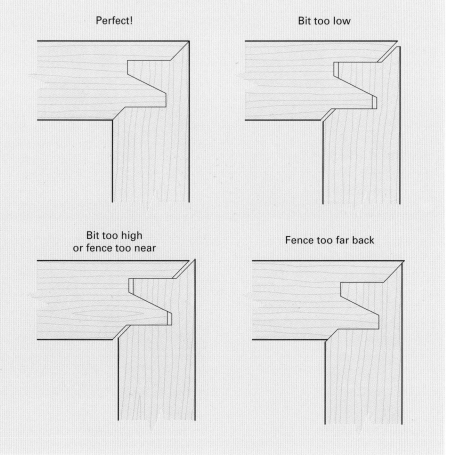

Perfect!

Bit too low

Bit too high or fence too near

Fence too far back

Practice Project

While there's no particular practice project in the book, for inspiration I've included a look at a piece I made that uses this joint. (See photo, below.) Please go ahead and take the challenge, and design a square or rectangular box, then give the joint a try. Depending on the height you make the box, you could use it for umbrellas or silk flowers.

Flower Vase
Maple and walnut
3 in. sq. x 8 in. tall
Corners joined with
lock miter

COPE AND STICK

APPLICATIONS

Cope-and-stick joints are used to make paneled or glass doors and frames for wall paneling. Panels can be flat or raised. You may even have a set of cope-and-stick doors in your own kitchen!

WHAT'S NOT COVERED

Arched rails are not covered because there are so many different arch styles and each demands its own template. In addition, the individual door width affects the arch profile. For more on arched rails, refer to router bit catalogs, which sometimes offer sets of arch templates.

WHAT YOU NEED TO KNOW

- door style (inset, half overlay, or overlay)
- distance from inside stile to inside stile
- finished rail and stile width
- wood panel or glass?
- type of cutter (reversible, one-piece, or matched set)

JIGS

- push stick (page 49)
- push sled (page 49)

BITS AND TOOLS

- cope-and-stick bit
- router table

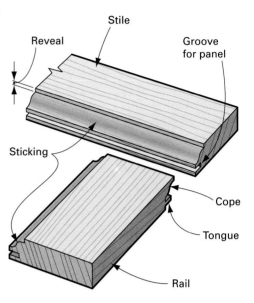

Cope and Stick

The cope-and-stick joint is created with a special router bit, or a set of bits, often referred to as rail-and-stile cutters. The routed joint consists of a decorative edge milled with a groove to accept the tongue of a panel or a pane of glass. "Stick" refers to the *sticking*, which is the profiled cut and its groove cut in the stiles and rails. The *cope* is the matching negative profile, always cut into the end of a rail, and it includes a short tongue. The coped area of the rail fits around the sticking in the stile, while its tongue fits the stile's groove.

There are three kinds of cope-and-stick router bits: a reversible bit, a one-piece bit, and a matched pair of bits. (See Three Types of Bits, opposite page.) The operations here show

using a reversible bit (my personal favorite), but you can select the bit of your choice, since setup and machining is generally the same for all types of cutters.

Stock Preparation

Rip all your material, including practice stock, ⅛ in. wider than final size. Cut each rail ¾ in. longer than the inside distance between the stiles. This takes into account the extra ⅜ in. at each end of the rail that gets coped and fits into the sticking.

Cut the stile stock ¼ in. over length so this, combined with the extra width, will help protect edges and corners from banging around during clamping. This extra material also allows you to trim the assembled door to square it up or to fit it to a slightly out-of-square opening.

Lay out the pieces in the order they'll go in the frame, and mark their relative positions as stiles and rails. Make sure to mark inside edges and outside faces as well. Generally, I like to match the grain on paired stiles and rails. On the stiles, I orient any flame patterns, or cathedrals, so they point up.

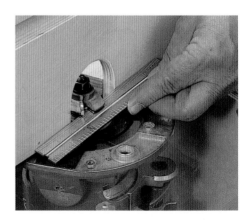

Height and depth. Once you've set the bit height, use a straightedge to align the fence flush with the bit's bearing.

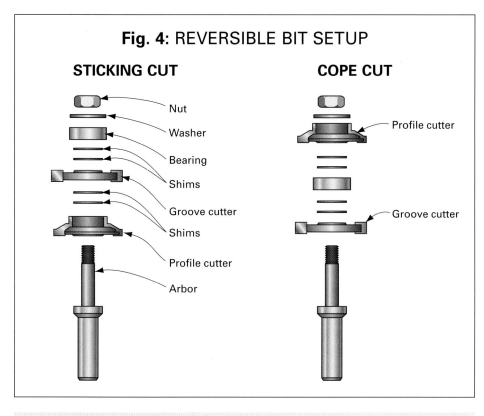

Fig. 4: REVERSIBLE BIT SETUP

STICKING CUT

- Nut
- Washer
- Bearing
- Shims
- Groove cutter
- Shims
- Profile cutter
- Arbor

COPE CUT

- Profile cutter
- Groove cutter

Sticking first. Orient the stock with its outside face down on the table and rout the sticking in two practice pieces.

Three Types of Bits

There are three basic cope-and-stick bits you can choose from for making standard cope-and-stick doors. All three have their pros and cons, and all three come in a variety of profiles for different decorative effects, from the common ogee and roundover to beads and bevels. Make sure to choose your profile carefully since you'll live with it for a long time.

MATCHED BITS

Advantage
- no adjustment needed between stick and cope cuts

Disadvantage
- most costly

Tips for use
- rout sticking with outside facing down router table
- cope ends with outside facing up

REVERSIBLE BIT

Advantages
- least expensive
- adjustable with shims for routing irregular stock (such as undersized plywood)

Disadvantage
- reversing and reassembling bit can be tricky

Tips for use
- rout sticking with outside facing down on router table
- cope ends with outside facing up

ONE-PIECE BIT

Advantage
- no pieces to reassemble

Disadvantage
- no adjustability for irregular stock

Tips for use
- rout all pieces with outsides facing up

Routing a Cope-and-Stick Joint

1. You'll make the stick cut first on the inside edges of all the rails and stiles. Check the catalog and/or the instructions that came with the bit, and make sure to assemble the reversible bit in the correct order for the sticking cut. (See fig. 4.) Chuck the bit in the router and then install the motor in the router table. Raise the bit to the desired reveal, which is usually 3/32 to 1/8 in. Mount the fence, and swing it flush with the bit's bearing. (See photo, opposite page.)

2. Remember, you'll rout with the stock's outside facing down, except when using a one-piece bit. Carry out the router flight check and rout the sticking on two practice pieces using a push stick. (See photo, above.)

Check that you've routed a full profile, and measure to make sure the depth of the groove is 3/8 in., indicating the fence is set correctly. Also inspect the depth of the reveal to confirm the look you want. When all is well, rout the inside edges of all the rails and stiles.

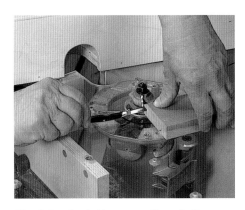

Flush by feel. Use a small penknife blade to feel when the groove on the test piece lines up with the tongue-cutting area on the bit.

Like a glove. Check to see that the routed joint fits well, with tight shoulders and a seamless miter.

No tearout. When the rail's sticking is oriented towards the back of the cut and against the push block, nestle a coped piece into the sticking to back up the cut and prevent blowout.

3. Unplug the router and reset or replace the bit for the cope cut. You'll cope the ends of all the rails with their outside faces up on the table, regardless of the type of bit you're using. The profile section of the bit should be upside down, except when using a one-piece bit. Set the bit to the correct height by placing the stick-cut practice piece next to the bit, outside surface facing down, and adjust the bit until the tongue-cutting section of the cutter aligns precisely with the groove in the stick piece. You can get this match accurately by feel. I use the smallest blade in my penknife, rubbing its back edge across the bit and groove

Cope like this. Use a push sled when making the cope cuts and orient the stock facing up.

to feel when the parts are dead flush. (See top photo, left.)

4. Swing the fence flush to the bit bearing. Place the end of the rail against the fence with its edge against a push sled. Perform the router flight check, and then cope the end of one of your practice pieces, as shown in the bottom photo, left.

5. Now insert the cope cut into the sticking piece. Look to see that the intersection is flush and the coped corners come together in a crisp miter. (See photo, above.) If the fit is off, make the necessary adjustments now. (See Making the Joint Fit, right.)

6. When the fit is to your liking, complete the router flight check, and rout a cope cut into the long grain edge of a third practice piece. Use this piece to prevent blowout when running one half of all your cope cuts on the rails. Simply insert the coped piece into the sticking on your rail, flush up the ends, and rout the two pieces as one. (See top photo, right.)

Making the Joint Fit

There are six possible scenarios you may run into that can result in a poor-fitting joint. Follow one of the suggestions below, depending on the type of problem you encounter.

1. Rail and stile aren't flush: Adjust bit height.

2. Gap between rail and stile: Adjust the fence.

3. Gap between the end of the tongue and the bottom of the groove: Adjust the fence.

4. Tongue is too thick (using a reversible bit): Reduce number of shims between groove cutter and profile cutter.

5. Tongue is too skinny (using a reversible bit): Add shims between groove cutter and profile cutter.

6. Door is too narrow for case opening: You forgot to add ¾ in. to the length of the rails!

RAISED PANEL

WHAT YOU NEED TO KNOW

- inside dimensions of the frame
- depth of the frame's groove
- thickness of the panel

BITS AND TOOLS

- vertical raised-panel bit
- push block
- router with variable speed
- horizontal router table setup (page 38)

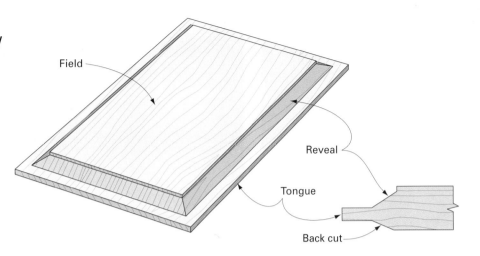

Field

Reveal

Tongue

Back cut

Raised Panel

Raising a solid-wood panel, and then assembling it within a frame, produces an attractive, well-crafted door. Although plywood can certainly be used for a panel, most of us like to see a raised-panel door, such as we see in a lot of kitchens and fine furniture. Raising a solid panel is an opportunity to display unique wood characteristics, carvings, and even contrasting woods. While the routed edges of the panel, called the *reveals*, are quite attractive, their practical purpose is to be thin enough on their edges to form a tongue that fits into the grooves milled into the frame members.

The secret to raising a panel is to acquire a panel-raising bit. There are three kinds of cutters to choose from, and they all work on the router table. (See Three Types of Bits, page 126.) Once you've selected the type of cutter, you can pick from a variety of profiles to create a number of distinctive reveals, from an assortment of bevels and ogees to matching cope-and-stick profiles and other

curves. And you can raise both the front and the back of the panel if you wish. Since it's one of my favorites, I'll focus on using a vertical panel-raising bit for raising a panel on both sides to fit into a cope-and-stick frame. Once you get familiar with the basic technique, you can use any of the panel raisers mentioned here for making beautiful solid wood doors.

Stock Preparation

If you have access to wide boards, by all means use them for your panels. If not, edge join your stock until the desired panel width is achieved. Surface the panel smooth, and don't forget to include a practice board surfaced to the same thickness. For a standard ¾-in.-thick frame, you may want to reduce your panel's thickness to ⅝ in. to avoid having to remove material from the back of the panel. The procedure shown here is for a full ¾-in.-thick panel.

When making raised-panel doors, I always make the frame first. To determine the size of the panel, lightly clamp the frame together and

measure its inside dimensions. To find the panel's length, measure the inside height of the frame, add twice the depth of the groove, and then subtract ¹⁄₁₆ in. To find the panel's width, measure the inside width of the frame, add two groove depths, and then subtract ¼ in. Subtracting more across the width in this manner takes into account the planned expansion and contraction of the panel across its grain. (See photo, below.) Keep in mind that subtracting ¼ in. is the right amount for a panel that's about 12 in. wide. If you double the panel's width, then

Measure for movement. Dry-assemble the frame and measure across its width to determine how wide to make your panel.

Three Types of Bits

You can choose from three types of panel raisers, all of which are available in a variety of profiles. Your choice depends on the factors described below.

STANDARD HORIZONTAL BIT

This is the most recognizable type of bit. It sports a bearing to control the width of the reveal, and its large diameter necessitates that you use a large, variable-speed router, set to its slowest speed. As with any panel-raising bit, cuts must be made in increments. You do this by raising the bit a little each time. When using this type of bit with a ¾ in. panel, the back requires a separate operation to keep the front in the same plane as the frame. You can use the same bit to do this, removing only enough material to create the tongue that fits into the groove in the frame.

HORIZONTAL BIT WITH BACK CUTTER

This type of cutter is the most expensive, and is typically found on big bits. Like the standard horizontal bit, this cutter comes with a bearing. The notable difference is the addition of a back cutter. This arrangement allows

you to mill the front and back of the panel in the same pass, which saves time. This procedure is very demanding, so make sure you have a powerful, variable-speed router. Unlike the standard bit, taking incremental cuts involves adjusting the bit to its final height to begin with and adjusting the fence into the bit to expose only a small portion of its cutting edges. Then you move the fence back in small amounts, taking successive passes until the entire profile is cut.

VERTICAL BIT

My favorite of the three, the vertical bit is the least expensive and is available in the same common profiles. Its relatively small diameter makes it much easier on the router and safer to use. There isn't a bearing on this style of bit. Instead, you rely on the fence to control the cut. While this type of bit can be used in a standard router table equipped with a tall fence, it's a tipsy affair since you hold the stock on edge to make the cut. You're better off installing the bit in a horizontal router table setup so you can comfortably guide the work flat on the table.

double the amount you subtract, and so on. This rule of thumb ensures your doors don't blow apart due to the panel swelling and pushing on the joints in the frame.

Mark the outside face of the panel in the middle where you won't rout it off, and indicate which end is up.

Routing a Raised Panel

To build a door where the panel is flush with the outside surface of the frame, you'll need to keep in mind that the tongue on the panel won't necessarily be centered on the stock's thickness. You can get an idea of where to locate the tongue by placing the panel stock on a flat surface adjacent to the groove in a frame piece.

1. Set up the horizontal table setup, install a vertical bit in a variable-speed router, and secure the router to the metal plate.

2. Extend the bit to the desired reveal. Then raise the plate so the bit is high enough above the table to remove about ⅛ in. of stock. (See photo, below.)

Three types of raisers, same profile. Panel-raising bits come in three different styles, shown from left to right: standard horizontal bit; horizontal bit with back cutter; and vertical bit

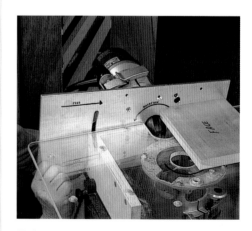

Raise it a little. Plan to make cuts in small, ⅛ in. increments, starting with the bit about ⅛ in. above the table.

End grain first. Start by routing the end of the panel, using a push block to guide the work past the bit.

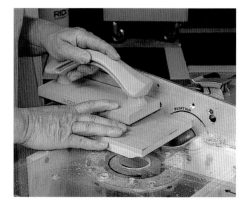

Long grain second. Mill the adjacent long-grain edge, and continue this rotation to rout the remaining two edges. This approach reduces tearout on the delicate end-grain edges.

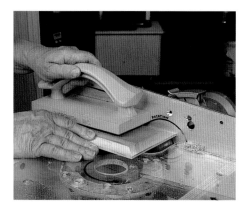

Get the back, too. To produce a panel that's flush with the frame, make a few passes on the back side to create an off-centered tongue.

Slide-in fit. The finished tongue should slip into the groove by hand. You shouldn't have to hammer it home, and there shouldn't be any rattle between the groove and the panel.

3. Plan to rout the end grain first, then the long grain of one edge, then the opposite end grain, and finally the opposite long-grain edge. Begin by performing the router flight check, and rout the practice stock with its outside surface down on the table. Be sure to use a push block for safety. (See top photo, left.)

4. Proceed to cut all around the panel, making your second cut on the adjacent long-grain edge, as shown in the middle photo, left. Make the third cut on the opposite end, and the fourth cut on the remaining long-grain edge.

5. Remember to take incremental cuts during the routing procedure, moving the bit up about ⅛ in. after each pass. On the first couple of passes, flip the stock over to cut the back face. (See photo, left.) After cutting around the panel at each bit setting, lay the panel on your bench next to a grooved frame piece and check that the tongue is shaping up to the right size and in the right place.

6. Once the back of the panel is flush with the back of the frame, continue making passes on the outside face only, again orienting the stock with its outside face down on the table. Remember to maintain the correct rotation of the panel as you make your cuts, and work slowly up to the final tongue thickness. As the reveal gets wider, reduce the amount that you raise the bit. The last pass should be very light; I call it a "kiss" pass. Aim for removing 1/64 in. or less for a smooth and burn-free last cut. The final check is to test-fit the panel in the groove. It should slide in easily but without rattling. (See photo, above.)

Practice Project

If you've gone this far and successfully completed a cope-and-stick frame and a raised panel to fit, you deserve a hand. Congratulations! You're ready to make the Frame-and-Panel Door on page 153 that swings on the Router Bit Cabinet (see page 150).

SECTION 3:
Special Stuff

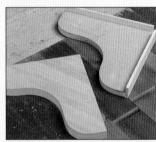

Routing with Templates

Consider this section a bonus. You've patiently learned the joinery skills presented in this book—now it's time to have some fun. There are three techniques you can practice that utilize templates for making all sorts of shapes: template routing, complementary template routing, and template inlay. Although technically not joinery, each of these router skills will let you cut complex shapes, adding interest and dimension to your woodworking. Template routing will let you duplicate parts quickly and efficiently, such as routing a shop-full of push sticks or making items to sell at your local craft fair. Complementary template routing lets you make complementary curved shapes that nest together, opening up a whole world of interesting projects for you to explore. And learning to rout inlays with a template will help you fix defects, stabilize cracks, or simply beautify your projects by adding interesting designs into your work.

Template makes the shape. Once you make a wooden template (right), it's a snap to rout one or more parts, such as the wooden bracket shown here.

Template Routing

Building furniture often requires matching details such as brackets, corbels, or any number of curved surfaces or edges. And making crafts for sale usually requires making copies—and making them at regular intervals. Template routing is the easiest method for making these curves and for producing them in mass. In addition, using template routing allows you to make parts more predictably and with greater speed. Perhaps the best attribute of all is that, when done carefully, this technique practically eliminates sanding!

Template routing works by making a template to the exact shape you want and attaching it to a piece of wood that's been cut to the rough final shape. You then use a router and flush-trimming bit with a bearing that follows the shape of the template to mill a perfect copy in the stock. Luckily, there are only few rules that apply, and you'll need a minimum of tools to get started.

Making the Template

Figure 1 shows a typical template in the shape of a curved bracket for the corbels I produce in my work. I recommend medium-density fiberboard (MDF) for your templates because it's inexpensive, flat, and stable. Panels that are ½ in. thick work best and present a smooth edge for the bit's bearing to follow.

Draw your desired design on the panel, then use a bandsaw to cut out the shape. Smooth the sawn edges with medium-grit sandpaper, taking your time to remove any small dips or bumps, as the bearing will roll over every imperfection and faithfully reproduce it in your work. It's a good idea to paint or apply a coat or two of finish to the surface of the template. This lets you fasten the panel to your stock multiple times without damaging it. Hot glue is my preferred method of attaching the template to the stock (see The Secret of Hot Glue, page 65) and a painted surface will easily pop off the routed piece once the cutting is done.

Fig. 1: TEMPLATE ANATOMY

¼ in. plywood
Make wide enough to register against straight edges of workpiece. Glue and nail to MDF.

½ in. MDF

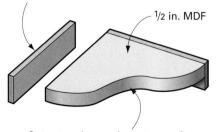

Cut out and smooth contours of template to exact desired shape.

TEMPLATE ROUTING

WHAT YOU NEED TO KNOW

- desired shape of piece
- stock thickness

JIGS

- router table

BITS AND TOOLS

- flush-trimming bit
- bandsaw, jigsaw, scrollsaw, or coping saw

MATERIALS AND HARDWARE

- ¼ in. plywood (as needed)
- ½ in. MDF

When drawing the shape of your template, keep in mind that the only limitation you have is the diameter of the bearing on your flush-trimming bit. Make sure that all inside radii on the template are larger than the bit's bearing; my rule of thumb is at least ⅛ in. bigger. A slightly larger radius allows you to feed the bit more smoothly into and out of the curve, reducing the chance of hesitation and burning.

If the pattern you wish to make has one or more straight edges, attach a small plywood fence to each edge of the template so you can quickly align the workpiece and help keep the template in place throughout the routing process.

Routing with a Template

1. Choose a stock thickness that won't exceed the capacity of your flush-trimming bit. Then use the

Trace it first. Follow the template with a pencil to draw the contour onto your stock. Fences on the edge of the template make it easy to align with the work.

template as a pattern to trace the shape onto the stock, as shown in the photo, above.

2. Cut out the shape on the bandsaw, scrollsaw, jigsaw, or coping saw, staying outside, or to the waste side, of your pencil line by $\frac{1}{16}$ to $\frac{1}{8}$ in. (See photo, below.)

Saw out the rough shape. It's fast and easy to cut out the contours by staying about $\frac{1}{8}$ in. outside your pencil line.

Stick 'em together. Use hot glue to secure the template to the sawn stock, making sure the edge of the stock extends at least $\frac{1}{16}$ in. beyond the template along its curved areas.

3. Use hot glue to attach the template to the rough-cut stock, checking that the sawn edge extends beyond the edges of the template. (See photo, above.)

4. Install a flush-trimming bit in the router table. Place the template and workpiece on the table with the template side facing up, and adjust the bit height so the bearing is roughly centered on the template's edge. To ensure the entire edge of the workpiece is cut, check that the top of the bit's cutting flutes are slightly above the stock and at the level of the template. (See top photo, right.)

5. Execute the router flight check (see page 76). Use the heel of your hand to start the cut (see Routing Without a Fence, page 73), and employ the skiing technique (see Skiing Into the Cut, page 75) to rout the shape in a smooth, continuous motion. (See middle photo, right.)

6. Pop off the template, clean away any glue residue, and you're done!

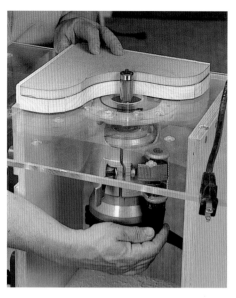

Center the bearing. Raise the bit so the bearing makes good contact with the edge of the template, with the cutting edges of the bit slightly above the stock.

Bearing follows the template. Move the template onto the bearing to begin the cut, then ride the bearing around the contours of the template.

Practice Project

Now that you've got the hang of it, there are two jig handles—one for the offset baseplate (page 52) and one for the push stick (page 50)—that offer ideal and useful opportunities to practice template routing.

Complementary Template Routing

Complementary template routing takes standard template routing to the next level by allowing you to duplicate two (or more) parts that fit together along an irregular edge. One example is the cabinet shown in the photo, right, where a series of curving drawer fronts fit together. Using this technique you can glue together all sorts of undulating edges to make a variety of interesting projects, such as tabletops, door panels, breadboards, pizza paddles—your imagination is the only limit. The best part is that the finished product will have your woodworking buddies asking, "How'd you do that?"

Matching curves using complementary template routing is easy to do and requires few tools. However, it does require a bit of concentration—and a lot of careful labeling. You start by making a master pattern, which is an exact copy of your desired design. You use this pattern and a special washer to make a master template. Next, you use the master template and a straight bit fitted with a stop collar and an oversized bearing to make matching left and right templates. Then you use a flush-trimming bit and the left and right templates to mill the two workpieces. Once you've routed the curved design in the workpieces, you can glue them together, wavy edge to wavy edge.

One useful tool to have for this procedure, and not mentioned elsewhere in the book, is a French curve. This is a plastic template (available at art-supply stores) that helps you draw *fair lines*. A fair line is a term borrowed from boatbuilding, and

Nesting curves. Furniture maker Dan Gindling used complementary template routing to rout the wavy sycamore drawer fronts on his award-winning CD cabinet. *Photo by Martin Mann*

refers to an undulating line that seamlessly transitions from one curve to another—an important feature when making templates. You can easily judge a fair line by simply running your fingers along its edge to determine that it's fair. The transitions should be perfectly smooth, without bumps or dips.

Make the Master Pattern

The first step is to make a master pattern, from which you'll create the master template. There are only two limitations when making the master pattern. You're limited to ⅞ in. diam-

eters when drawing inside (concave) curves, and sharp corners are not possible. Otherwise, you can fashion any curved line you like.

Sketch your design on posterboard or thin cardboard for transferring onto plywood or MDF, or pencil your line directly onto the pattern material. Make sure your line is about 1 in. longer than the desired pattern on each end of the panel, and use a French curve to help with drawing smooth fair lines. (See top left photo, opposite page.)

COMPLEMENTARY TEMPLATE ROUTING

WHAT YOU NEED TO KNOW

- desired shape of piece
- stock thickness

JIGS

- offset baseplate (page 52)
- router table

BITS AND TOOLS

- ¼ x 2½ in. spiral bit with ¾ in. bearing and ¼ in. stop collar
- ½ in. flush-trimming bit
- French curve
- hot-glue gun
- bandsaw, jigsaw, scrollsaw, or coping saw
- router with ¼ and ½ in. collets

MATERIALS AND HARDWARE

- "magic" washer
- ½ in. MDF
- scrap MDF or similar

Draw the design. Use a French curve to help create smooth lines on the pattern material.

Cut out the pattern on the bandsaw, or use a jigsaw, scrollsaw, or coping saw. Smooth the edges with sandpaper and files, or use an oscillating spindle sander, being careful to keep the edges as perpendicular as possible. Keep in mind that this is the line that the bearing will follow, so a smooth and continuous edge counts. Once you've faired and smoothed the edge, mark this as the master pattern.

Make the Master Template

You will need a "magic washer" to make the master template. This is simply a flat washer where the difference between its outside and inside diameter equals ¼ in., and it's the secret to successful complementary template routing. If you can't find one in your shop, take your dial calipers to the hardware store and rummage through the washers sold loose in a bin.

Once you have your magic washer in hand, use hot glue to adhere the master pattern to a piece of ½ in. MDF that's the same length as the pattern and at least 6 in. wide at the narrowest point of the design. Place the magic washer against the master pattern, insert a sharp pencil into the

washer's hole, and trace a perfect ¼ in. offset line by riding the washer along the edge of the template. (See photo, right.) Set the master pattern aside; you won't need it again. Cut out the MDF and sand to the line, just as you did for the master pattern, and mark the panel as the master template.

Make the Left and Right Templates

Now you can make the "working" templates that will let you rout the actual workpieces. Start by sticking the master template on top of and to one side of another piece of ½ in. MDF with hot glue, making sure this next piece of MDF is twice as wide as the master template. Mark the exposed side with an "X."

Secure a ¾ in. bearing and a stop collar on the shank of a ¼ in. spiral bit,

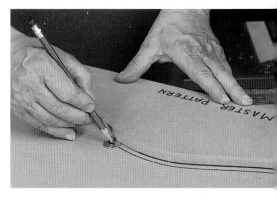

The perfect offset. Place the tip of a pencil on the inner edge of the magic washer and ride it along the template to create a line that's offset by precisely ¼ in.

and install the bit in your router. Attach an offset baseplate to the router base, then set the bit depth so the bearing will ride against the edge of the master template, the bit will cut the bottom MDF piece in two, and the stop collar doesn't interfere with anything. (See photo, below.) Once you've set up the router and

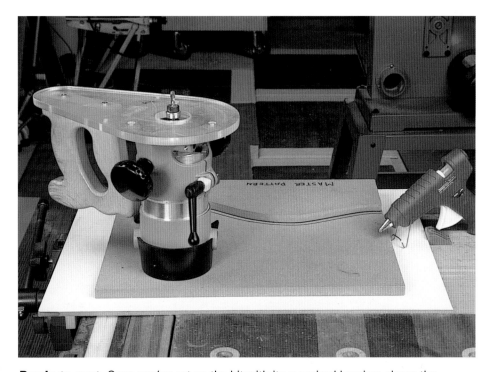

Ready to rout. Once you've set up the bit with its oversized bearing, clamp the assembly to the benchtop, making sure there's a scrap piece underneath to avoid routing into your bench.

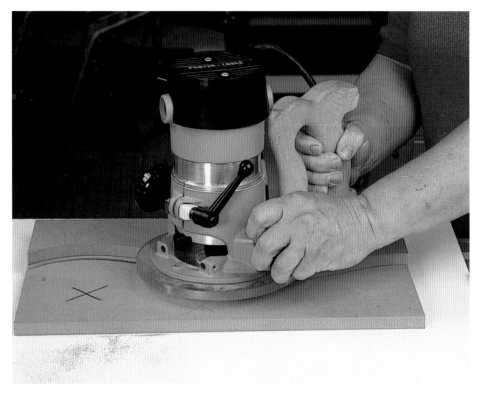

Mill the left template. Concentrate on keeping the bearing on the bit against the edge of the master template as you rout the piece into two parts.

Label it "left." Mark the piece directly under the master template as the left template. Save the "X" piece for making the right template.

bit, temporarily glue or clamp the whole assembly on top of a scrap piece of MDF or similar material (so you won't rout into your bench!), and clamp the scrap to your benchtop.

Complete the router flight check. Keeping the bearing firmly against the master template, rout the MDF in two. Beware that any deviation of the bearing with the edge of the template will result in a "new" design, so make this cut as smoothly and as evenly as possible. (See photo, left.) Remove the master template and label the piece under it as the left template, as shown in the bottom photo, left.

Use the remaining piece marked with an "X" to make the matching right template. Use hot glue again to attach the piece to a fresh piece of ½ in. MDF. Set up the router table with the same bit and bearing, then rout the offset cut, as shown in the top left photo, opposite page. Pop off the "X" piece and set it aside; you won't need it again. Label the newly cut piece as the right template, and check your work by nesting the left and right templates together to make sure they fit along their curved edges. (See middle left photo, opposite page.)

Routing Right and Left Workpieces

1. Lay the right template on top of a piece of stock marked "right workpiece" and trace its outline along the shaped edge, then repeat with the left template on a piece of stock marked "left workpiece." For fun, try using contrasting wood for the two parts, as shown in the bottom left photo, opposite page.

2. Using the bandsaw or a similar tool, saw out the two blanks proud of

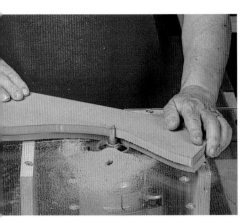

Rout the right. With the "X" piece glued to a new piece of MDF, use the router table to cut the right template.

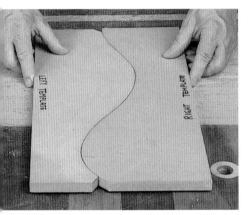

A perfect joint. Hold the two templates together and check that their undulating edges meet perfectly.

Lay out the joints. Use the right and left templates to mark the joint lines on the workpieces. Using contrasting woods can add an element of fun to your work.

the pencil lines by about 1/16 to 1/8 in. Then use hot glue to secure each template to its corresponding blank, aligning the template to the pencil line on the stock. There should be 1/16 to 1/8 in. of extra material beyond the edge of each template. Install a flush-trimming bit in the router table and rout each workpiece flush with its template. (See photo, right.)

3. Spread glue along the curved edges of the work, and draw the joint together with clamps. (See photo, below.) Once the glue has dried, scrape and smooth the panel. Keep in mind that your curving designs can repeat several times across a wide panel, and you can make alternating workpieces from several different species of wood for extra impact.

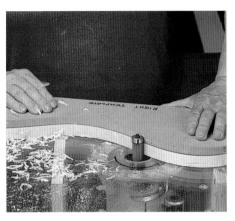

Rout it flush. Use a flush-trimming bit with a bearing to mill the edges of the stock even with the template.

Practice Project

Now go and have some fun making the Breadboard (page 141). Don't forget to be creative and let your imagination run free!

Put it together. Use bar clamps to pull the glued joint line together. After the glue dries, smooth the panel and apply your favorite finish!

Cool cover. This inlaid piece of walnut is a great way to add exciting designs to your work, or simply cover up natural defects in your stock.

TEMPLATE INLAY

WHAT YOU NEED TO KNOW

- thickness of inlay material
- desired shape of inlay

BITS AND TOOLS

- ⅛ x 2 in. spiral bit or end mill with adapter
- inlay kit (page 28)
- router with baseplate that accepts template guide
- bandsaw, jigsaw, scrollsaw, or coping saw

MATERIALS AND HARDWARE

- 5⁄16 or ⅜ in. MDF or similar
- solid wood for inlay, maximum ¼ in. thick

Template Inlay

Inlays can enhance your woodworking, provide structural support, or cover defects or mistakes. If you're dealing with inlays that have straight, parallel edges (such as wood bandings), it's simple enough to mill a dado or groove into the stock (see Dadoes, Grooves, and Slots, page 85), and then glue the inlay into the recess. For irregular shapes, however, a template is needed to guide the cut.

Template inlay is a two-part process that utilizes a shop-made template and an inlay kit, which is a specialized type of template guide bushing. Using a template, first you mill a cavity in the wood's surface, then you make an inlay patch that fits into the cavity perfectly. One common application is to make football-shaped "Dutchman" inlays that cover

defects. Another approach is to stabilize cracks by spanning them with a bow tie-shaped patch. Inlay can also be strictly decorative, such as inlaying ribbons of contrasting or decorative wood patterns into tabletops and other surfaces.

Keep in mind that if you want sharp points or corners in your design, you'll need to chisel these out by hand, because a router bit can't negotiate the sharp areas. All other shapes are possible as long as inside (concave) curves are greater than a ⅝ in. diameter.

Choosing the Inlay Material and the Bit

Dimension your inlay material first, milling it at least 4 in. longer and wider than your desired pattern. For a special effect, try choosing a wood

that contrasts with the stock that's receiving it. Typical stock thickness is ⅛ to ¼ in., depending on the type of inlay you wish to make and the working length of your bit, as described below.

Secure the inlay kit to your router's baseplate, installing the nut on the inside of the plate and the bushing, or collar, on the outside. Then slip the special removable bushing over the collar. A rubber O-ring keeps the bushing in place.

Chuck an ⅛ in. bit in the collet. Keep in mind that these small diameter bits can break easily. I prefer using a less-expensive end mill for this operation, so I'm not out too much money if the bit snaps during routing. The overall length of your bit is also critical. You'll need to factor the depth of the cavity you wish to rout (which equals the thickness of your inlay stock), the required bit depth in your collet (see Router Bits, page 13), the thickness of your template, plus a clearance factor between the collet and the guide bushing of about ⅛ in. For example, on my router, a 2-in.-long bit can cut as deep as ¼ in. Of course, at that depth, great care must be taken to avoid breaking the bit.

Making the Pattern

The first thing you'll do is make a template, which is a cutout of the approximate shape of the inlay you want. While any length of inlay is possible using this technique, the width of your design is limited to about 2½ in., thus the opening in your template will be no more than 2½ in. This provides adequate support for the router as you move it across the opening in the template, especially when excavating the inlay.

You can use practically any material for the template, but keep in mind that the edges of the template must be smooth enough for the bushing to ride on. Plywood will work if you do a good job of sanding it, but I prefer medium-density fiberboard (MDF) or

melamine-coated particleboard (MCP). Thin templates work best, but make sure the template material is slightly thicker than the bushing so the bushing won't drag on the surface of your stock. Template material 5/16 to 3/8 in. thick is usually about right. Also, make the template at least 4 in. wider all the way around the pattern's shape to safely support the router.

Once you've chosen your template material, draw the desired shape of the inlay directly onto it. You'll need to offset the line and make the opening smaller by the amount of offset in your bushing, typically ⅛ in. For an exact pattern, you can use the same technique used in complementary template routing and acquire the appropriate size "magic" washer (see page 32), where the difference between the inside and outside diameter of the washer equals the necessary offset. A high-tech way would be to draw the shape in a computer-aided design (CAD) program on your computer. Or simplify things and do as I do: First draw or trace your design onto the template material, then sketch freehand inside the pattern to create the necessary offset, as shown in the bottom photo, left.

After marking the template, carefully cut out the pattern by first drilling a hole through the template and then inserting a jigsaw, scrollsaw, or coping saw blade through the hole and guiding the saw along the inside line. Sand the edges smooth.

Routing the Recess

1. With the removable bushing installed on the router, set the bit depth equal to the thickness of your inlay material. The best way to adjust the depth is to place the template on the router's baseplate, then

Set the bit upside down. Position the template on the baseplate and the inlay material on the template, and raise the bit until it's even with the surface of the inlay stock.

position the inlay material on top of the template and set the bit flush with the top of the stock. (See photo, above.)

2. Use hot glue to attach the template to the surface of the stock in which the inlay will be applied.

Make it smaller by hand. Mark the cutout in the template by drawing the desired shape of the inlay, then offsetting the line by eye by ⅛ in.

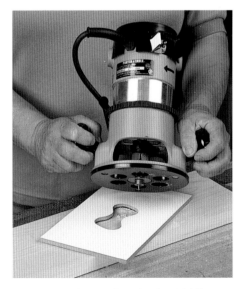

Rout the recess. Start in the middle, then move to the edges of the template to rout the offset cavity.

3. Perform the router flight check, and check that the removable bushing is still attached to the router. With the router tilted slightly on the template so the bit isn't in contact, turn on the router, then carefully lower the bit into the opening in the template and into the stock. Alternatively, you can use a plunge router and plunge the bit into the stock. Work from the center out, taking small cuts in a circular fashion. (See bottom right photo, previous page.) Continue routing, riding the bushing against the edges of the template to mill the entire recess, leaving a flat bottom. Make a final pass in a clockwise direction, holding the bushing firmly against the pattern template edge.

4. Pop the template loose and remove any glue residue from both the wood and the template.

Routing the Inlay

1. If your inlay material is particularly small, attach it to a larger scrap panel with hot glue. Then secure the template on top of the inlay stock, again using hot glue. If necessary, temporarily glue some scrap blocks equal in thickness to the inlay on the panel to support the router and prevent it from tipping.

2. Remove the bushing from the template guide, and carry out the router flight check. Place the router over the template, with the edge of the bushing firmly against the opening in the template. Tilt the bit up, turn on the router, and then plunge the bit into the stock. Now rout around the opening, maintaining firm contact between the bushing and the edge of the template. Any deviation will result in an imperfect inlay. (See top photos.)

Mill the inlay. Remove the outer bushing, then rout the inlay by carefully following the edges of the template.

3. Test-fit the inlay into the cavity. (See photo, right.) If you see any imperfections or if you need to cut any sharp points, now is the time to clean them up by hand with a chisel.

4. Once you're satisfied with the fit, apply an even coat of glue to the bottom and to the walls of the recess, line up the inlay over the opening, and then tap it fully into the recess using a soft hammer. (See right photo, below.) Once the glue has dried, scrape and sand the surface and apply the finish of your choice.

Practice Project

There are no specific projects in the book that require inlay, but now that you've got the knack of it, don't hesitate to use this technique for fixing defects or for adding a decorative effect to your furniture. Above all, have fun!

Check out the fit. Before gluing the inlay in place, test its fit in the cavity by pushing it in only $\frac{1}{16}$ in. or so.

Tap it home. Coat the walls and the bottom of the recess with glue, then tap the inlay into place with firm blows from a soft-faced hammer.

SECTION 4:
Practice Projects

Projects That Test Your Joinery Skills

There are seven great projects in this chapter that I've chosen especially for you to practice the joints presented in this book. I hope you find them fun, practical, a little challenging, and immensely satisfying.

Three thoughts before you proceed. There is no tool in the shop more underestimated than the lowly square. No project can be successfully completed without a truly square square. What could be more frustrating than investing a lot of time and effort in a project, only to find that it is out of square and your doors don't fit, your drawers bind, and the piece won't sit flat on the floor? So check your square often, and square it if it needs it. (See Squaring a Square, page 25.) Keep in mind that once you're working with a reliable square, don't assume the cut you're about to make will be square. Check your setup. Experienced craftspeople check often and check automatically, without even thinking about it. You should get in the habit, too. Woodworking is supposed to be fun—and square cuts are the key to that fun.

The second point is that I'd like you to consider the projects shown here as stepping stones on the path towards even more rewarding work. Hopefully, when you've completed these small projects, you'll have a good grasp on making similar furniture, in different and more challenging sizes.

The third note is about the drawings and the cutting lists. Take your time to study the drawings, since they have most of the building information in them. And please use the cutting lists as guides only. As is the case with most lists, the dimensions are listed in the order of thickness x width x length. If you would like to change the size of a project to suit your own needs and tastes, by all means feel free to do so. Just make

sure you alter the dimensions to reflect your changes. Along the same lines, don't think the listed dimensions are the final word, and above all don't cut your parts straight from each list. Usually it's best to cut the major components of any one project and assemble those pieces first, then take direct measurements from your assembly to determine the actual sizes you'll need for subsequent parts. This is a smart and more realistic way of woodworking, and prevents headaches and mistakes.

Good luck. Proceed carefully, not just for your own safety, but also for the success of your project. Most importantly, have fun!

Breadboard

This jazzy breadboard employs complementary template routing for creating undulating waves of contrasting strips of wood in its construction. (See Complementary Template Routing, page 132.) Once you've made the necessary templates, the project is easy to build and makes good use of small or skinny leftover stock that's too expensive to burn or throw away.

The patterns, or curves, on the board shown here repeat themselves, but at slightly different angles. Because of this, you only need to make one template, then attach it at different angles to make irregular-looking strips. This is one of those great gift projects. Make several and stash them until you need a present. Making them will be a lot more fun, less expensive, and more relaxing than going to the mall!

Building Steps

1. Make left and right templates by first constructing a master pattern and then making a master template. Make sure your templates are about an inch to two longer than the finished breadboard.

2. Use the left and right templates to trace their outlines onto your mating stock pieces, and saw out the strips to rough shape, staying about ⅛ in. away from your lines. Remember to select two of your strips for the long edges of the board, leaving their outer edges straight.

5. Attach each template to its corresponding stock piece, carry out the router flight check (see page 76), and rout the stock to final shape using a flush-trimming bit.

Waves of wood. Serve your bread in style on this board made from edge-glued strips cut to precise shapes using complementary templates.

6. Spread glue on the edges of each strip (except for the two outer edges, of course!), and clamp the assembly.

7. Once the glue has dried, scrape and sand the joints and rip and crosscut the panel to finished size.

8. Break all the sharp edges either with a block and sandpaper or round them over with a roundover bit. Leave the board bare if you like, or apply your favorite finish.

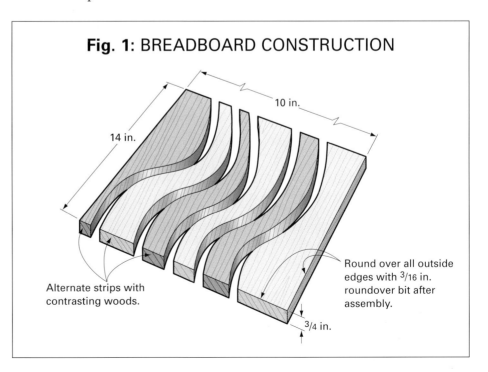

Fig. 1: BREADBOARD CONSTRUCTION

14 in.

10 in.

3/4 in.

Alternate strips with contrasting woods.

Round over all outside edges with 3/16 in. roundover bit after assembly.

Totebox

This totebox features partitions that divide the box into compartments, making it a handy box to store and carry different items. You can use it for holding shop supplies, storing silverware for the dining room table, or any number of other uses you can dream up. I made the box shown here from red oak, but go ahead and choose your favorite hardwood if you like.

Box joints join the corners of the box. (See Box Joint, page 92.) I used a ½ in. spiral bit to rout the notches, and designed the box's height in a multiple of ½ in. to make laying out and cutting these joints a snap. If you want to use a different bit and alter the box's height, remember to change the width of the sides so they're multiples of the new bit's diameter. Here's a hint. Once you have your box joint jig dialed in, make several boxes. They make wonderful gifts, and you, dear friend, will be somebody's woodworking hero!

Tote in style. The carry-all features box-jointed corners and dividers that keep all your gear organized.

Building Steps

1. Mill all the stock to thickness. If you want your box to hold heavy items, such as nails, use ¾ in. thick material.

2. Cut the sides to length. Check that the ends are square, and that the sides opposite each other are exactly the same length.

3. Set up the box joint jig (see page 46), and rout the corners. Dry-assemble the box and mark the inside faces and the bottom edges.

4. Disassemble the box and mark the grooves for the bottom. Take note that two of the grooves are stopped

so they don't show on the outside of the finished box. Mark the appropriate stops, then go ahead and rout the grooves in all four sides. (See Dadoes, Grooves, and Slots, page 85.)

5. Reassemble the box and measure for the bottom. Cut the bottom ¹⁄₁₆ in. smaller than your measurement to allow for easier assembly and glue-up. Test-fit the bottom, then set it aside.

Totebox

CUTTING LIST

Description	Qty.	Dimensions (in.)	Material
Sides	4	½ x 3 x 8	¼ stock
Handle divider	1	½ x 6¾ x 7¼	¼ stock
Short dividers	2	½ x 4¾ x 7¼	¼ stock
Bottom	1	¼ x 7³⁄₁₆ x 7³⁄₁₆	plywood

Fig. 2: TOTEBOX CONSTRUCTION

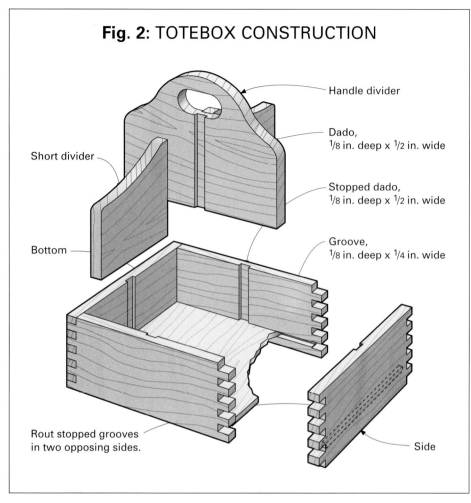

Handle divider

Dado,
1/8 in. deep x 1/2 in. wide

Stopped dado,
1/8 in. deep x 1/2 in. wide

Groove,
1/8 in. deep x 1/4 in. wide

Short divider

Bottom

Rout stopped grooves
in two opposing sides.

Side

Fig. 3: DIVIDER PATTERNS

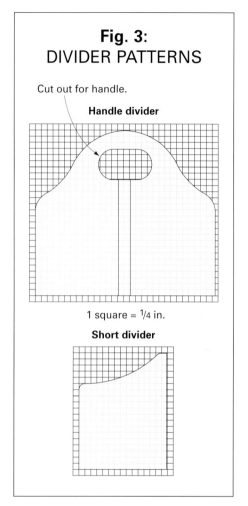

Cut out for handle.

Handle divider

1 square = 1/4 in.

Short divider

Fig. 4: BOX ELEVATIONS

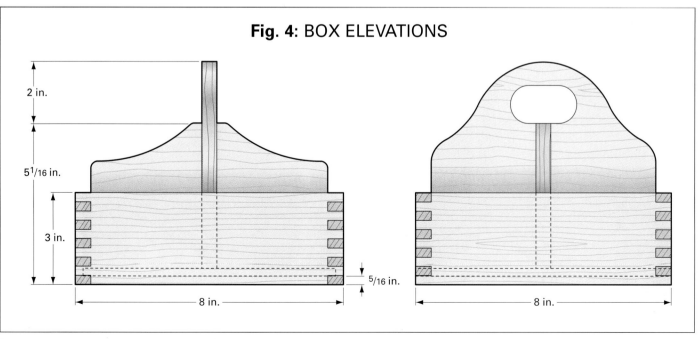

2 in.

5 1/16 in.

3 in.

5/16 in.

8 in.

8 in.

6. Mark the stopped dadoes in the middle of each side, and then rout the dadoes.

7. Make the dividers, cutting out the profiles using a bandsaw, scrollsaw, jigsaw, or coping saw. Drill a few holes in the handle area in the handle divider, then finish the cutout with a jigsaw or coping saw. Rout a dado centered on either side of the handle divider.

8. Dry-assemble and clamp the parts together to check the fit. This is especially important because the trickiest part of this project is gluing it up. Disassemble and sand all interior surfaces.

9. Glue-up requires you to work quickly and smoothly. Have all your supplies on hand, including clamps and your gluing tools (I use an old toothbrush, a damp rag, and a dish of water.) Ordinary yellow glue will give you enough open time, but if you feel you need a little extra time, use white glue. It will be plenty strong.

Start the glue-up by joining one corner. Next, insert the bottom, glue one short divider into the handle divider, and then insert the dividers into their respective dadoes with glue. Add the side on the opposite end of the handle divider, then install the second short divider. Finally, add the last side. Make sure the dividers are sitting firmly on the bottom. Square up the box, and clamp. Check for square and clean up any glue squeeze-out, especially on the inside joints. Allow the box to dry overnight.

10. Finish-sand the exterior surfaces, breaking all sharp edges with a sanding block. Apply the finish of your choice.

Basic books. This small cabinet is just right for storing a specialized library, plus its small size is ideal for practicing your hand at routing rabbets and dadoes.

Small Bookcase

This small bookcase is useful for storing and displaying cookbooks, children's books, computer books, or any small collection of special-interest reading material. Glued dadoes and rabbets hold the parts together. A nice touch is the router-made molding that wraps around the top and bottom of the case. Perhaps the best part of this project is that it utilizes the same construction techniques used on large bookcases so you'll learn some valuable tips for making larger units.

Building Steps

1. Cut the two sides to exactly the same length and width. Mark the insides, the bottom edge, and the front edge.

2. Place the sides back edge–to–back edge, and measure from the bottom of the sides to mark the centerlines

of each dado location. If you plan on storing taller books on the bottom shelf, adjust the fixed shelf's location accordingly by measuring your tallest book and adding 1 in. Make sure to mark the stopped dado for the fixed shelf ¼ in. in from the front edge of the sides.

3. Execute the router flight check, mill the dadoes, and then square the stopped ends with a sharp chisel. (See Dadoes, Grooves, and Slots, page 85.)

4. Rip the top and bottom shelves to exactly the same width, and rip the fixed shelf ¼ in. narrower to accommodate the back. Then crosscut all three parts to precisely the same length. Lay out and notch the front corners of the fixed shelf to fit the stopped dadoes in the sides, using a fine handsaw.

5. Dry-assemble and clamp the sides to the top and bottom in preparation for routing the rabbet for the back. Set the fixed shelf aside for now.

Made to order. This router-made molding is easy to make and miters neatly around the front to finish off the case.

Small Bookcase

CUTTING LIST

Description	Qty.	Dimensions (in.)	Material
Sides	2	¾ x 10½ x 24	4/4 stock
Top	1	¾ x 10½ x 14	4/4 stock
Bottom	1	¾ x 10½ x 14	4/4 stock
Fixed shelf	1	¾ x 10¼ x 14	4/4 stock
Back	1	¼ x 14¼ x 22	plywood
Cleats	2	¾ x ¾ x 13½	4/4 stock
Molding	1	¾ x 1½ x 48	4/4 stock x 3¼ in. wide *

* Note: Rout both edges of stock, then rip in half to produce individual molding strips.

Check for square by taking diagonal measurements, and make any necessary adjustments. Cut some 2 in. long scraps to fit into the rear of the fixed-shelf dadoes, using masking tape to hold them in place for the next step.

6. Set up and install a rabbetting bit in your router with a bearing that allows for a ⅜ in. wide rabbet. (See Rabbets, page 78.) Secure an offset baseplate to your router and set the bit depth to the thickness of your back material. The idea is to ride the router on the back edges of the assembled cabinet to rout the rabbet, which is a tricky balancing act. For more support, I make an oversized baseplate that spans the width of the bookcase and sports two handles for more control. Once you've set up the router, execute the router flight check and rabbet the back by riding the bearing all around the inside of the case. (See photo, right.) Finish by squaring up the rounded corners with a few cuts from a chisel.

7. With the assembly still clamped together, measure for the back. Then cut the back to size, making sure the sides are square to each other since a square back helps square up the case during assembly. Test-fit the back before removing the clamps.

8. Sand all inside surfaces. Brush the dadoes with glue and clamp the

Rigid rabbetting. The author secures her router to an oversize baseplate for better support when routing the rabbets for the back into the edges of the case.

Fig. 5: BOOKCASE CONSTRUCTION

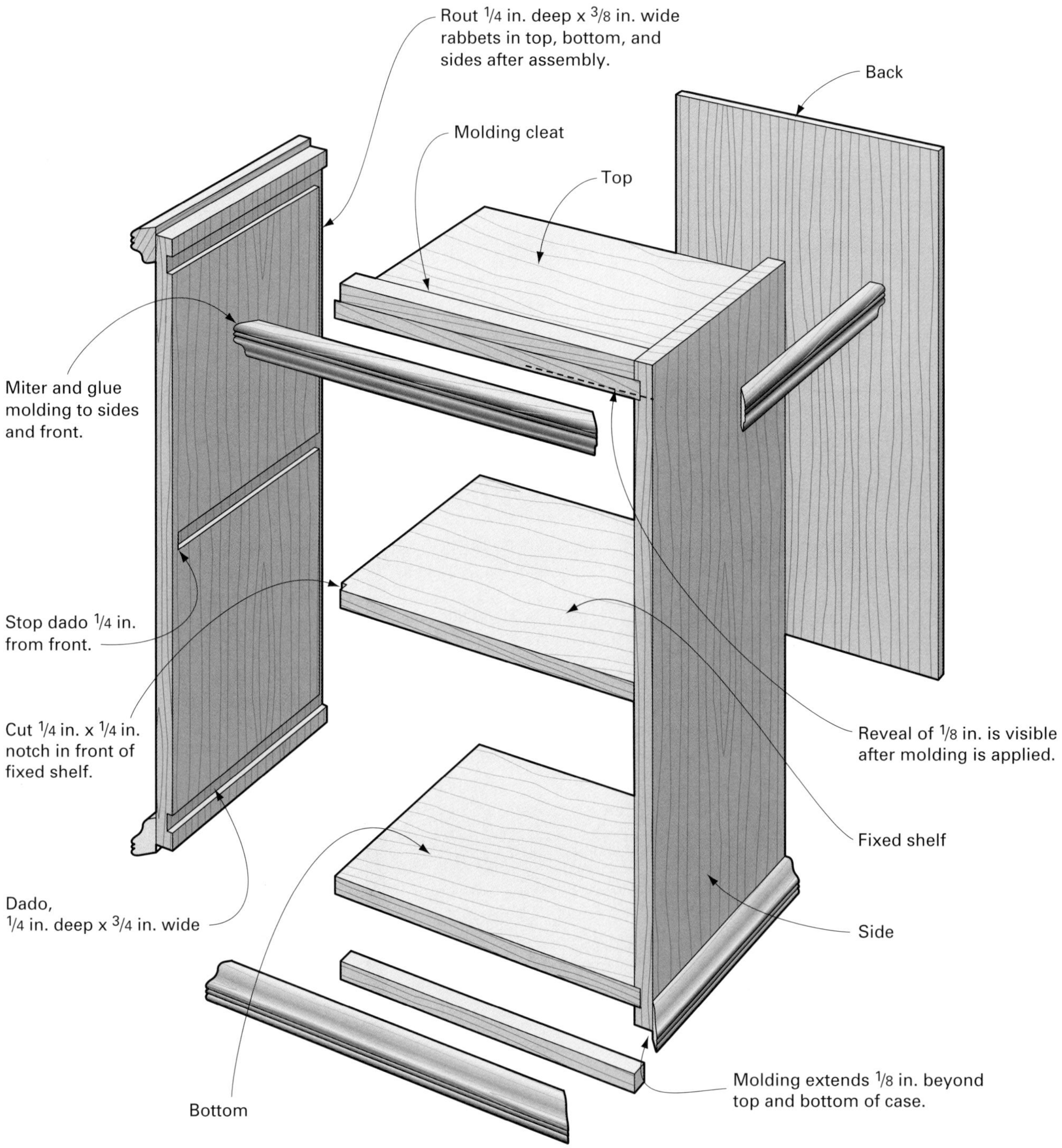

Rout $\frac{1}{4}$ in. deep x $\frac{3}{8}$ in. wide rabbets in top, bottom, and sides after assembly.

Back

Molding cleat

Top

Miter and glue molding to sides and front.

Stop dado $\frac{1}{4}$ in. from front.

Cut $\frac{1}{4}$ in. x $\frac{1}{4}$ in. notch in front of fixed shelf.

Reveal of $\frac{1}{8}$ in. is visible after molding is applied.

Fixed shelf

Dado, $\frac{1}{4}$ in. deep x $\frac{3}{4}$ in. wide

Side

Bottom

Molding extends $\frac{1}{8}$ in. beyond top and bottom of case.

Fig. 6: CASE ELEVATIONS

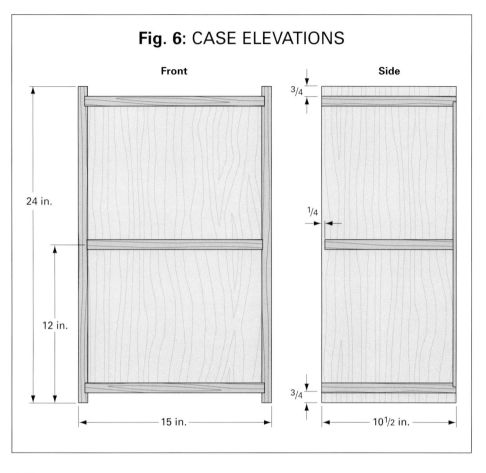

Front

Side

3/4

24 in.

1/4

12 in.

3/4

15 in.

10 1/2 in.

Fig. 7: BOOKCASE MOLDING

Begin with 3/4 x 3 1/4 x 45 in. stock.

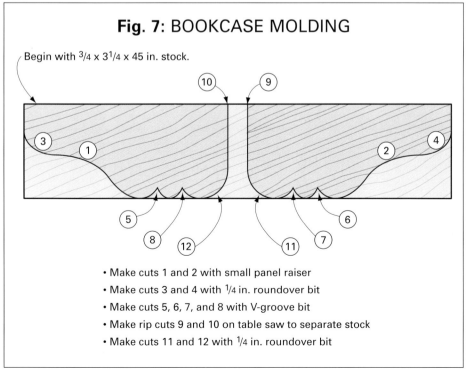

- Make cuts 1 and 2 with small panel raiser
- Make cuts 3 and 4 with 1/4 in. roundover bit
- Make cuts 5, 6, 7, and 8 with V-groove bit
- Make rip cuts 9 and 10 on table saw to separate stock
- Make cuts 11 and 12 with 1/4 in. roundover bit

assembly together. Insert the back and test for square, but don't glue or fasten the back just yet.

9. Measure between the sides, mill the two cleats, and glue and clamp them in place. Allow the assembly to dry undisturbed overnight.

10. While the bookcase is drying, it's time to make the molding. One approach is to use a large profile cutter to mill the molding in one shot. But these bits are pricey, and can be difficult to obtain. An easier method is to use a selection of cutters and mill the profile in stages, as shown in figure 7. Carry out the router flight check, and make all your molding cuts on the router table.

11. Miter the molding at 45° and clamp all three pieces to the case to check the fit of the miters. Adjust as necessary, then trim the molding flush to the back edges of the case. Glue and clamp the front molding first, aligning it with the top to leave an 1/8 in. reveal. (See fig. 5.) Then add the side moldings in the same manner.

12. Remove the clamps, clean up any excess glue, and finish-sand the outside of the case. Apply the finish of your choice, including the uninstalled back panel.

13. After the finishing work is done, fasten the back with small brass screws or brads. If you choose to hang the cabinet on a wall, check out the specialty hardware made for this purpose in your favorite woodworking catalog.

Small Table

This small table with a solid-wood top offers a chance to hone your hands on making mortise-and-tenon joints, as well as having a bit of fun making a top with contrasting strips of wood. To keep the top stable as it expands and contracts across its width, shop-made wooden buttons secure it to the table frame. The table shown here has tapered legs to give it a more graceful stance, but like most of the projects shown here, this is an option and you can keep the legs square if you prefer.

Building Steps

1. Start by constructing the top. You can make the top from one piece of wood (if you can find such a wide piece), or edge-glue narrower strips to make up the necessary width. Try adding a few contrasting strips of wood in a different color to add a decorative effect, as I did on the top shown here. Once you've glued up the top, scrape and sand its surfaces, and then cut it to final size.

2. The next step is to draw a side view of the table on a piece of graph paper. This lets you calculate the overhangs of the top and the shoulder-to-shoulder distance of the aprons between the legs. The table here is designed with 1½ in. overhangs on the sides and 4 in. overhangs at each end. Once you know the dimensions of the aprons (don't forget to add the combined length of the tenons!), cut the leg and apron stock to size.

3. Mark the mortise locations on the legs, perform the router flight check, and mill the mortises in all four legs. (See Mortises and Tenons, page 96.)

Small Table

CUTTING LIST

Description	Qty.	Dimensions (in.)	Material
Top	1	¾ x 16 x 24	4/4 stock
Legs	4	1½ x 1½ x 23	6/4 stock
Short aprons	2	¾ x 3¼ x 12 *	4/4 stock
Long aprons	2	¾ x 3¼ x 15 *	4/4 stock
Wood buttons	8	½ x 1 x 1	4/4 stock

* Note: Length includes 1 in. long tenons

Tasty table. Made from solid wood with contrasting strips of cherry in its top, this little maple table relies on traditional mortise-and-tenon joinery for strength and durability.

4. Carry out the router flight check and rout a groove in each apron piece for the wood buttons. (See Dadoes, Grooves, and Slots, page 85.)

5. Set up the router table, go through the router flight check, and cut a practice tenon to fit a leg mortise. Once you're happy with the fit, mill all the tenons on the ends of the aprons. The leg thickness along with the tenon length demands that you miter the ends of the tenons so they don't interfere with each other. After mitering, shave the sides of the tenons round to fit the rounded ends of the mortises.

6. Measure the distance from the bottom edge of one of the grooves in an apron to its top edge, and then mill an overlong piece of button stock slightly less than this measurement, or just under ½ in. Set up the router table, perform the router flight check, and rabbet the long edge of the stock to create the tongue on the button. (Note the grain orientation in fig. 8, and see Rabbets, page 78.) Mark off individual buttons, then lay out and drill ³⁄₁₆ in. holes through the stock for screws, angling the bit back and forth to elongate each hole. After drilling, crosscut individual buttons from the strip.

7. Now is a good time to finish-sand the legs and aprons. Then glue the tenons into the mortises, keeping everything square and flat. My approach is to put some protective paper over a reliably flat surface (my tablesaw works great for this), clamp across the joints, and check the diagonals for square. Wipe away any excess glue with a damp cloth and let the assembly dry overnight.

8. After the glue has dried, remove the clamps and scrape and sand

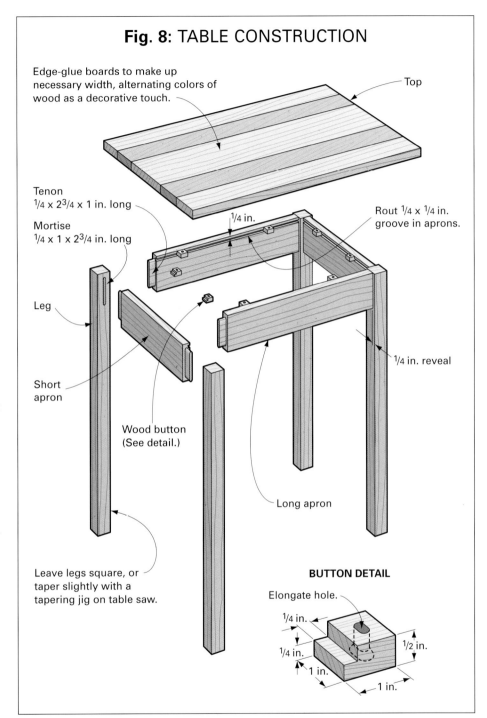

Fig. 8: TABLE CONSTRUCTION

Edge-glue boards to make up necessary width, alternating colors of wood as a decorative touch.

Top

Tenon
¼ x 2¾ x 1 in. long

Mortise
¼ x 1 x 2¾ in. long

Leg

Short apron

Wood button
(See detail.)

Long apron

¼ in.

Rout ¼ x ¼ in. groove in aprons.

¼ in. reveal

Leave legs square, or taper slightly with a tapering jig on table saw.

BUTTON DETAIL

Elongate hole.

¼ in.

¼ in.

1 in.

½ in.

1 in.

around the joints, plus any other areas that may need touching up. Apply a few coats of your favorite finish to the frame and the top. Once the finish is dry, lay the top upside down on your bench and center the frame over it. Slip the buttons into the grooves in the aprons, and drive screws through the buttons and into the top to secure it to the frame.

Router Bit Cabinet

Here's a small cabinet that's been specifically designed to hold your router bit collection. The same joints used on the small bookcase—dadoes and rabbets—hold this case together, although you'll lay them out somewhat differently. Pick your favorite hardwood to build the cabinet. I used some colorful carob wood that I had laying around. The cabinet accepts a drawer for router accessories and five trays for bits (see page 155), and a raised-panel door to keep the interior clean (see page 153). An alternative is to forgo router bit storage and simply make the cabinet for knickknacks in your home. In this case, you can go ahead and install the drawer and door if you like, but don't make the trays or mill the corresponding dadoes in the sides. Like the Small Bookcase (see page 144), this cabinet can be hung on a wall, which makes accessing your bits much easier.

Beauty and function. The author's router bit cabinet, made from carob wood, looks great on the outside. Below the door is a drawer for router accessories, and inside is a series of clever trays for stashing bits.

Router Bit Cabinet

CUTTING LIST

Description	Qty.	Dimensions (in.)	Material
Sides	2	¾ x 6½ x 22½	4/4 stock
Top	1	¾ x 8 x 17	4/4 stock
Bottom	1	¾ x 8 x 17	4/4 stock
Fixed shelf	1	¾ x 6¼ x 14	4/4 stock
Back	1	¼ x 14¼ x 22¾	plywood

Fig. 9: ROUTER BIT CABINET CONSTRUCTION

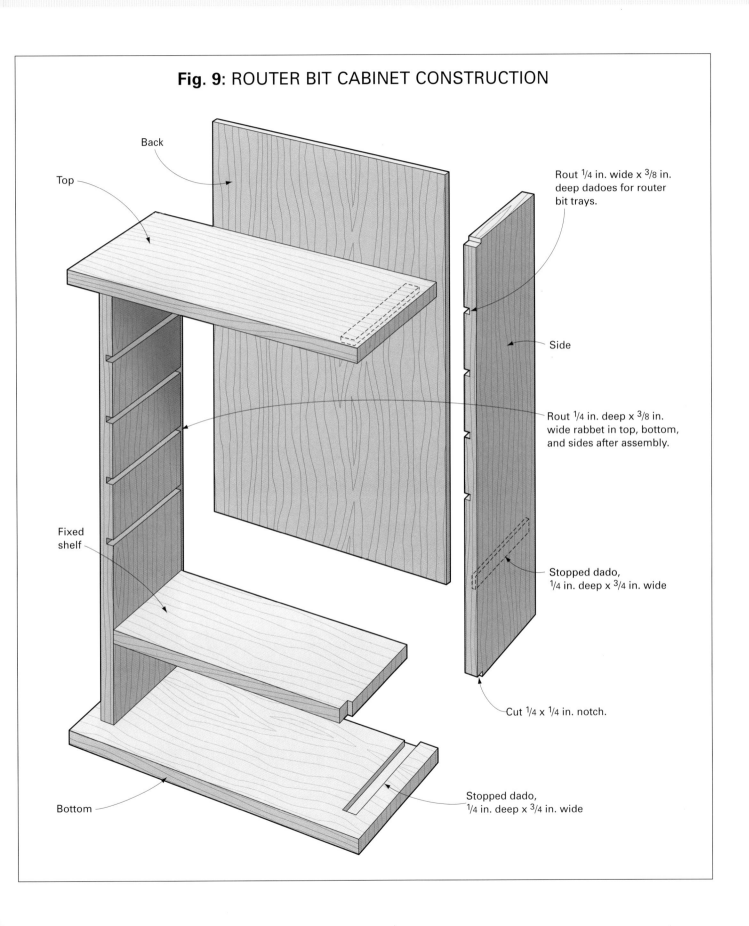

Back

Top

Rout $1/4$ in. wide x $3/8$ in. deep dadoes for router bit trays.

Side

Rout $1/4$ in. deep x $3/8$ in. wide rabbet in top, bottom, and sides after assembly.

Fixed shelf

Stopped dado, $1/4$ in. deep x $3/4$ in. wide

Cut $1/4$ x $1/4$ in. notch.

Bottom

Stopped dado, $1/4$ in. deep x $3/4$ in. wide

Building Steps

1. Mill the sides to dimension, making sure to account for the depth of the dadoes in the top and bottom that receive them. Label each piece for its top, bottom, inside face, and front edge.

2. Lay out the dadoes in the sides for the fixed shelf and the trays, placing the sides back edge–to–back edge and marking across both sides. Don't forget to mark the stopped dado for the shelf. I spaced the dadoes for the trays to accommodate my specific bits, and you should do the same. Once you've laid out the centerline for the fixed shelf, move up from that line by measuring your longest bit, then adding ½ in., so your biggest bits are towards the bottom of the case.

3. Carry out the router flight check, and rout the dadoes in the sides with the appropriate-sized router bit. (See Dadoes, Grooves, and Slots, page 85.)

4. Mill the top and bottom and, as before, mark its edges and surfaces.

5. Lay out the stopped dadoes in the top and bottom, measuring from the center of each piece and out to its ends for accuracy. Remember to account for the 1 in. overhang at each end.

6. Perform the router flight check, and rout the stopped dadoes in the top and bottom pieces. Square up the rounded ends with a chisel.

7. Set a side into one of its corresponding dadoes, making sure it seats firmly in the bottom, and use a craft knife to mark the depth of the notch cut. Use this measurement to mark all the notches in sides, then cut them out with a fine handsaw.

8. Clamp the case together and measure for the length of the fixed shelf, then cut the shelf to dimension and notch it as you did the sides.

9. With the case still clamped together (measure the diagonals to check that it's square!), use a rabbetting bit and the same setup used on the small bookcase (see page 144) to rout a rabbet in the top, bottom, and sides. After routing, use a sharp chisel to square up the rounded corners left by the bit.

10. Measure for the back, cut it to size, and test its fit. When all is as it should be, unclamp everything and sand all the interior surfaces.

11. Glue and clamp the case together. Don't forget to square the case, setting the back into its rabbets to help with this. (Your back *is* square, right?) Do not glue the back in, since it's easier to finish it on its own.

Now go and build the drawer, bit trays, and door. (See opposite page.) Once everything has been made and fitted, you can finish-sand all the parts and apply your finish of choice.

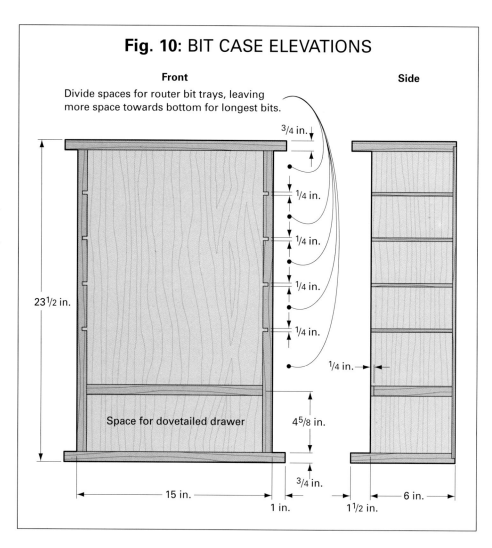

Fig. 10: BIT CASE ELEVATIONS

Front · Side

Divide spaces for router bit trays, leaving more space towards bottom for longest bits.

3/4 in.
1/4 in.
1/4 in.
1/4 in.
1/4 in.
1/4 in.

23 1/2 in.

Space for dovetailed drawer

4 5/8 in.

3/4 in.

15 in.

1 in.

1 1/2 in.

6 in.

Framed panel. This frame-and-panel door dresses up the front of the cabinet and features a raised panel that's shaped on its front and back face.

Frame-and-Panel Door

CUTTING LIST

Description	Qty.	Dimensions (in.)	Material
Stiles	2	¾ x 2¼ x 17	¼ stock
Rails	2	¾ x 2¼ x *	¼ stock
Panel	1	¾ x ** x **	¼ stock

* Note: Length depends on specific type of cope-and-stick cutter being used.

**Note: First construct the frame with a cope-and-stick bit, dry-assemble, then measure for the width and length of the panel.

Frame-and-Panel Door

This frame-and-panel door with a cope-and-stick frame accents the router bit cabinet beautifully (see page 150), and does a good job of sealing out dust and debris. Making the door is a great exercise in cutting cope-and-stick joinery (see page 122) and raising a solid-wood panel (see page 125). Brass butt hinges complete the look, and offer solid and long-wearing connections to the case.

Building Steps

1. With the drawer in the cabinet, measure the door opening. Dimension the frame stock to fit, taking special care to review the section on stock preparation in the cope-and-stick section.

2. Set up the router table with a cope-and-stick bit, perform the router flight check, and take practice cuts until they fit perfectly. Then rout the cope and stick on the rails and stiles.

3. Dry-assemble the frame and calculate the size of the panel by measuring the combined depth of the grooves. Subtract about ¼ in. from the panel's width and about ¹⁄₁₆ in. from its height to allow for wood movement and to ease assembly. If necessary, edge-glue some boards to make up the necessary width, then cut the panel to size and mark its outside face and bottom edge in an area that won't be routed off in the next step.

4. Set up a vertical panel-raising bit in your router table and perform the router flight check. Taking incremental cuts, raise the panel on all four

Bevels and brass. The back of the panel is beveled to keep it flush with the frame, and the door swings open on butt hinges.

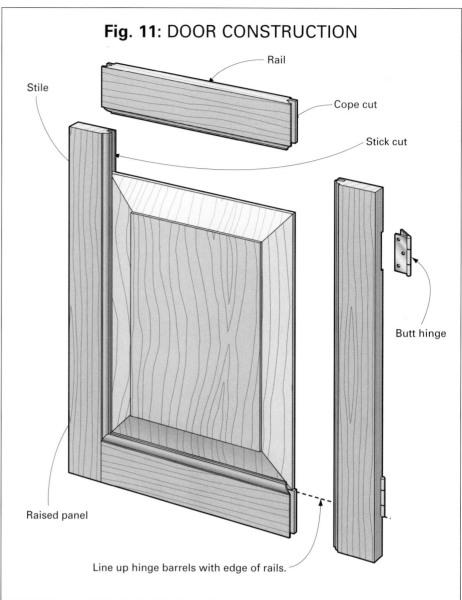

Fig. 11: DOOR CONSTRUCTION

Rail

Stile

Cope cut

Stick cut

Butt hinge

Raised panel

Line up hinge barrels with edge of rails.

edges and on both sides, taking cuts on the back side of the panel until the back surface sits flush with the back of the frame.

5. Dry-fit the assembly, making certain the coped ends of the rails fit tight to the stiles. Disassemble, then sand and apply finish to the panel and allow it to dry. Finishing the panel now prevents unsightly edges showing up later when the door expands and contracts with seasonal moisture changes.

6. Glue and clamp the door, squaring the assembly carefully by measuring the diagonals.

7. After the glue has dried, center the panel from left to right, then turn the door over and pin the panel in place by driving small brads or tiny brass screws through the rails and into the panel at the center of the door.

8. Fit the door to the case by trimming a little off the top and bottom edges with a hand plane until a gap of about $\frac{1}{32}$ in. is achieved between the drawer front below and the overhanging case above. Then center the door in the opening and trim the edges of the stiles until the door is even with the sides of the cabinet.

9. Rout the hinge mortises (see Hinge Mortise, page 100), install the hinges on the door, and then drive one screw per leaf into the case and test the fit of the door. Make any necessary adjustments and, when the fit is perfect, add the remaining screws. Remove the door and the hardware, finish-sand the door, apply your favorite finish, and reinstall the door once the finish has dried.

Dovetailed Drawer and Router Bit Trays

This small, dovetailed drawer with an overlay front and five router bit trays are great practice projects in and of themselves. You'll master two types of dovetail joints when making the drawer: half-blind dovetails and sliding dovetails. The bonus is that the drawer and trays are designed to fit and work with the Router Bit Cabinet (see page 150) for storing bits and other router-associated gear, such as wrenches, gauges, and the like. Start by making the drawer, and then build the trays.

Making the Drawer: Building Steps

1. Start by measuring the drawer opening in the cabinet, then mill all the drawer parts to size, except for the bottom. For now, keep the back and the sides over length. Because the sides will be joined using $\frac{1}{2}$ in. half-blind dovetails, their width must be a multiple of $\frac{7}{8}$ in. to accommodate the requirements of the dovetail jig's template. (See Half-Blind Dovetails, page 106.) Mark all the inside faces and bottom edges.

2. Lay out the stopped dovetail sockets on inside of the front, drawing a centerline for each $\frac{1}{2}$ in. socket. (See Sliding Dovetail, page 111.) The front should extend past the sides by $\frac{3}{4}$ in. For clearance, move the centerlines another $\frac{1}{32}$ in. per side, providing a total clearance between the sides of the drawer and the case of $\frac{1}{16}$ in. Mark a stop line on the front $\frac{1}{2}$ in. below what will be the top edge of the drawer side.

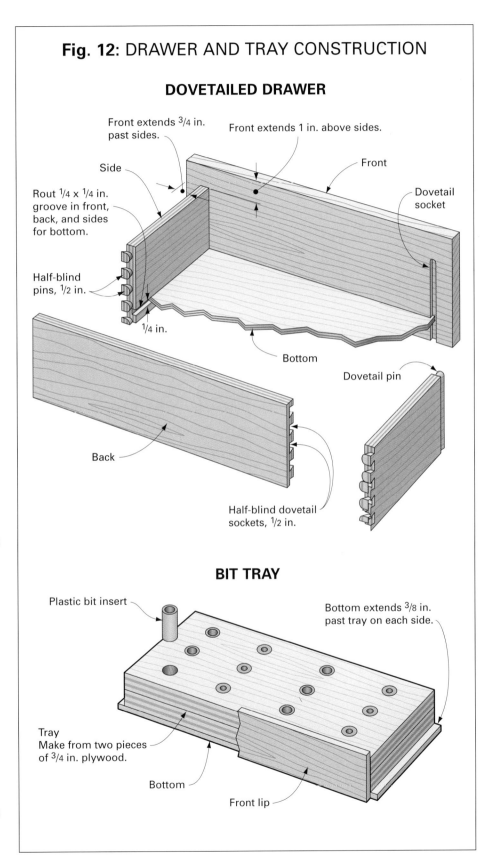

Fig. 12: DRAWER AND TRAY CONSTRUCTION

DOVETAILED DRAWER

Front extends $\frac{3}{4}$ in. past sides.

Front extends 1 in. above sides.

Side

Front

Rout $\frac{1}{4}$ x $\frac{1}{4}$ in. groove in front, back, and sides for bottom.

Dovetail socket

Half-blind pins, $\frac{1}{2}$ in.

$\frac{1}{4}$ in.

Bottom

Dovetail pin

Back

Half-blind dovetail sockets, $\frac{1}{2}$ in.

BIT TRAY

Plastic bit insert

Bottom extends $\frac{3}{8}$ in. past tray on each side.

Tray
Make from two pieces of $\frac{3}{4}$ in. plywood.

Bottom

Front lip

Bits and pieces. A series of trays fitted with plastic inserts holds a large collection of router bits, while a traditional dovetailed drawer keeps accessories neatly organized.

3. Fit a router with a ½ in. dovetail bit and set up the machine with the router tracking system (see page 54), go through the router flight check, and rout the sockets in the front.

4. Rout the mating pins in the sides on the router table, performing the router flight check and using the same dovetail bit. After routing the pins, notch them with a fine hand-saw to fit the stopped dovetail socket, checking that each side is flush with the bottom edge of the front.

5. Dry-assemble the sides to the front, and working as close as you can to the inside face of the front, measure the side-to-side distance. Cut the back to this measurement. With the sides still attached, mark and crosscut them to final length by measuring from the inside of the front and adding the depth of the drawer opening, minus ¹⁄₁₆ in. for clearance.

6. Set up your half-blind dovetail jig, execute the router flight check, and make practice joints until they fit perfectly. Disassemble the sides and front, and rout the dovetails for each back corner. Dry-assemble the drawer again and fit it into its opening. It should slide smoothly in and out and be ¹⁄₁₆ in. short of the rabbet for the cabinet back.

7. Disassemble the drawer again, carry out the router flight check, and rout the grooves in the front, back, and sides for the drawer bottom. (See Dadoes, Grooves, and Slots, page 85.) Remember to rout stopped grooves between the dovetail sockets on the front and between the pins on the back. Cut the bottom to fit. I like to use white melamine-coated particle-board (MCP) for drawer bottoms because it's clean and looks nice (both

Dovetailed Drawer and Router Bit Trays

CUTTING LIST FOR DOVETAILED DRAWER

Description	Qty.	Dimensions (in.)	Material
Front	1	¾ x 5 x 15	4/4 stock
Sides	2	½ x 3½ x 6 11/16	Baltic birch plywood
Back	1	½ x 3½ x 13 7/16	Baltic birch plywood
Bottom	1	¼ x 5 11/16 x 12 15/16	plywood or MCP

CUTTING LIST FOR BIT TRAY (1 TRAY)

Description	Qty.	Dimensions (in.)	Material
Tray	1	1½ x 6 x 13 7/16	plywood *
Front lip	1	¼ x 2 x 13 7/16	plywood
Bottom	1	¼ x 6 x 14 3/16	plywood

* Note: Laminate two pieces of ¾ in. plywood to create necessary thickness.

attributes that win a lady's heart), but plywood will do just fine, too.

8. If you want to add a drawer pull, drill the hole for it in the front now before assembly. Finish-sand all the parts, especially the interior surfaces, as they will be difficult to reach after glue-up.

9. Glue up the drawer by inserting each sliding dovetail pin into its corresponding socket, applying glue only to the last ½ in. of the pin. Then slide the bottom into the grooves, and glue and assemble the back to the sides. You'll have to spread the sides slightly to get the back in, but it can be done. Place waxed paper in the cabinet opening so any glue squeeze-out won't stick, and insert the drawer into the opening. Clamp the front to the sides. From the back, wedge the sides so the drawer box is centered. Allow to dry overnight. Ease over any sharp edges with a block and sandpaper, then apply your favorite finish.

Making a Tray: Building Steps

Note: The following procedure describes how to make one tray. When making the lower tray which slides on the fixed shelf, glue the oversized bottom to the tray and then trim it flush to the sides of the tray.

1. Measure the drawer opening in the cabinet and then cut all the parts to size. Make sure the bottom slides easily into the dadoes in the case, and trim if necessary. Cut two ¾ in. tray pieces slightly oversize, glue them together, then trim them to final size.

2. Mark the location of each bit on the tray, making sure the bits won't touch each other. You can simply drill holes through the tray to match your bit diameters, or you can buy a set of plastic bit inserts from a woodworking catalog and drill larger holes for the inserts to slip into.

I prefer the inserts because they're available for ¼ and ½ in. shanks, they require a common and inexpensive ⅞ in. drill bit for installation, and they protect bit shanks from corrosion and discoloration. If you opt for drilling plain shank holes, you'll need slightly oversized holes for a good fit. Bits with ¼ in. shanks require a special lettered "F" bit; ½ in. shanks will fit in holes drilled with a 33/64 in. bit. Be sure to apply some finish inside the raw shank holes to protect the bits, especially if you live by the sea or in a high-humidity community.

To fit each insert, drill to a depth that matches the insert's length, then drill a ⅝ in. through hole. (The plywood bottom you attach in the next step prevents the bits from falling out.)

3. Glue and clamp the bottom to the tray, making sure the bottom extends evenly and about 5/32 in. beyond each short side of the tray.

4. Add the front lip by gluing and clamping it to the front of the tray. The bottom of the lip should be flush with the bottom of the tray, with its top ¼ in. or so above the tray top. Sand any sharp edges and apply a coat or two of finish.

Acknowledgments

Over the years, dozens and dozens of students, joined by members of half a dozen woodworking clubs, have spurred me on to write this book. Discovering so many people who had the same frustrations as I did when using routers was a big motivation to write this step-by-step manual. Thanks to all who said, "So, when you gonna write a book?"

No book comes to you, the reader, without the work of dozens of people, including photographers, graphic illustrators, art directors, proofreaders, and editors. Lark Books has provided some of the best there are. I am especially indebted to Sandor Nagyszalanczy, a noted author and woodworker in his own right, and a brilliant photographer. I am pleased to call him friend for many years, and I'm sure you'll love his photos.

Some tool suppliers lent support and tools. I appreciate the generosity of Chris Carlson at S-B Power Tool Co., Dave Hazelwood, Director of Marketing at Emerson Tool Co., Bob McFarlin at Router Technologies, Inc., and Marc Sommerfeld at Sommerfeld Tools and CMT Cutters.

During the actual writing process no one was more helpful to me than friend, fellow woodworker, and book reviewer Barb Siddiqui. Her encouragement, editorial insight, and insistence on clarity and usefulness to the less experienced router user played a huge hand. If you find the book useful, it's due in no small part to her patience and her probing questions.

And, lastly, thanks to my dear, departed grandpa who put the first manual router in my hands a half century ago. Manual router? A hand plane, of course! I learned to make pine curlicues at age seven. It was in grandpa's primitive shop that I first learned that rabbets were not just small furry animals. The excitement of cutting wood into new shapes took birth there—a love I will have forever.

This book is dedicated to all those woodworkers who have held a router in their hands and thought "Now what?"

Index

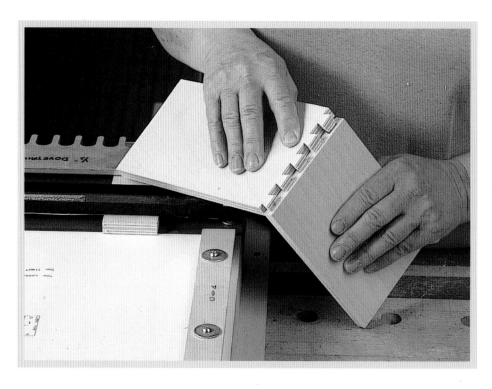